Teacher's Edition

WORLD ENGLISH Intro

SECOND EDITION

Real People • Real Places • Real Language

NATIONAL GEOGRAPHIC LEARNING | **CENGAGE Learning**

Australia • Brazil • Japan • Korea • Mexico • Singapore • Spain • United Kingdom • United States

World English Intro Teacher's Edition
Real People • Real Places • Real Language
Kristin Johannsen

Publisher: Sherrise Roehr

Executive Editor: Sarah Kenney

Senior Development Editor: Margarita Matte

Development Editor: Brenden Layte

Assistant Editor: Alison Bruno

Editorial Assistant: Patricia Giunta

Media Researcher: Leila Hishmeh

Senior Technology Product Managers:
Lauren Krolick, Scott Rule

Director of Global Marketing: Ian Martin

Senior Product Marketing Manager:
Caitlin Thomas

Sr. Director, ELT & World Languages:
Michael Burggren

Production Manager: Daisy Sosa

Content Project Manager: Andrea Bobotas

Senior Print Buyer: Mary Beth Hennebury

Cover Designer: Aaron Opie

Art Director: Scott Baker

Creative Director: Chris Roy

Cover Image: Martin Roemers/Panos Pictures

Compositor: MPS Limited

Cover Image

Taksim Square, Istanbul, Turkey

World English Intro Teacher's Edition: 978-1-285-84838-9

National Geographic Learning
20 Channel Center Street
Boston, MA 02210
USA

Cengage Learning is a leading provider of customized learning solutions with office locations around the globe, including Singapore, the United Kingdom, Australia, Mexico, Brazil, and Japan.

Cengage Learning products are represented in Canada by Nelson Education, Ltd.

Visit National Geographic Learning online at ngl.cengage.com

Visit our corporate website at www.cengage.com

Printed in Canada
1 2 3 4 5 6 7 13 12 11 10 09

CONTENTS

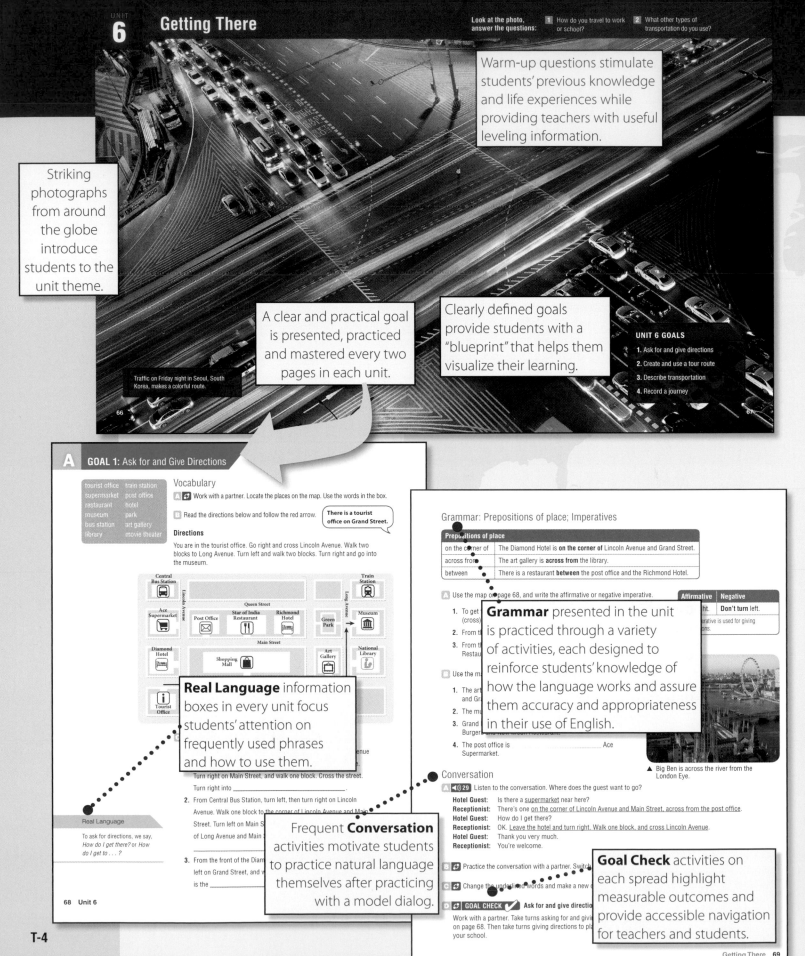

UNIT 6 — Getting There

Look at the photo, answer the questions:
1 How do you travel to work or school?
2 What other types of transportation do you use?

Warm-up questions stimulate students' previous knowledge and life experiences while providing teachers with useful leveling information.

Striking photographs from around the globe introduce students to the unit theme.

Traffic on Friday night in Seoul, South Korea, makes a colorful route.

A clear and practical goal is presented, practiced and mastered every two pages in each unit.

Clearly defined goals provide students with a "blueprint" that helps them visualize their learning.

UNIT 6 GOALS
1. Ask for and give directions
2. Create and use a tour route
3. Describe transportation
4. Record a journey

A GOAL 1: Ask for and Give Directions

Vocabulary

tourist office / train station / supermarket / post office / restaurant / hotel / museum / park / bus station / art gallery / library / movie theater

A. Work with a partner. Locate the places on the map. Use the words in the box.

B. Read the directions below and follow the red arrow.

There is a tourist office on Grand Street.

Directions

You are in the tourist office. Go right and cross Lincoln Avenue. Walk two blocks to Long Avenue. Turn left and walk two blocks. Turn right and go into the museum.

Central Bus Station / Train Station / Ace Supermarket / Queen Street / Post Office / Star of India Restaurant / Richmond Hotel / Green Park / Museum / Diamond Hotel / Main Street / Shopping Mall / Art Gallery / National Library / Tourist Office

Real Language information boxes in every unit focus students' attention on frequently used phrases and how to use them.

Real Language

To ask for directions, we say, How do I get there? or How do I get to . . . ?

Turn right on Main Street, and walk one block. Cross the street. Turn right into _____.

2. From Central Bus Station, turn left, then turn right on Lincoln Avenue. Walk one block to the corner of Lincoln Avenue and Main Street. Turn left on Main S... of Long Avenue and Main _____.

3. From the front of the Diam... left on Grand Street, and ... is the _____.

68 Unit 6

T-4

Grammar: Prepositions of place; Imperatives

Prepositions of place	
on the corner of	The Diamond Hotel is **on the corner of** Lincoln Avenue and Grand Street.
across from	The art gallery is **across from** the library.
between	There is a restaurant **between** the post office and the Richmond Hotel.

A. Use the map on page 68, and write the affirmative or negative imperative.

	Affirmative	Negative
	...ht.	**Don't turn** left.

...rative is used for giving ...ons.

1. To get ... (cross)...
2. From t...
3. From t... Restau...

Grammar presented in the unit is practiced through a variety of activities, each designed to reinforce students' knowledge of how the language works and assure them accuracy and appropriateness in their use of English.

B. Use the ma...

1. The art... and Gr...
2. The mu...
3. Grand ... Burger...
4. The post office is _____ Ace Supermarket.

▲ Big Ben is across the river from the London Eye.

Conversation

A. 🔊 29 Listen to the conversation. Where does the guest want to go?

Hotel Guest: Is there a <u>supermarket</u> near here?
Receptionist: There's one <u>on the corner of Lincoln Avenue and Main Street, across from the post office.</u>
Hotel Guest: How do I get there?
Receptionist: OK. <u>Leave the hotel and turn right. Walk one block, and cross Lincoln Avenue.</u>
Hotel Guest: Thank you very much.
Receptionist: You're welcome.

B. Practice the conversation with a partner. Switch...

C. Change the underlined words and make a new c...

Frequent **Conversation** activities motivate students to practice natural language themselves after practicing with a model dialog.

D. **GOAL CHECK** ✓ Ask for and give directi...
Work with a partner. Take turns asking for and givi... on page 68. Then take turns giving directions to pla... your school.

Goal Check activities on each spread highlight measurable outcomes and provide accessible navigation for teachers and students.

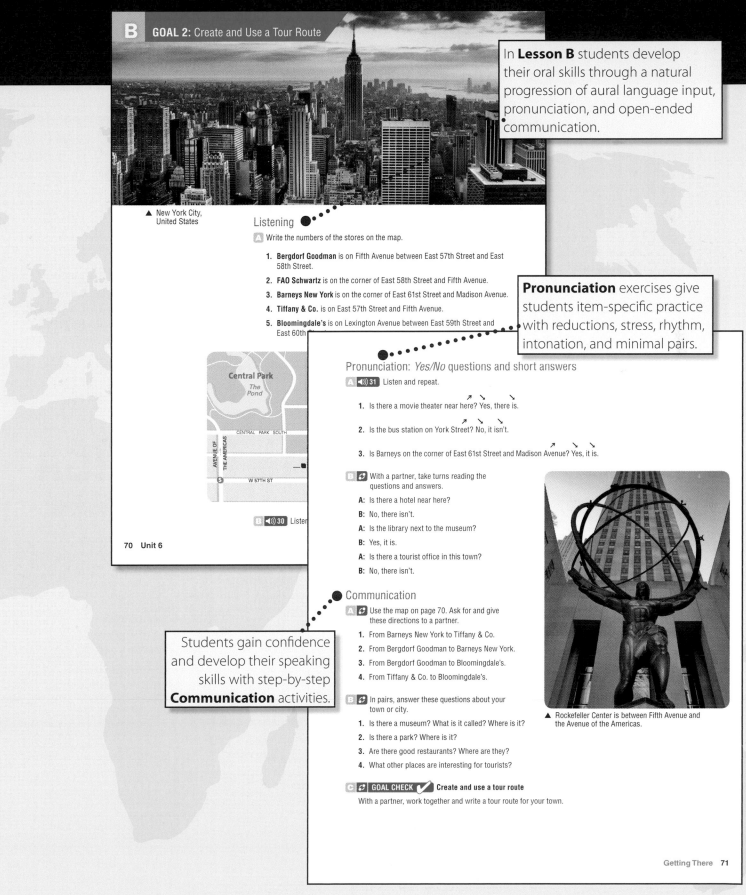

In **Lesson B** students develop their oral skills through a natural progression of aural language input, pronunciation, and open-ended communication.

▲ New York City, United States

Listening

A Write the numbers of the stores on the map.

1. **Bergdorf Goodman** is on Fifth Avenue between East 57th Street and East 58th Street.
2. **FAO Schwartz** is on the corner of East 58th Street and Fifth Avenue.
3. **Barneys New York** is on the corner of East 61st Street and Madison Avenue.
4. **Tiffany & Co.** is on East 57th Street and Fifth Avenue.
5. **Bloomingdale's** is on Lexington Avenue between East 59th Street and East 60th

Pronunciation exercises give students item-specific practice with reductions, stress, rhythm, intonation, and minimal pairs.

Central Park
The Pond

CENTRAL PARK SOUTH

AVENUE OF THE AMERICAS

W 57TH ST

Pronunciation: *Yes/No* questions and short answers

A ◀))) 31 Listen and repeat.

1. Is there a movie theater near here? Yes, there is.
2. Is the bus station on York Street? No, it isn't.
3. Is Barneys on the corner of East 61st Street and Madison Avenue? Yes, it is.

B With a partner, take turns reading the questions and answers.

A: Is there a hotel near here?
B: No, there isn't.
A: Is the library next to the museum?
B: Yes, it is.
A: Is there a tourist office in this town?
B: No, there isn't.

B ◀))) 30 Listen

70 Unit 6

Communication

Students gain confidence and develop their speaking skills with step-by-step **Communication** activities.

A Use the map on page 70. Ask for and give these directions to a partner.

1. From Barneys New York to Tiffany & Co.
2. From Bergdorf Goodman to Barneys New York.
3. From Bergdorf Goodman to Bloomingdale's.
4. From Tiffany & Co. to Bloomingdale's.

B In pairs, answer these questions about your town or city.

1. Is there a museum? What is it called? Where is it?
2. Is there a park? Where is it?
3. Are there good restaurants? Where are they?
4. What other places are interesting for tourists?

C **GOAL CHECK** ✔ **Create and use a tour route**

With a partner, work together and write a tour route for your town.

▲ Rockefeller Center is between Fifth Avenue and the Avenue of the Americas.

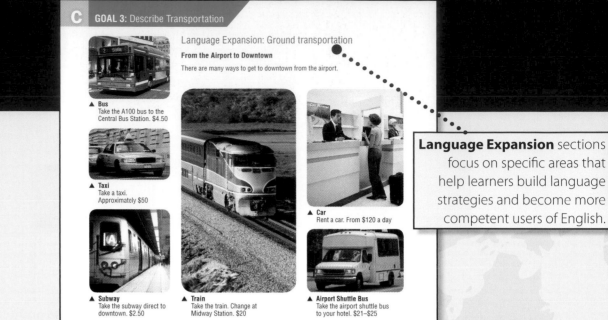

Language Expansion: Ground transportation

From the Airport to Downtown

There are many ways to get to downtown from the airport.

▲ **Bus**
Take the A100 bus to the
Central Bus Station. $4.50

▲ **Taxi**
Take a taxi.
Approximately $50

▲ **Subway**
Take the subway direct to
downtown. $2.50

▲ **Train**
Take the train. Change at
Midway Station. $20

▲ **Car**
Rent a car. From $120 a day

▲ **Airport Shuttle Bus**
Take the airport shuttle bus
to your hotel. $21–$25

A Complete the chart with the names of different types of ground transportation.

Rental car $120
Expensive

Subway $2.50

> **Language Expansion** sections focus on specific areas that help learners build language strategies and become more competent users of English.

Reading

A Read the diary and look at the pictures.

B Choose the correct answer.

1. The journey starts in _____ .
   a. Elephant Island   c. South Georgia
   b. London

2. The *Endurance* breaks up on _____ .
   a. October 26, 1914
   b. October 26, 1915
   c. October 26, 1916

3. _____ men leave Elephant Island on a small boat.
   a. four   c. six
   b. five

4. It takes _____ to go from Elephant Island to South Georgia.
   a. one week   c. three weeks
   b. two weeks

5. Shackleton finds help in _____ .
   a. Stromness   c. London
   b. Elephant Island

The ship *Endurance*, with men playing soccer on the ice.

Word Focus

break up = fall to pieces
help = assistance
rescue = save

JOURNEY TO
ANTARCTICA

1914
August 8 Ernest Shackleton and his men leave London on their ship *Endurance*.

1915
January 18 The *Endurance* is trapped in the ice. The men play soccer on the ice.

October 26 It's very cold. The *Endurance* **breaks up.** The men have to leave the *Endurance*. They camp on the ice.

1916
April 9 The ice starts to break up. The men have to get into the small boats.

April 15 They land on Elephant Island.

April 24 Shackleton and five men leave Elephant Island in a small boat to find **help.** The other men stay on Elephant Island.

May 8 Shackleton lands in South Georgia.

May 19 Shackleton leaves three men with the boat. He crosses the mountains of South Georgia with two men to find help.

May 20 They arrive in Stromness, the main town in South Georgia. They find help.

August 30 Shackleton **rescues** the men on Elephant Island.

> Magazine-style readings are a springboard for opinion sharing and personalization, and provide opportunities for students to use the grammar and vocabulary presented earlier in the unit.

London, England

lava lake
crater
eruption
lava
magma

▲ rocks and soil

Writing Strategy

To put events in order, we use: **first, next, then,** and **finally.**

First we go to Sydney, **then** we go to Melbourne, and **finally** to Perth.

Where do we want to go?

How long will we stay?

What do we want to visit there?

What will we do each day?

Communication

A 🔁 Read the European Tour plan below. With a partner, [...] another part of the world. Think about the questi[...]

European To[ur]

Tour itinerary:

June 3: Arrive in Paris. First w[...] the Louvre, next the Eiffel Tow[...] finally we have dinner on the C[...] Elysées.

June 4: Leave Paris. Take the t[...] London. First we visit the Lond[...] and then the Tower of London, [...] evening we take a boat tour on [...] Thames to see the city at night[...]

B 🔁 Tell another pair about yo[...]

> Students conclude the unit by watching an authentic but carefully-graded National Geographic video clip. This application of students' newly acquired language skills is a part of the on-going unit assessment system and serves as a motivating consolidation task.

Writing

A 🔁 Now write your itinerary in your notebook.

B **GOAL CHECK** ✔ **Record a journey**

Think about your itinerary. In your notebook, write a diary entry about the trip. Share your diary entry with the class.

Before You Watch

A Study the picture. Use the labels in the picture to complete the text.

A volcano is a mountain with a large hole at the top. This hole is called a _____. A volcano produces very hot, melted rock. When it is underground, this hot, melted rock is called _____. When it leaves, [...] the volcano, it is called _____. When the lava stays [...] orms a _____. When lava leaves a volcano, we say [...]ots. We call it an _____.

[...]tch

[...]ideo. Match the sentence parts.

[...]s _____

[...] _____

[...]es out of the earth _____

[...]nds hours _____

[...] to stand near the crat[...]

6. The professors are _____

> The video can be watched in class from the **Classroom DVD** or students can watch it individually on the **Student CD-ROM**.

After You Watch

A 🔁 Discuss these questions with a partner.

1. Do you want to explore a volcano? Why or why not?
2. How can people travel to difficult places?

Writing activities reinforce the structures, vocabulary and expressions learned in the unit.

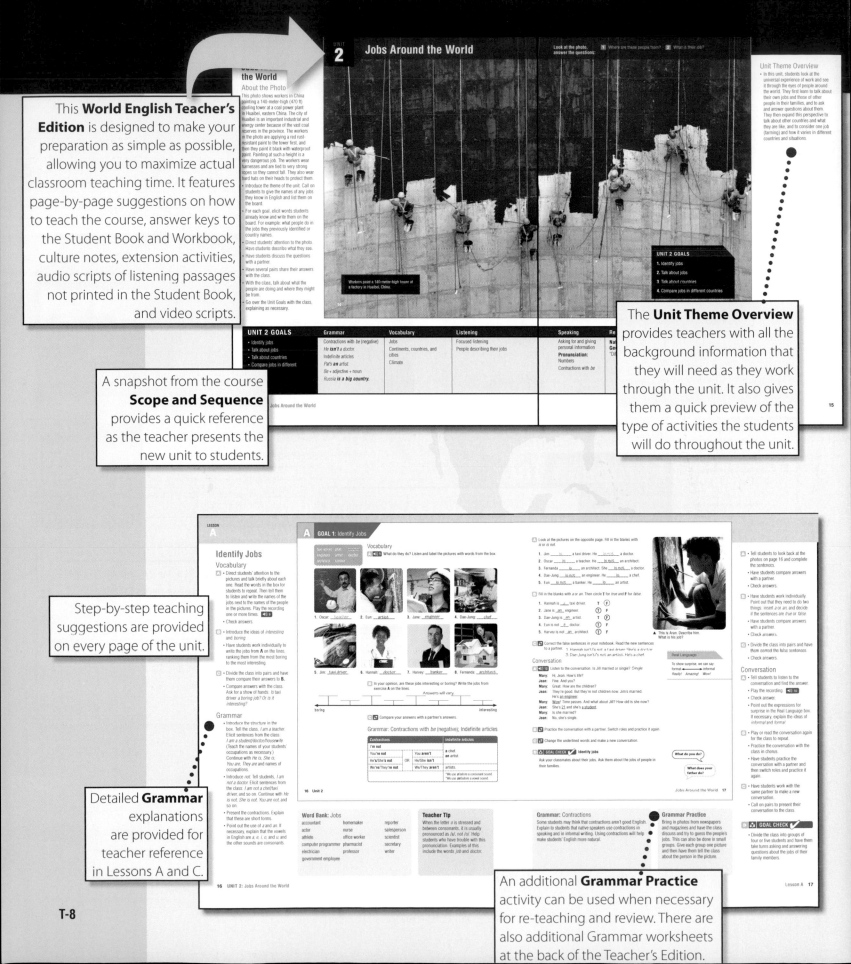

This **World English Teacher's Edition** is designed to make your preparation as simple as possible, allowing you to maximize actual classroom teaching time. It features page-by-page suggestions on how to teach the course, answer keys to the Student Book and Workbook, culture notes, extension activities, audio scripts of listening passages not printed in the Student Book, and video scripts.

A snapshot from the course **Scope and Sequence** provides a quick reference as the teacher presents the new unit to students.

The **Unit Theme Overview** provides teachers with all the background information that they will need as they work through the unit. It also gives them a quick preview of the type of activities the students will do throughout the unit.

Step-by-step teaching suggestions are provided on every page of the unit.

Detailed **Grammar** explanations are provided for teacher reference in Lessons A and C.

An additional **Grammar Practice** activity can be used when necessary for re-teaching and review. There are also additional Grammar worksheets at the back of the Teacher's Edition.

	Communication Goals	Language Focus
UNIT 1 Friends and Family	• Describe a person	She/He's young, with straight _____ hair. His/Her name is _____.
UNIT 2 Jobs Around the World	• Asking for and giving personal information • Talking about jobs • Talking about countries	What's your name? How old are you? Where are you from?
UNIT 3 Houses and Apartments	• Describing a house	What's in the big bedroom? There are two beds.
Unit 4	• Talking about the personal possessions	These earrings look cool. She already has earrings. What about this ___?

This Teacher's Edition provides additional Communication and Writing practice through classroom materials that can be photocopied. **Communication Activities** include information gap, group work, interview worksheets, simulations and role-plays.

Unit 5: Daily Activities
Lesson A

A Complete the sentences. Use the verbs in parentheses.
1. Jorge and Linda _have dinner_ (have dinner) at six o'clock.
2. Farah _____ (take a shower) every morning.
3. We _____ (start work) at nine o'clock in the morning.
4. Kira _____ (get up) at six o'clock every morning.
5. Isabel _____ (have lunch) every day.

B Write the sentences. Make them negative.
1. They finish work at five o'clock. _They don't finish work at five o'clock._
2. We eat lunch at one o'clock. _____
3. Tina takes a shower in the evening. _____

The **Grammar Worksheets,** new for this edition, provide additional support and practice for the grammar points presented in Lessons A and C in the Student Book units.

	Writing Tasks	Language Focus
Unit 1 Describe Your Family	• Use *be* in a conversation. • Draw and describe family members.	Hi, my name is Michael. This is Toby. He is my brother.
Unit 2 Describe a Country	• Answer questions about yourself. • Write sentences about countries.	No, I'm not a doctor. Brazil is a large country.
Unit 3 Describe a Room	• Finish sentences about a house and an apartment. • Write sentences about a room.	There are three bedrooms in my house. There is a lamp on the table.
Unit 4 A Short Story	• Finish senten___ • Write question___ • Finish senten___	

UNIT 5 DAILY ACTIVITIES
DAILY SCHEDULE

A Look at Jillian's schedule.

Monday	Tuesday	Wednesday	Thursday	Friday
7:30 get up	7:30 get up	7:30 get up	7:30 get up	7:30 get up
9:00 start work	9:00 start work	9:00 start work	9:00 start work	9:00 start work
12:30 have lunch	12:30 have lunch	12:30 have lunch	12:30 have lunch	12:30 have lunch
	3:00 finish work		3:00 finish work	
5:00 finish work		5:00 finish work		5:00 finish work
11:00 go to bed	11:00 go to bed	11:00 go to bed	11:00 go to bed	11:00 go to bed

✓ Use the words below to write sentences about Jillian's schedule.
1. get up/every morning _Jillian gets up at 7:30 every morning._
2. start work/every day _____
3. have lunch/every day _____
4. finish work/Tuesdays and Thursdays _____
5. finish work/Mondays, Wednesdays, and Fridays _____
6. go to bed/every night _____

✓ Compare your sentences with a partner.

B What do you do every day? Fill in the schedule with your information.

Monday	Tuesday	Wednesday	Thursday	Friday

The **Writing Program** reinforces and complements the lessons in the Student Book. Writing gives students a chance to reflect on the English they've learned and to develop an indispensable academic skill.

GETTING THERE
UNIT 6

Lesson A GRAMMAR AND VOCABULARY

Label the pictures.

tourist office   train station   supermarket   post office   library   park
restaurant   hotel   museum   bus stop

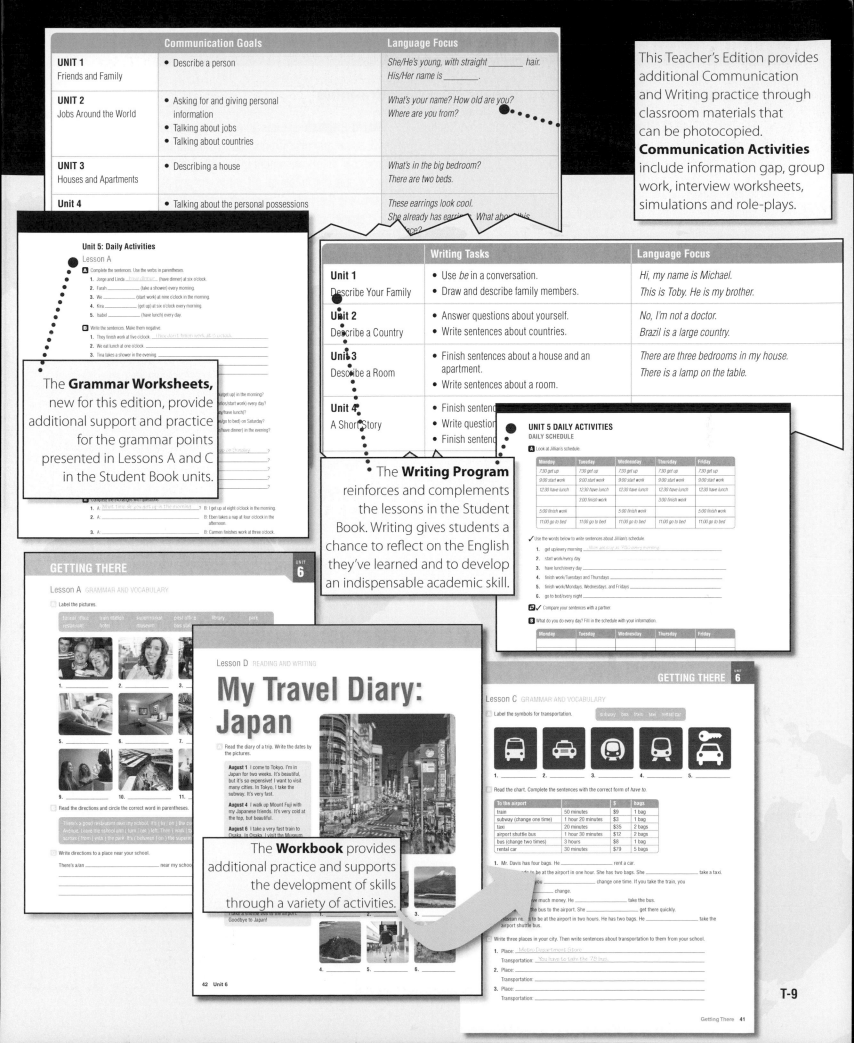

1. _____ 2. _____ 3. _____

5. _____ 6. _____ 7. _____

9. _____ 10. _____ 11. _____

Read the directions and circle the correct word in parentheses.

There's a good restaurant near my school. It's (in / on) Oak Avenue. Leave the school and (turn / go) left. Then I walk (across / from) the park. It's (between / on) the supermarket.

Write directions to a place near your school.

There's a/an _____ near my school.

Lesson D READING AND WRITING

My Travel Diary: Japan

A Read the diary of a trip. Write the dates by the pictures.

August 1 I come to Tokyo. I'm in Japan for two weeks. It's beautiful, but it's so expensive! I want to visit many cities. In Tokyo, I take the subway. It's very fast.

August 4 I walk up Mount Fuji with my Japanese friends. It's very cold at the top, but beautiful.

August 6 I take a very fast train to Osaka. In Osaka, I visit the Museum.

I take a shuttle bus to the airport. Goodbye to Japan!

42 Unit 6

The **Workbook** provides additional practice and supports the development of skills through a variety of activities.

GETTING THERE
UNIT 6

Lesson C GRAMMAR AND VOCABULARY

Label the symbols for transportation.

subway   bus   train   taxi   rental car

1. _____ 2. _____ 3. _____ 4. _____ 5. _____

Read the chart. Complete the sentences with the correct form of *have to*.

To the airport		$	bags
train	50 minutes	$9	1 bag
subway (change one time)	1 hour 20 minutes	$3	1 bag
taxi	20 minutes	$35	2 bags
airport shuttle bus	1 hour 30 minutes	$12	2 bags
bus (change two times)	3 hours	$8	1 bag
rental car	30 minutes	$79	5 bags

1. Mr. Davis has four bags. He _____ rent a car.
2. _____ needs to be at the airport in one hour. She has two bags. She _____ take a taxi.
3. If you _____ you _____ change one time. If you take the train, you _____ change.
4. _____ have much money. He _____ take the bus.
5. _____ the bus to the airport. She _____ get there quickly.
6. Hassan ne___ to be at the airport in two hours. He has two bags. He _____ take the airport shuttle bus.

Write three places in your city. Then write sentences about transportation to them from your school.
1. Place: _Metro Department Store_
   Transportation: _You have to take the 78 bus._
2. Place: _____
   Transportation: _____
3. Place: _____
   Transportation: _____

Overview

The new edition of **World English** uses rich, engrossing National Geographic text, photos, art, and videos to involve students in learning about real people, real places, and real language.

In this edition, newly added TED Talks and Readings also bring some of the world's most important and interesting speakers to the classroom.

Each unit is divided into three two-page lessons, a three-page Reading, Writing, and Communication lesson, and a Video Journal.

A concrete objective at the beginning of every lesson focuses students' attention on what they will be learning. At the end of the lesson, a personalization activity gives students an opportunity to apply what they've learned and lets both teachers and students check student progress.

Unit Opener

Each unit opens with a two-page spread featuring a striking photo. These photos have been chosen both to illustrate the unit theme and to provide material for discussion. Before beginning the unit, teacher and students can describe the picture, name as many things as they can in it, and make guesses about when and where the photo was taken. The two discussion questions then lead students into the topic and introduce several key vocabulary items.

In this Teacher's Edition, a Unit Theme Overview is provided to orient you to the scope of the unit and to give additional information that may be useful in discussing the unit theme. Throughout the lesson notes, For Your Information boxes contain additional facts about the topic of a listening passage, reading, or video.

Vocabulary

Lessons A and C both begin with a short activity presenting lexical items related to the unit theme. In Lesson A, the vocabulary section introduces the core words that students will need to discuss and learn about the unit topic. These are presented in context, with text or pictures to aid students in understanding. After completing the exercises in this section, students have a written record of the meanings of the words, which they can refer to later. The lesson notes in this Teacher's Edition contain a Word Bank of supplementary vocabulary that can be used in activities or taught as enrichment.

Grammar

World English features an explicit grammar syllabus, with individual grammar points tied to the unit theme. Two different grammar points are taught in Lesson A and Lesson C. They are used in the opening presentation of the lessons along with the vocabulary items and then explicitly presented in a box with examples, rules, and usage notes.

Students first do controlled practice with the structure in writing, then freer production in writing, and finally use the structure in controlled speaking practice. Every grammar point is followed by a Conversation section that gives further practice in the use of the structure.

The lesson notes in this Teacher's Edition contain a brief summary of each grammar point for teacher reference, as well an additional Grammar Practice Activity.

New to this edition are Grammar worksheets in the back of the Teacher's Edition. Each unit has two worksheets, one for each of the grammar points in Lessons A and C.

Conversation

Each unit contains two model conversations highlighting both the vocabulary and the grammar for the lesson. Students first listen to the conversation with their books closed and answer one general comprehension question. Next, they listen again while reading the conversation. They are then ready to practice the conversation, taking turns with both roles before making their own conversations based on the model and incorporating specified information along with their own ideas.

Listening

Lesson B starts off with a listening activity. After a warm-up to introduce the subject of the activity, students listen to a conversation, radio program, or interview multiple times, completing a series of written tasks of graded difficulty. The first time, they are asked to listen for the gist or main ideas; subsequent activities ask them to find numbers, details, or further information. A post-listening task helps students to explore and personalize what they've heard.

Audioscripts for all listening activities begin on page T-169.

Pronunciation

The pronunciation component of **World English** emphasizes stress, intonation, reductions, and other features to make learners' English more natural and comprehensible to a wide international audience. Students first learn to recognize a feature of English pronunciation and then to produce it. Examples are presented on the audio recording in the context of the unit theme. Students begin by listening, then repeat with the audio recording, and then practice freer production of the features while interacting with a partner.

If a particular pronunciation point is especially challenging for your students, it can be practiced in a number of ways. You can have the entire class repeat the items in chorus, then the two halves of the class, then rows or columns of students, and finally you can call on individual students to pronounce the items. When students practice in pairs, circulate around the room listening and correcting.

Communication

In contrast to the controlled speaking practice in the Conversation sections, the Communication activities give freer practice with the structures and vocabulary that the students have learned. These activities are designed to allow personal expression, but still within a controlled field of language, so that all students can feel confident of success. While students are doing these activities, you should circulate around the class to help with vocabulary and ideas as needed and to make note of errors and interesting responses to discuss with the class after the end of the activity.

The lesson notes in this Teacher's Edition include Expansion activities for further discussion around the theme of the listening passage. For classes where more practice of free communication is desired, this book also contains 12 Communication Activity Worksheets, which may be photocopied, one for each unit. The activities, which require 15 to 30 minutes of class time each, reinforce the vocabulary and structures from the unit while giving students another opportunity to express their own ideas in English.

Language Expansion

The first part of Lesson C is a Language Expansion activity that is meant to broaden students' vocabulary around the unit theme by introducing a closely related group of lexical items. These are presented in context and are used immediately in writing and then speaking, giving students more options when doing the Grammar and Conversation activities that follow in Lesson C.

Reading

Lesson D is centered around a reading passage, which is followed by a Communication activity that prepares students for writing. All of the reading passages in **World English** are abridged and adapted from authentic articles in National Geographic publications or TED Talks. To help students read for interest and enjoyment, unfamiliar vocabulary is explained either with glosses in a Word Focus box or in a picture dictionary illustration.

The lesson notes in this Teacher's Edition include a Web search activity and a suggestion for a simple project that can be done as a follow-up for each reading passage.

Writing

The writing activities in Lesson D of **World English** flow from the subject of the reading passage and are always preceded by a Communication activity in which students discuss and explore the topic further. This generates ideas and forms a natural prewriting sequence. Writing tasks are short and simple and range from writing single sentences in the lower levels, through writing groups of sentences, on up to writing an entire paragraph.

The writing activities in the units emphasize helping students put their ideas into written form. Where a more structured approach to writing is desired, this Teacher's Edition contains a complete Writing Program, which may be photocopied. These optional writing worksheets, one for each unit, provide instruction and practice in a sequence of writing skills graded to the level of the course.

Video Journal

Each unit of **World English** concludes with an authentic National Geographic three- to four-minute video, with a voice-over that has been specially edited for language learners. The video segments recycle the themes and language of the main unit, bringing them to life in colorful locations around the globe. A Before You Watch activity presents new words that students will hear and gives information about the setting of the video. Students watch the video several times while completing While You Watch activities that ask them first to find general themes and then to locate specific information. They give their response to the video in an After You Watch activity.

The responses to the video draw the strands of the unit together and allow students to demonstrate what they've learned.

TED Talks

In this new edition, students also watch a TED Talk every three units. These videos are accompanied by four-page sections which review the vocabulary and grammar content of the previous three units and also allow students to build upon prior instruction to communicate about issues that affect their community and the world.

Special Features in the Student Book

Real Language This feature highlights high-frequency expressions from everyday language that will make students' speech sound natural and confident. To present them, point out their use in the activity and discuss other situations when they might be useful. If desired, have students work in pairs to create conversations using the expressions.

Word Focus These boxes present and explain additional vocabulary used in an activity, as well as introduce commonly used collocations.

WORLD ENGLISH Intro

SECOND EDITION

Real People • Real Places • Real Language

Martin Milner, Author

Rob Jenkins, Series Editor

Australia • Brazil • Japan • Korea • Mexico • Singapore • Spain • United Kingdom • United States

World English Intro
Real People, Real Places, Real Language
Martin Milner, Author
Rob Jenkins, Series Editor

Publisher: Sherrise Roehr

Executive Editor: Sarah Kenney

Senior Development Editor: Margarita Matte

Development Editor: Brenden Layte

Assistant Editor: Alison Bruno

Editorial Assistant: Patricia Giunta

Media Researcher: Leila Hishmeh

Senior Technology Product Manager: Scott Rule

Director of Global Marketing: Ian Martin

Senior Product Marketing Manager:
    Caitlin Thomas

Sr. Director, ELT & World Languages:
    Michael Burggren

Production Manager: Daisy Sosa

Content Project Manager: Andrea Bobotas

Senior Print Buyer: Mary Beth Hennebury

Cover Designer: Aaron Opie

Art Director: Scott Baker

Creative Director: Chris Roy

Cover Image: Martin Roemers/Panos Pictures

Compositor: MPS Limited

For product information and technology assistance, contact us at
Cengage Learning Customer & Sales Support, 1-800-354-9706

For permission to use material from this text or product,
submit all requests online at **cengage.com/permissions**
Further permissions questions can be emailed to
permissionrequest@cengage.com

World English Intro ISBN: 978-1-285-84868-6
World English Intro + CD-ROM ISBN: 978-1-285-84834-1
World English Intro + Online Workbook ISBN: 978-1-305-08955-6

National Geographic Learning
20 Channel Center Street
Boston, MA 02210
USA

Cengage Learning is a leading provider of customized learning solutions with office locations around the globe, including Singapore, the United Kingdom, Austrailia, Mexico, Brazil, and Japan.

Cengage Learning products are represented in Canada by Nelson Education, Ltd.

Visit National Geographic Learning online at ngl.cengage.com

Visit our corporate website at www.cengage.com

Printed in Canada
1 2 3 4 5 6 7 8 9 10   16 15 14 13

Thank you to the educators who provided invaluable feedback during the development of the second edition of the *World English* series:

AMERICAS

Brazil

Renata Cardoso, Universidade de Brasília, Brasília
Gladys De Sousa, Universidade Federal de Minas Gerais, Belo Horizonte
Marilena Fernandes, Associação Alumni, São Paulo
Mary Ruth Popov, Ingles Express, Ltda., Belo Horizonte
Ana Rosa, Speed, Vila Velha
Danny Sheps, English4u2, Natal
Renata Zainotte, Go Up Idiomas, Rio de Janeiro

Colombia

Eida Caicedo, Universidad de San Buenaventura Cali, Cali
Andres Felipe Echeverri Patiño, Corporación Universitaria Lasallista, Envigado
Luz Libia Rey, Centro Colombo Americano, Bogota

Dominican Republic

Aida Rosales, Instituto Cultural Dominico-Americano, Santo Domingo

Ecuador

Elizabeth Ortiz, COPEI-Copol English Institute, Guayaquil

Mexico

Ramon Aguilar, LEC Languages and Education Consulting, Hermosillo
Claudia García-Moreno Ávila, Universidad Autónoma del Estado de México, Toluca
Ana María Benton, Universidad Anahuac Mexico Norte, Huixquilucan
Martha Del Angel, Tecnológico de Monterrey, Monterrey
Sachenka García B., Universidad Kino, Hermosillo
Cinthia I. Navarrete García, Universidad Autónoma del Estado de México, Toluca
Alonso Gaxiola, Universidad Autonoma de Sinaloa, Guasave
Raquel Hernandez, Tecnológico de Monterrey, Monterrey
Beatriz Cuenca Hernández, Universidad Autónoma del Estado de México, Toluca
Luz María Lara Hernández, Universidad Autónoma del Estado de México, Toluca
Esthela Ramírez Hernández, Universidad Autónoma del Estado de México, Toluca
Ma Guadalupe Peña Huerta, Universidad Autónoma del Estado de México, Toluca
Elsa Iruegas, Prepa Tec Campus Cumbres, Monterrey
María del Carmen Turral Maya, Universidad Autónoma del Estado de México, Toluca
Lima Melani Ayala Olvera, Universidad Autónoma del Estado de México, Toluca
Suraya Ordorica Reyes, Universidad Autónoma del Estado de México, Toluca
Leonor Rosales, Tecnológico de Monterrey, Monterrey
Leticia Adelina Ruiz Guerrero, ITESO, Jesuit University, Tlaquepaque

United States

Nancy Alaks, College of DuPage, Glen Ellyn, IL
Annette Barker, College of DuPage, Aurora, IL
Joyce Gatto, College of Lake County, Grayslake, IL
Donna Glade-Tau, Harper College, Palatine, IL
Mary "Katie" Hu, Lone Star College – North Harris, Houston, TX
Christy Naghitorabi, University of South Florida, St. Petersburg, FL

ASIA

Beri Ali, Cleverlearn (American Academy), Ho Chi Minh City
Ronald Anderson, Chonnam National University, Yeosu Campus, Jeollanam
Michael Brown, Canadian Secondary Wenzhou No. 22 School, Wenzhou
Leyi Cao, Macau University of Science and Technology, Macau
Maneerat Chuaychoowong, Mae Fah Luang University, Chiang Rai
Sooah Chung, Hwarang Elementary School, Seoul
Edgar Du, Vanung University, Taoyuan County
David Fairweather, Asahikawa Daigaku, Asahikawa
Andrew Garth, Chonnam National University, Yeosu Campus, Jeollanam
Brian Gaynor, Muroran Institute of Technology, Muroran-shi
Emma Gould, Chonnam National University, Yeosu Campus, Jeollanam
David Grant, Kochi National College of Technology, Nankoku
Michael Halloran, Chonnam National University, Yeosu Campus, Jeollanam
Nina Ainun Hamdan, University Malaysia, Kuala Lumpur
Richard Hatcher, Chonnam National University, Yeosu Campus, Jeollanam
Edward Tze-Lu Ho, Chihlee Institute of Technology, New Taipei City
Soontae Hong, Yonsei University, Seoul
Chaiyatip Katsura, Mae Fah Luang University, Chiang Rai
Byoug-Kyo Lee, Yonsei University, Seoul
Han Li, Aceleader International Language Center, Beijing
Michael McGuire, Kansai Gaidai University, Osaka
Yu Jin Ng, Universiti Tenaga Nasional, Kajang, Selangor
Somaly Pan, Royal University of Phnom Penh, Phnom Penh
HyunSuk Park, Halla University, Wonju
Bunroeun Pich, Build Bright University, Phnom Penh
Renee Sawazaki, Surugadai University, Annaka-shi
Adam Schofield, Cleverlearn (American Academy), Ho Chi Minh City
Pawadee Srisang, Burapha University, Chanthaburi Campus, Ta-Mai District
Douglas Sweetlove, Kinjo Gakuin University, Nagoya
Tari Lee Sykes, National Taiwan University of Science and Technology, Taipei
Monika Szirmai, Hiroshima International University, Hiroshima
Sherry Wen, Yan Ping High School, Taipei
Chris Wilson, Okinawa University, Naha City, Okinawa
Christopher Wood, Meijo University, Nagoya
Evelyn Wu, Minghsin University of Science and Technology, Xinfeng, Hsinchu County
Aroma Xiang, Macau University of Science and Technology, Macau
Zoe Xie, Macau University of Science and Technology, Macau
Juan Xu, Macau University of Science and Technology, Macau
Florence Yap, Chang Gung University, Taoyuan
Sukanda Yatprom, Mae Fah Luang University, Chiang Rai
Echo Yu, Macau University of Science and Technology, Macau

The publisher would like to extend a special thank you to Raúl Billini, English Coordinator, Mi Colegio, Dominican Republic, for his contributions to the series.

Listening	Speaking and Pronunciation	Reading	Writing	Video Journal
Listening for general understanding and specific information People describing their families	Talking about your family The /r/ sound	**National Geographic:** "Families around the World"	Writing sentences to describe your family	**National Geographic:** "Animal Families"
Focused listening People describing their jobs	Asking for and giving personal information Numbers Contractions with *be*	**National Geographic:** "Different Farmers"	Writing a paragraph to describe a person's job	**National Geographic:** "A Job for Children"
Listening for general understanding and specific details People talking about their houses	Describing your house Final −*s*	**TED**TALKS "Kent Larson: Brilliant Designs to Fit More People in Every City"	Writing descriptions of houses Writing Strategy: Topic Sentence	**National Geographic:** "A Very Special Village"
Listening for specific information People proving ownership	Talking about the personal possessions of others /iː/ and /ɪ/ sounds	**National Geographic:** "Jewelry"	Summarizing a class survey Using commas	**National Geographic:** "Uncovering the Past"
Listening for general understanding and specific details Describing a photographer's work	Asking and answering questions about work or school activities Falling intonation on statements and information questions	**TED**TALKS "Karen Bass: Unseen Footage, Untamed Nature"	Writing a job description	**National Geographic:** "Zoo Dentists"
Listening for specific information Radio ad for a tour	Ask for and give directions *Yes/no* questions and short answers	**National Geographic:** "Journey to Antarctica"	Writing a travel itinerary	**National Geographic:** "Volcano Trek"

	Unit Goals	Grammar	Vocabulary
UNIT 7 **Free Time** Page 82	• Identify activities that are happening now • Make a phone call • Talk about abilities • Talk about sports	Present continuous tense *I'm **not watching** TV. I'm **reading.*** *Can* (for ability) *He **can't** play the guitar. He **can** sing.*	Pastimes Games and sports
UNIT 8 **Clothes** Page 94	• Identify and shop for clothes • Buy clothes • Express likes and dislikes • Learn about clothes and colors	*Can/could* (for polite requests) ***Can** I try on these shoes?* Likes and dislikes *I **love** your sweater! She **hates** pink.*	Colors Clothes
UNIT 9 **Eat Well** Page 106	• Order a meal • Plan a party • Describe your diet • Talk about a healthy diet	*Some, any* *There's **some** ice cream in the fridge.* *How much/how many* ***How many** oranges do we need?* ***How much** chocolate do we have?*	Food types Meals Quantities Count/non-count nouns

TEDTALKS Video Page 118 **Ron Finley: A Guerilla Gardener in South Central L.A.** Video Strategy: Using Visual Cues

	Unit Goals	Grammar	Vocabulary
UNIT 10 **Health** Page 122	• Identify parts of the body to say how you feel • Ask about and describe symptoms • Identify remedies and give advice • Describe how to prevent health problems	Review of simple present tense *My back **hurts**.* *Look* + adjective *Feel* + adjective *John **looks** terrible. I **feel** sick.* *Should* (for advice) *You **should** take an aspirin.*	Parts of the body Common illnesses Remedies
UNIT 11 **Making Plans** Page 134	• Plan special days • Describe holiday traditions • Make life plans • Express wishes and plans	*Be going to* *What **are** you **going to** do?* *We **are going to** have a party.* *Would like to* (for wishes) *I **would like to** be a doctor.*	Special plans American holidays Professions
UNIT 12 **On the Move** Page 146	• Use the simple past • Give biographical information • Describe a move • Discuss migrations	Simple past tense *We **went** to the mountains.* *He **moved** from San Francisco to New York.*	Verbs + prepositions of movement Preparing to move

TEDTALKS Video Page 158 **Derek Sivers: Weird or Different?**

Listening	Speaking and Pronunciation	Reading	Writing	Video Journal
Listening for specific information Telephone conversation	Have a phone conversation /ʃ/ and /tʃ/ sounds *Can* and *can't*	**National Geographic:** "Soccer—The Beautiful Game"	Writing sentences about your abilities	**National Geographic:** "Danny's Challenge"
Listening for specific details Listening to people shopping for clothes	Describing people's clothes *Could you*	**National Geographic:** "Chameleon Clothes"	Writing about what people are wearing	**National Geographic:** "Traditional Silk-Making"
Listening for specific details Conversation to confirm a shopping list	Planning a dinner *And*	**TED**TALKS "Ron Finley: A Guerilla Gardener in South Central L.A."	Writing sentences about eating habits Writing Strategy: Self-Correct	**National Geographic:** "Slow Food"
Listening for general understanding and specific details Describing symptoms to a doctor	Describing symptoms and illnesses; giving advice Sentence stress	**National Geographic:** "Preventing Disease"	Writing a paragraph on disease prevention	**National Geographic:** "Farley, the Red Panda"
Listening for general understanding and specific details American holiday traditions	Talking about celebrating holidays *Be going to* (reduced form)	**TED**TALKS "Derek Sivers: Keep Your Goals to Yourself"	Writing about one's plans for the future	**National Geographic:** "Making a Thai Boxing Champion"
Listening for general understanding and specific details Biographies of famous immigrants	Discussing moving *—ed* endings	**National Geographic:** "Human Migration"	Writing a vacation postcard	**National Geographic:** "Monarch Migration"

BACKGROUND – LEARNING AND INSTRUCTION

Learning has been described as acquiring knowledge. Obtaining knowledge does not guarantee understanding, however. A math student, for example, could replicate any number of algebraic formulas, but never come to an *understanding* of how they could be used or for what purpose he or she has learned them. If understanding is defined as the ability to use knowledge, then learning could be defined differently and more accurately. The ability of the student to use knowledge instead of merely receiving information therefore becomes the goal and the standard by which learning is assessed.

This revelation has led to classrooms that are no longer teacher-centric or lecture driven. Instead, students are asked to think, ponder, and make decisions based on the information received or, even more productive, students are asked to construct learning or discover information in personal pursuits, or with help from an instructor, with partners, or in groups. The practice they get from such approaches stimulates learning with a purpose. The purpose becomes a tangible goal or objective that provides opportunities for students to transfer skills and experiences to future learning.

In the context of language development, this approach becomes essential to real learning and understanding. Learning a language is a skill that is developed only after significant practice. Students can learn the mechanics of a language but when confronted with real-world situations, they are not capable of communication. Therefore, it might be better to shift the discussion from "Language Learning" to "Communication Building." Communication should not be limited to only the productive skills. Reading and listening serve important avenues for communication as well.

FOUR PRINCIPLES TO DEVELOPING LEARNING ENVIRONMENTS

Mission: The goal or mission of a language course might adequately be stated as the pursuit of providing sufficient information and practice to allow students to communicate accurately and effectively to a reasonable extent given the level, student experiences, and time on task provided. This goal can be reflected in potential student learning outcomes identified by what students will be able to do through performance indicators.

World English provides a clear chart within the table of contents to show the expected outcomes of the course. The books are designed to capture student imagination and allow students ample opportunities to communicate. A study of the table of contents identifies the process of communication building that will go on during the course.

Context: It is important to identify what vehicle will be used to provide instruction. If students are to learn through practice, language cannot be introduced as isolated verb forms, nouns, and modifiers. It must have context. To reach the learners and to provide opportunities to communicate, the context must be interesting and relevant to learners' lives and expectations. In other words, there must be a purpose and students must have a clear understanding of what that purpose is.

World English provides a meaningful context that allows students to connect with the world. Research has demonstrated pictures and illustrations are best suited for creating interest and motivation within learners. National Geographic has a long history of providing magnificent learning environments through pictures, illustrations, true accounts, and video. The pictures, stories, and video capture the learners' imagination and "hook" them to learning in such a way that students have significant reasons to communicate promoting interaction and critical thinking. The context will also present students with a desire to know more, leading to life-long learning.

Objectives (Goals)

With the understanding that a purpose for communicating is essential, identifying precisely what the purpose is in each instance becomes crucial even before specifics of instruction have been defined. This is often called "backward design." Backward design means in the context of classroom lesson planning that first desired outcomes, goals, or objectives are defined and then lessons are mapped out with the end in mind, the end being what students will be able to do after sufficient instruction and practice. Having well-crafted objectives or goals provides the standard by which learners' performance can be assessed or self-assessed.

World English lessons are designed on two-page spreads so students can easily see what is expected and what the context is. The goal that directly relates to the final application activity is identified at the beginning. Students, as well as instructors, can easily evaluate their performance as they attempt the final activity. Students can also readily see what tools they will practice to prepare them for the application activity. The application activity is a task where students can demonstrate their ability to perform what the lesson goal requires. This information provides direction and purpose for the learner. Students, who know what is expected, where they are going, and how they will get there, are more apt to reach success. Each success builds confidence and additional communication skills.

Tools and Skills

Once the lesson objective has been identified and a context established, the lesson developer must choose the tools the learner will need to successfully perform the task or objective. The developer can choose among various areas in communication building including vocabulary, grammar and pronunciation. The developer must also choose skills and strategies including reading, writing, listening, and speaking. The receptive skills of reading and listening are essential components to communication. All of these tools and skills must be placed in a balanced way into a context providing practice that can be transferred to their final application or learner demonstration which ultimately becomes evidence of communication building.

World English units are divided into "lessons" that each consists of a two-page spread. Each spread focuses on different skills and strategies and is labeled by a letter (A-E). The units contain the following lesson sequence:

> A: Vocabulary
> B: Listening and Pronunciation
> C: Language Expansion
> D: Reading/Writing
> E: Video Journal

Additional grammar and vocabulary are introduced as tools throughout to provide practice for the final application activity. Each activity in a page spread has the purpose of developing adequate skills to perform the final application task.

LAST WORD

The philosophy of World English is to provide motivating context to connect students to the world through which they build communication skills. These skills are developed, practiced, and assessed from lesson to lesson through initially identifying the objective and giving learners the tools they need to complete a final application task. The concept of performance is highlighted over merely learning new information and performance comes from communicating about meaningful and useful context. An accumulation of small communication skills leads to true and effective communication outside of the classroom in real-world environments.

Friends and Family

About the Photo

Martin Schoeller is a photographer who specializes in portraits of people. His work has captured celebrities, families, and in the series these photos are from, the changing face of the United States. For an October 2013 story in *National Geographic* magazine, Schoeller took photos showing the changing look of the population of the United States as more and more people from around the world live together in the country.

- Introduce the words *friends* and *family*.
- Direct students' attention to the photos. With the class, look at each one and talk about the people in them.
- Write words students already know on the board. For example: *boy, woman, young*.
- Answer the questions with the class.

Answers: Answers will vary.

- Go over the Unit Goals with the class, explaining as necessary.
- For each goal, elicit any words students already know and write them on the board.

Teacher Tip:
Activate prior knowledge

It is helpful to activate students' prior knowledge before beginning a theme by asking questions and writing on the board any ideas students have, as suggested above. This helps prepare students for the new knowledge, as they can relate it to what they already know (in both their first language and English).

Around the world, people have friends and family that come from many different age groups and backgrounds.

2

UNIT 1 GOALS	Grammar	Vocabulary	Listening
• Meet and introduce people • Identify family members • Describe people • Present your family	Present tense *be* *I'm Kim. / They're Maria and Lola.* *Be* + adjective *They're young. / I am tall.* Questions with *be* and short answers *Are you married?* *Yes, I am/No, I'm not.*	Greetings and introductions Family members Adjectives to describe people	Listening for general understanding and specific information

Unit Theme Overview

- In this unit, students learn to introduce themselves and their families and friends. Even such a seemingly basic activity has interesting cultural variations.

- Customs for names vary greatly in different regions. English speakers commonly refer to their first name (given name) and last name (family name). In Asian countries, the family name is often written first. For example, in the Korean name Pak Jin-Ho, the man's family name is Pak and his given name is Jin-Ho. In Spanish-speaking countries, some people use both their father's and mother's family names. For example, in the name Francisco Cruz Rios, Francisco is his given name, Cruz is his father's family name, and Rios is his mother's family name. Informally, he is Francisco Cruz. In Islamic countries, some people use their father's given name after their own given name. For example, in the Islamic name Laila Ali Al-Ayubi, Laila is her given name, Ali is her father's name, and Al-Ayubi is her family name.

- There are also interesting differences in terminology for family relationships. English has comparatively few terms for different relationships. For example, the word *brother* is used for both an older brother and a younger brother (many languages have two different words). As even these simple examples show, learning a new language involves learning about other ways to see the world.

UNIT 1 GOALS

1. Meet and introduce people

2. Identify family members

3. Describe people

4. Present your family

3

Speaking	Reading	Writing	Video Journal
Talking about your family Describing people **Pronunciation:** The /r/ sound	**National Geographic:** "Families Around the World"	Writing a description of your family	**National Geographic:** "Animal Families"

Planning Ahead

Have students gather photos of their family. At least one photo should include as many members of their family as possible. They will need their family photos for the Communication activity on page 7 and for the Writing activity on page 12.

Meet and Introduce People

Vocabulary

A • Direct students' attention to the picture on the left. Ask: *Do they know each other? Are they friends?*

• Play the recording and have students listen. 🔊 2

• Point out the other expressions in the box. Draw faces to show words with similar meanings. *great* and *fine* = ☺ *OK* and *so-so* = ☺

• Then direct students' attention to the picture on the right. Ask: *Do they know each other?* Explain that we talk informally to friends and formally to people we don't know well.

• Point out the other expressions in the box. Explain the times of day when we use each greeting.

B • Tell students to walk around and greet three classmates informally.

C • Call on individual students to greet you formally.

D • Direct students' attention to the pictures and talk about the people.

• Play the recording and have students listen. Then play it again for the class to repeat. 🔊 3

E • Direct students' attention to the Real Language box. Have them repeat the question and answer. Have students introduce themselves to, and spell their names for, three classmates.

F • Divide the class into pairs to role-play introducing themselves formally.

G • Divide the class into groups of three to introduce each other.

• Call on students to introduce a group member to the whole class.

Word Focus

• Go over the letters in the English alphabet. Play the recording. Have students practice saying the alphabet to a partner. 🔊 4

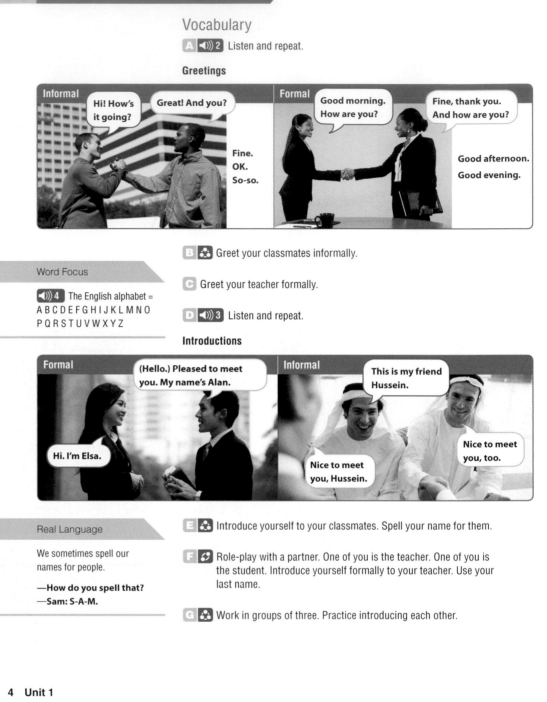

A   GOAL 1: Meet and Introduce People

Vocabulary

A 🔊 2 Listen and repeat.

Greetings

Informal
Hi! How's it going?
Great! And you?
Fine.
OK.
So-so.

Formal
Good morning. How are you?
Fine, thank you. And how are you?
Good afternoon.
Good evening.

B Greet your classmates informally.

C Greet your teacher formally.

Word Focus

🔊 4 The English alphabet =
A B C D E F G H I J K L M N O
P Q R S T U V W X Y Z

D 🔊 3 Listen and repeat.

Introductions

Formal
(Hello.) Pleased to meet you. My name's Alan.
Hi. I'm Elsa.

Informal
This is my friend Hussein.
Nice to meet you, too.
Nice to meet you, Hussein.

Real Language

We sometimes spell our names for people.

—**How do you spell that?**
—**Sam: S-A-M.**

E Introduce yourself to your classmates. Spell your name for them.

F Role-play with a partner. One of you is the teacher. One of you is the student. Introduce yourself formally to your teacher. Use your last name.

G Work in groups of three. Practice introducing each other.

4   Unit 1

For Your Information: Names in the classroom

This is a good opportunity to ask students to think about what they'd like to be called in class. Many will use their given names. Some may have a nickname or short version of their name that they want to use. Some learners may prefer a title like *Mr.* or *Ms.* followed by a surname. In turn, you can tell students how they should address you.

Grammar: Present tense *be*

The verb *be* may be difficult for learners whose languages do not have a similar structure. They may produce incorrect sentences such as *He John,* or *She a student.* If necessary, explain to the class that every English sentence must contain a verb and that *be* is a verb.

Grammar: Present tense *be*

Subject pronoun	Be	
I	am	
You	are	Kim.
He/She	is	
We	are	Lucas and Ed.
They	are	Maria and Claudia.

Contractions with *be*
I'm
you're
he's/she's
we're
they're

Possessive adjectives	
My	name is Mario.
Your	name is Rachel.
His	name is Robert.
Her	name is Liujun.
Their	names are Ben and Dan.

A Write the correct form of the verb *be*.

1. Their names ___are___ Julie and Les.
2. My name ___is___ Irwin.
3. I ___am___ Said.
4. We ___are___ Rigo and Rosana.
5. His name ___is___ Arata.
6. Your name ___is___ Yan-Ching.

B Unscramble the sentences.

1. Ron. name My is ___My name is Ron.___
2. Leila. is name Her ___Her name is Leila.___
3. is name Mr. Aoki. His ___His name is Mr. Aoki.___
4. Tim. Their Jan names are and ___Their names are Jan and Tim.___

C Write the sentences again. Use contractions.

1. He is Ruben. ___He's Ruben.___
2. I am Diego. ___I'm Diego.___
3. You are Rebecca. ___You're Rebecca.___
4. They are Ashley and Hana. ___They're Ashley and Hana.___

> **Real Language**
>
> When we introduce ourselves formally, we sometimes use our last name as well.
>
> Hello. My name's Peter Derby.

Conversation

A 🔊 5 Listen to the conversation.

Donna: Hi, Nick. How are you?
Nick: Great. And you?
Donna: Fine.
Nick: Donna, this is my friend Hiroshi.
Donna: Nice to meet you, Hir . . . sorry?
Hiroshi: It's Hiroshi. H-I-R-O-S-H-I. Nice to meet you, Donna.

B Practice the conversation in groups of three.

C Practice the conversation again. Use your own names.

D **GOAL CHECK** ✔ **Meet and introduce people**

Work in pairs. Find another pair and introduce each other.

Friends and Family **5**

Grammar

- Go over the first chart with the class. Read the sentences for them to repeat.
- Go over the chart of contractions.
- Introduce the possessive adjectives. Hold up your book and say, *It's my book,* and so forth.
- Some students will pronounce the word *is* as /ɪs/ rather than /ɪz/. Practice the pronunciation of this frequently used word with the class. Likewise, show that the *s* in *he's* and *she's* is pronounced /z/, but the *s* in *it's* sounds like /s/.

A
- Tell students to work individually.
- Have students compare answers with a partner.
- Check answers.

B
- Tell students to work individually. Explain the position of capital letters and punctuation within sentences.
- Check answers.

C
- Tell students to work individually.
- Check answers.
- Direct students' attention to the Real Language box. Call on a few students to introduce themselves.

Conversation

A
- Have students close their books. Play the recording. 🔊 5

B
- Play or read the conversation again for the class to repeat.
- Have students practice the conversation in groups and then switch roles and practice it again.

C
- Have students practice the conversation in groups of three using their own names.

D **GOAL CHECK** ✔

- Divide the class into pairs. Have them introduce themselves. Then combine student pairs to form groups of four, and have them take turns introducing their partners.

Grammar Practice: Name circle

Sit with the class in a circle. Begin by saying, *My name is _____ .* The student on your right then says, *Her/His name is _____ . My name is _____* OR *I'm _____ .* The next student says the names of all of those who have come before (using complete sentences). If a student forgets a name, he or she begins again with *My name is _____ .* Play until all students have had several turns and have learned most of the names of their classmates.

Identify Family Members

- Go over the family tree with the class. Pronounce the words for family members and have students repeat them.
- Ask any students who know any other family words in English to share them with the class.

Listening

A
- Tell students they are going to hear about a family. Have them look at the pictures.
- Play the recording. Have them point to the people as they hear about them. 🔊 6

B
- Tell students to work individually.
- Tell students to listen again and read the sentences. Have them answer *true* or *false*. 🔊 6
- Play the recording one or more times.
- Check answers.

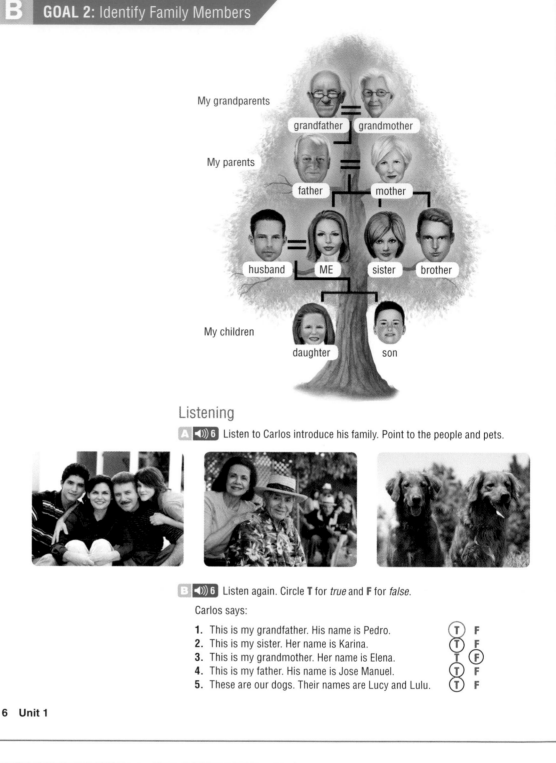

My grandparents
grandfather grandmother

My parents
father mother

husband ME sister brother

My children
daughter son

Listening

A 🔊 6 Listen to Carlos introduce his family. Point to the people and pets.

B 🔊 6 Listen again. Circle **T** for *true* and **F** for *false*.

Carlos says:

1. This is my grandfather. His name is Pedro.   (T) F
2. This is my sister. Her name is Karina.   (T) F
3. This is my grandmother. Her name is Elena.   T (F)
4. This is my father. His name is Jose Manuel.   (T) F
5. These are our dogs. Their names are Lucy and Lulu.   (T) F

6   Unit 1

For Your Information: Family members

In English, the word *brother* is used to refer to both an older and a younger male sibling, and *sister* can refer to an older or younger female sibling. This may differ from your students' language. Likewise, in English, *grandfather* refers to both the father's father and the mother's father, and *grandmother* refers to both the father's mother and the mother's mother. (Native speakers say, *my grandfather on my father's/mother's side*.) Be sure to clarify this for your students if necessary.

C 🔁 Correct any *false* sentences. Take turns to read all the sentences to a partner.

3. This is my mother. Her name is Elena.

D Fill in the blanks in Carlos's family tree.

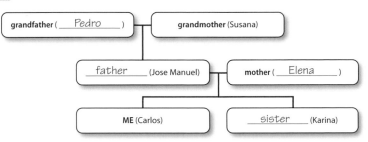

grandfather (_Pedro_)　　grandmother (Susana)

father (Jose Manuel)　　mother (_Elena_)

ME (Carlos)　　_sister_ (Karina)

E Complete the sentences.

1. Karina is Jose Manuel's _daughter_ .
2. Jose Manuel is Elena's _husband_ .
3. Susana and Pedro are Carlos's _grandparents_.
4. Karina is Carlos's _sister_ .
5. Karina's parents are _Jose Manuel_ and _Elena_ .

Pronunciation: The /r/ sound

A 🔊 7 Underline the letter *r*. Listen to the /r/ sound and repeat the word.

fathe<u>r</u>	siste<u>r</u>	<u>R</u>ick	<u>R</u>obe<u>r</u>t B<u>r</u>own
mothe<u>r</u>	b<u>r</u>othe<u>r</u>	<u>R</u>ose	Ma<u>r</u>y B<u>r</u>own

B 🔁 Take turns reading the words to a partner.

Communication

A Draw your own family tree.

B 🔁 Describe your family tree to a partner.

C 🔗 **GOAL CHECK** ✔ **Identify family members**

Bring some family photos to class. Introduce your family to your classmates.

> This is my grandmother. Her name is Aiko.

Friends and Family　**7**

Expansion Activity

With the class, draw the family tree of a celebrity who students are familiar with. Then have them work with a partner to talk about the relationships in the family.

Lesson B　**7**

Describe People

Language Expansion

- Present the vocabulary in the pictures. Give/elicit more examples using students' names: *Who is tall? Who has curly hair?* and so on.

A • Have students complete the sentence to describe themselves.
- Call on students to share their sentence with the class.

B • Divide the class into pairs. Have students take turns describing themselves and other students. Remind them to use the verb *be* with adjectives and *with* when describing hair.

C • Tell students to write a description of someone in the class.
- Have students read their description aloud to the class. The rest of the class guesses who it is. **Note:** In large classes, this can be done in groups of four rather than as a whole group activity.
- Direct students' attention to the Real Language box.

Grammar

- Go over the information in the chart. Point out that we can say *he/she isn't* or *he's not/she's not.* The meaning is the same. If necessary, remind students that all sentences in English must have a verb, and *be* is a verb.
- Give/elicit more examples.
- Present the information about short answers in the box. Go around the class asking students, *Are you old/young/single/married?* and so forth, and have them give short answers.
- Go over the formation of questions with *be* and give/elicit the pattern (the *be* verb comes first).

Language Expansion: Adjectives

He is tall with short black hair.

▲ curly black hair

▲ straight gray hair   ▲ wavy red hair

▲ straight blond hair   ▲ curly brown hair

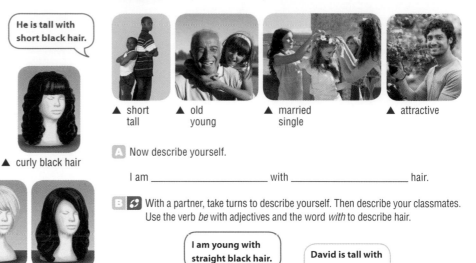

▲ short tall   ▲ old young   ▲ married single   ▲ attractive

A Now describe yourself.

I am _____ with _____ hair.

B 🔄 With a partner, take turns to describe yourself. Then describe your classmates. Use the verb *be* with adjectives and the word *with* to describe hair.

I am young with straight black hair.

David is tall with curly black hair.

C Describe a student to the class. The class guesses who you are describing.

Grammar: *Be* + adjective

Subject + *be* + adjective					
I	**am**	young.	Emily	**is**	young and short.
You	**are**	tall and handsome.	We	**are**	married.
John	**is**	old with gray hair.	They	**are**	tall with black curly hair.

Questions with *be* and short answers

Questions			Short answers	
Are	you	married?	Yes, I **am**.	No, I'**m not**.
Is	he/she	single?	Yes, he/she **is**.	No, he/she **isn't**. No, he'**s**/she'**s not**.
Are	they	married?	Yes, they **are**.	No, they'**re not**. No, they **aren't**.

Real Language

When we want to call someone *attractive*, we usually say *handsome* for a man, and *pretty* for a woman.

Word Bank:
More adjectives

divorced	sad
happy	thin
heavy	thirsty
hungry	tired
middle-aged	widowed

Teacher Tip: Group work

In order to promote as much student participation as possible, especially in large classes, it can be useful to have students work in small groups (three or four students), rather than with the whole class. For example, in **C** above, students can read their descriptions to their group rather than to the whole class. This will ensure that more students are participating at the same time.

A Match the questions and the answers.

Questions	Answers
1. Is your brother tall? _b_	a. Yes, she is.
2. Are your brothers married? _c_	b. No, he isn't. He's short.
3. Is Emma tall? _a_	c. Chen is married. Lee isn't.
4. Is your brother single? _e_	d. No, they're not.
5. Are your mother and father old? _d_	e. No, he isn't. He's married.

B Fill in the blanks with a question or an answer.

1. **Q:** Is she short _____?
   A: No, she isn't. She's tall.

2. **Q:** Is she tall with (red/black/brown/gray) hair _____?
   A: No, she isn't. She is short with blond hair.

3. **Q:** Is Alicia attractive?
   A: Yes, she is. / No, she isn't/she's not _____.

4. **Q:** Is she married _____?
   A: Yes, she is. Her husband's name is Marco.

Conversation

A  **8** Listen to the conversation.

Ana: Who's this in the photo?   **Ana:** Is <u>he</u> married?
Carol: It's my <u>brother</u>.   **Carol:** Yes, <u>he</u> is.
Ana: What's <u>his</u> name?   **Ana:** Too bad!
Carol: <u>Richard</u>.

B Practice the conversation with a partner. Switch roles and practice it again.

C Change the underlined words and make a new conversation.

D Take turns asking your partner questions about himself/herself. Then, introduce your partner to the class.

> This is Salma. That's S-A-L-M-A. She is young with curly brown hair.

E **GOAL CHECK** ✔ **Describe people**

Describe three people to your partner. They can be people you know or celebrities.

Friends and Family 9

A • Have students work individually to match the questions and answers.
   • Check answers.

B • Have students work individually to write questions or answers using the information provided and their own ideas.
   • Compare answers with the class.

Conversation

A • Tell students to listen to the conversation.
   • Play the recording. Explain that *Too bad!* means Ana is not happy. 🔊 **8**

B • Play or read the conversation again for the class to repeat. 🔊 **8**
   • Practice the conversation with the class in chorus.
   • Have students practice the conversation with a partner and then switch roles and practice it again.

C • Have students work with the same partner to change the underlined words to make a new conversation using their own ideas.
   • Call on student pairs to present their conversations to the class.

D • Have pairs take turns asking each other questions about themselves.
   • Then have students introduce their partners to the class.

E **GOAL CHECK** ✔

   • Divide the class into pairs and have them describe three people they know, or celebrities, to each other.

For Your Information: *Are you married?*

Students should be aware that *Are you married?* can be a sensitive question for English speakers. If a man asks a woman this question, it can sound as though he is romantically interested in her.

Grammar Practice: Questions with *be* and short answers

Bring in photos of famous people from newspapers and magazines. Ask the class questions about each person, such as *Is he/Are they young/old/married/single?* and have them give short answers. Then call on students to stand in front of the class and ask questions about the pictures.

Present Your Family

Reading

A
- Have students look at the two pictures. Call on different students to describe people in each family.
- Divide the class into pairs. Have them guess the family relations in each family.
- Have students read the article and confirm the family relations.

B
- Tell students to work individually and complete the sentences.
- Have students compare answers with a partner.
- Check the answers.

C
- Tell students to work individually and choose the correct answers.
- Have students compare answers with a partner.
- Check the answers.

Reading

A Look at the pictures. Guess the family relations.

> This man is married to this woman.

Now read and check your guesses.

B Complete the sentences with the words from the box.

> mother   long   son
> five   pretty   black

1. Rose is the ____mother____ of Bao.
2. Minh has ____black____ hair.
3. Trang and Thuy are ____pretty____.
4. Bachau and Mishri have ____five____ children.
5. Guddi and Aarti have ____long____ hair.
6. Anil is the ____son____ of Bachau.

C Circle the correct answers.

1. Her father is Anh Hoang.
   a. (Thuy)   **b.** Seema
2. His wife is Mishri.
   a. Anh   **b.** (Bachau)
3. Her brother is Bao.
   (**a.** Trang)   **b.** Guddi
4. Guddu is the brother of
   a. Minh   (**b.** Anil)
5. Their mother is Rose.
   a. (Thuy and Bao)   **b.** Guddi and Aarti

FAMILIES AROUND THE WORLD

This is the Hoang family. Let's start with the parents, Anh and Rose Hoang. They are married and have two sons and their names are Minh and Bao. Minh has short black hair. Bao's hair is a little longer. Anh's hair is longer than Minh's or Bao's. Anh and Rose have two daughters. Their names are Trang and Thuy. They are older than their brothers. They are both pretty and wear colorful clothing.

For Your Information: Family size

An important difference in families around the world is the number of children in a family. One way to measure this is by the average number of children that women give birth to within their lifetime. This number varies widely from country to country. In Mali, in West Africa, the average woman will have 6.2 children. The countries with the lowest numbers are Singapore (0.8 children), South Korea (1.2), and Lithuania (1.2). The world average is 2.5 children.

This is the Yadav family. Bachau and Mishri Yadav are married and they have five children. They have three girls: Guddi, Seema, and Aarti, and two boys: Guddu and Anil. Guddi and Aarti have long hair. The rest of the family has shorter hair. They spend a lot of time together. They are a happy family.

Friends and Family 11

After Reading
Divide the class into pairs and have them exchange information about their families, taking notes about what they hear. Then have them write sentences about their partner and his or her family.

Present Your Family

Communication

A • With the class, review adjectives for describing people.

• Divide the class into pairs. Have them take turns describing the pictures and guessing the names.

• Call on a student to describe one of the people. Have the class guess the name.

Writing

A • Have students take turns showing their photo to their partner and describing their family. Encourage them to ask each other questions. For example: *Who's this? What's his name? Is he married?*

B • Have students work individually and write descriptions of three members of their family.

• Have students exchange papers with a partner. Ask students to mark corrections and suggestions for improvements on their partner's paper.

• If desired, have students rewrite their papers, to be collected for marking.

C **GOAL CHECK** ✔

• Have students work with a different partner and take turns describing people in their families.

Communication

A Look at the pictures. Choose one picture. Describe that person to a partner. Your partner guesses who you are describing.

Martin Schoeller is famous for taking close-up photos. His subjects include famous people, twins, and the changing face of America. These are some of his photos.

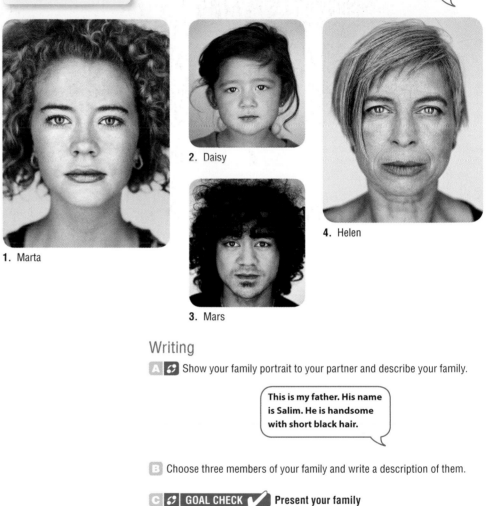

> She is tall with curly hair. She is young.

> Is it Marta?

> Yes, it is!

1. Marta

2. Daisy

3. Mars

4. Helen

Writing

A Show your family portrait to your partner and describe your family.

> This is my father. His name is Salim. He is handsome with short black hair.

B Choose three members of your family and write a description of them.

C **GOAL CHECK** ✔ **Present your family**

Work with a partner. Take turns describing your family.

12   Unit 1

Writing Tip

Whenever possible, it is helpful to give students some time to prepare their ideas before writing. This can be done by having them talk about the topic with a partner, as in **A** above, or by having them brainstorm ideas and write down key words and phrases.

Teacher Tip: Correcting writing

You can save a lot of time in marking student papers by using peer correction. Before students turn in a paper, have them exchange their work with a partner and mark any mistakes or problems they see on their partner's paper. Then have them make the corrections on their own papers before handing them in to you for marking.

VIDEO JOURNAL: *Animal Families* **E**

1. ___polar bears___

2. ___male gorilla___

3. ___meerkats___

4. ___female lion___

5. ___leopard___

Before You Watch

A Label the animals. Use the words in the box.

female lion	leopard
male gorilla	meerkats
polar bears	

While You Watch

A ▶ Watch the video. Circle **T** for *true* and **F** for *false*.

1. Polar bears have big families.   T (F)
2. Lions live in family groups.   (T) F
3. Meerkats are big.   T (F)
4. Female gorillas have gray (silver) hair on their backs.   T (F)

B ▶ Complete the sentences. Use the words in the box. Then watch the video again to check your answers.

| pretty | big | long | male |

1. A male lion has ___long___ hair on his neck.
2. Meerkats live in ___big___ groups.
3. Young meerkats are ___pretty___.
4. The ___male___ gorilla is the leader of the family.

After You Watch

A 🔄 What animals do you know that fit in these categories? With a partner, fill in the chart, then share your answers with the class.

	Big	Small
Live in groups	lions	bees
Live alone	polar bears	

Friends and Family **13**

Video Journal:
Animal Families
Before You Watch

A • Go over the pictures of animals and elicit any names the students already know.

• Then have students label the pictures using the words in the box.

• Check answers.

While You Watch

A • Tell students they are going to watch a video about animal families.

• Read the sentences with the class. Tell them to watch the video and answer *true* or *false*.

• Play the video.

• Have students compare answers with a partner.

• Check answers. Play the video again if necessary.

B • Tell students to watch the video again and complete the sentences. Have students read the sentences.

• Play the video.

• Have students compare answers with a partner.

• Check answers.

After You Watch

A • Tell students to work with a partner and write the names of other animals in the correct boxes of the chart. Remind students to ask themselves, *Is the animal big or small? Does it live alone or in groups?*

• Check answers. Answers will vary.

• Copy the chart onto the board and have students share answers by completing it together.

For Your Information: Meerkat

The meerkat is a small animal that lives in the deserts of Botswana and South Africa. Meerkats live in family groups called clans. A clan usually has about 25 members, but some have more than 50. Meerkats eat insects and work together to find them. One meerkat watches for predators while the others dig for insects. If a predator is near, the "guard" will bark a whistle to alert the clan. If everything is safe, the guard makes soft peeping sounds. Meerkats are social animals. They groom each other's fur, and female meerkats "babysit" each other's young.

Teacher Tip

Being given an opportunity to confirm and discuss answers with a peer can help students' understanding of a theme or language point and therefore increase their confidence in answering in front of the whole class.

Jobs Around the World

About the Photo

This photo shows workers in China painting a 140-meter-high (470 ft) cooling tower at a coal power plant in Huaibei, eastern China. The city of Huaibei is an important industrial and energy center because of the vast coal reserves in the province. The workers in the photo are applying a red rust-resistant paint to the tower first, and then they paint it black with waterproof paint. Painting at such a height is a very dangerous job. The workers wear harnesses and are tied to very strong ropes so they cannot fall. They also wear hard hats on their heads to protect them.

- Introduce the theme of the unit. Call on students to give the names of any jobs they know in English and list them on the board.

- For each goal, elicit words students already know and write them on the board. For example: what people do in the jobs they previously identified or country names.

- Direct students' attention to the photo. Have students describe what they see.

- Have students discuss the questions with a partner.

- Have several pairs share their answers with the class.

- With the class, talk about what the people are doing and where they might be from.

- Go over the Unit Goals with the class, explaining as necessary.

Workers paint a 140-meter-high tower at a factory in Huaibei, China.

14

UNIT 2 GOALS	Grammar	Vocabulary	Listening
• Identify jobs • Talk about jobs • Talk about countries • Compare jobs in different countries	Contractions with *be* (negative) He **isn't** a doctor. Indefinite articles Pat's **an** artist. *Be* + adjective + noun Russia **is a big country.**	Jobs Continents, countries, and cities Climate	Focused listening People describing their jobs

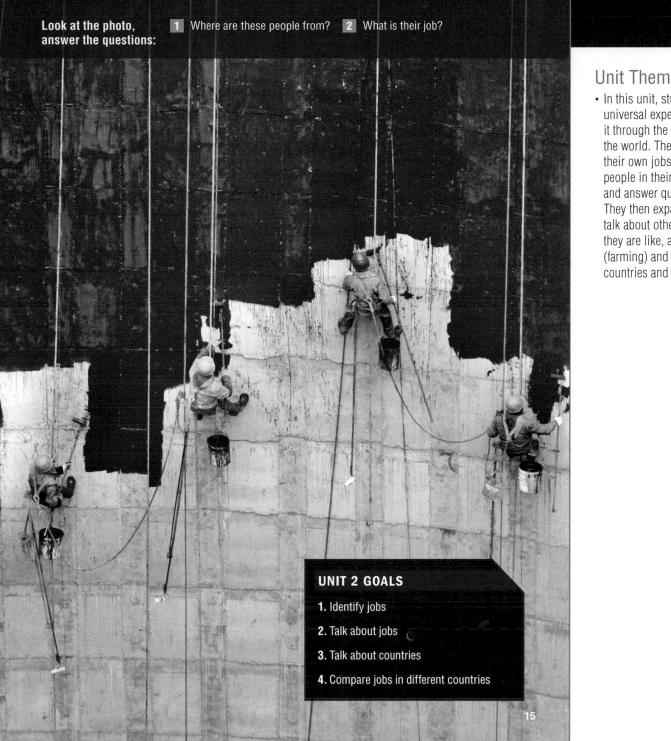

Unit Theme Overview

• In this unit, students look at the universal experience of work and see it through the eyes of people around the world. They first learn to talk about their own jobs and those of other people in their families, and to ask and answer questions about them. They then expand this perspective to talk about other countries and what they are like, and to consider one job (farming) and how it varies in different countries and situations.

UNIT 2 GOALS

1. Identify jobs

2. Talk about jobs

3. Talk about countries

4. Compare jobs in different countries

15

Speaking	Reading	Writing	Video Journal
Asking for and giving personal information **Pronunciation:** Numbers Contractions with *be*	**National Geographic:** "Different Farmers"	Writing sentences to describe people's jobs	**National Geographic:** "A Job for Children"

Identify Jobs

Vocabulary

A • Direct students' attention to the pictures and talk briefly about each one. Read the words in the box for students to repeat. Then tell them to listen and write the names of the jobs next to the names of the people in the pictures. Play the recording one or more times. 🔊 9

• Check answers.

B • Introduce the ideas of *interesting* and *boring*.

• Have students work individually to write the jobs from **A** on the lines, ranking them from the most boring to the most interesting.

C • Divide the class into pairs and have them compare their answers to **B**.

• Compare answers with the class. Ask for a show of hands: *Is* taxi driver *a boring job? Or is it interesting?*

Grammar

• Introduce the structure in the box. Tell the class, *I am a teacher.* Elicit sentences from the class: *I am a student/doctor/housewife.* (Teach the names of your students' occupations as necessary.) Continue with *He is, She is, You are, They are* and names of occupations.

• Introduce *not.* Tell students, *I am not a doctor.* Elicit sentences from the class: *I am not a chef/taxi driver,* and so on. Continue with *He is not, She is not, You are not,* and so on.

• Present the contractions. Explain that these are short forms.

• Point out the use of *a* and *an.* If necessary, explain that the vowels in English are *a, e, i, o,* and *u,* and the other sounds are consonants.

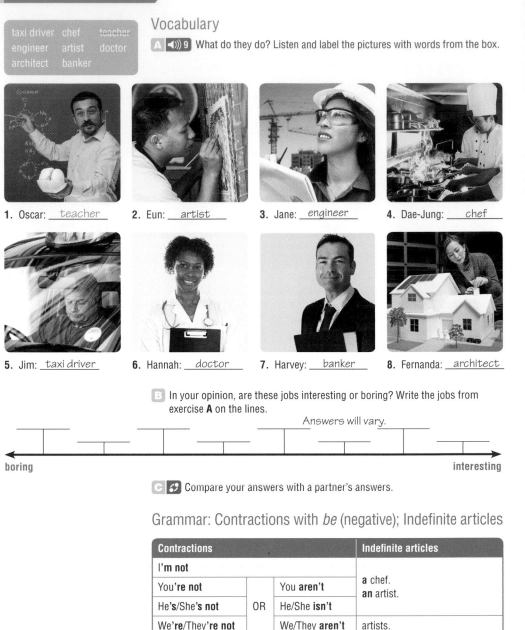

A GOAL 1: Identify Jobs

Vocabulary

taxi driver	chef	~~teacher~~
engineer	artist	doctor
architect	banker	

A 🔊 9 What do they do? Listen and label the pictures with words from the box.

1. Oscar: _teacher_   2. Eun: _artist_   3. Jane: _engineer_   4. Dae-Jung: _chef_

5. Jim: _taxi driver_   6. Hannah: _doctor_   7. Harvey: _banker_   8. Fernanda: _architect_

B In your opinion, are these jobs interesting or boring? Write the jobs from exercise **A** on the lines.

Answers will vary.

boring ←————————————————————————→ interesting

C 🔄 Compare your answers with a partner's answers.

Grammar: Contractions with *be* (negative); Indefinite articles

Contractions			Indefinite articles
I**'m not**			**a** chef.
You**'re not**	OR	You **aren't**	**an** artist.
He**'s**/She**'s not**		He/She **isn't**	
We**'re**/They**'re not**		We/They **aren't**	artists.
			*We use *a* before a consonant sound.
			*We use *an* before a vowel sound.

16   Unit 2

Word Bank: Jobs

accountant	homemaker	reporter
actor	nurse	salesperson
athlete	office worker	scientist
computer programmer	pharmacist	secretary
electrician	professor	writer
government employee		

Teacher Tip

When the letter *o* is stressed and between consonants, it is usually pronounced as /a/, not /o/. Help students who have trouble with this pronunciation. Examples of this include the words *job* and *doctor.*

A Look at the pictures on the opposite page. Fill in the blanks with *is* or *is not*.

1. Jim _____is_____ a taxi driver. He ___is not___ a doctor.
2. Oscar _____is_____ a teacher. He ___is not___ an architect.
3. Fernanda _____is_____ an architect. She ___is not___ a doctor.
4. Dae-Jung ___is not___ an engineer. He _____is_____ a chef.
5. Eun ___is not___ a banker. He _____is_____ an artist.

B Fill in the blanks with *a* or *an*. Then circle **T** for *true* and **F** for *false*.

1. Hannah is __a__ taxi driver.   T   (F)
2. Jane is __an__ engineer.   (T)   F
3. Dae-Jung is __an__ artist.   T   (F)
4. Eun is not __a__ doctor.   (T)   F
5. Harvey is not __an__ architect.   (T)   F

C 🔁 Correct the false sentences in your notebook. Read the new sentences to a partner. 1. Hannah isn't/'s not a taxi driver. She's a doctor.
3. Dae-Jung isn't/'s not an artist. He's a chef.

▲ This is Aran. Describe him. What is his job?

Conversation

A 🔊 **10** Listen to the conversation. Is Jill married or single? *Single*

Mary: Hi, Jean. How's life?
Jean: Fine. And you?
Mary: Great. How are the children?
Jean: They're good. But they're not children now. Jim's married. He's <u>an engineer</u>.
Mary: <u>Wow</u>! Time passes. And what about Jill? How old is she now?
Jean: She's <u>21</u> and she's <u>a student</u>.
Mary: Is she married?
Jean: No, she's single.

B 🔁 Practice the conversation with a partner. Switch roles and practice it again.

C 🔁 Change the underlined words and make a new conversation.

D ♻ **GOAL CHECK** ✔ **Identify jobs**

Ask your classmates about their jobs. Ask them about the jobs of people in their families.

> **Real Language**
>
> To show surprise, we can say:
> formal ◄———► informal
> *Really!   Amazing!   Wow!*

> **What do you do?**

> **What does your father do?**

Jobs Around the World   **17**

Grammar: Contractions

Some students may think that contractions aren't good English. Explain to students that native speakers use contractions in speaking and in informal writing. Using contractions will help make students' English more natural.

Grammar Practice

Bring in photos from newspapers and magazines and have the class discuss and try to guess the people's jobs. This can also be done in small groups. Give each group one picture and then have them tell the class about the person in the picture.

A • Tell students to look back at the photos on page 16 and complete the sentences.
• Have students compare answers with a partner.
• Check answers.

B • Have students work individually. Point out that they need to do two things: insert *a* or *an*, and decide if the sentences are *true* or *false*.
• Have students compare answers with a partner.
• Check answers.

C • Divide the class into pairs and have them correct the false sentences.
• Check answers.

Conversation

A • Tell students to listen to the conversation and find the answer.
• Play the recording. 🔊 **10**
• Check answer.
• Point out the expressions for surprise in the Real Language box. If necessary, explain the ideas of *informal* and *formal*.

B • Play or read the conversation again for the class to repeat.
• Practice the conversation with the class in chorus.
• Have students practice the conversation with a partner and then switch roles and practice it again.

C • Have students work with the same partner to make a new conversation.
• Call on pairs to present their conversation to the class.

D ♻ **GOAL CHECK** ✔

• Divide the class into groups of four or five students and have them take turns asking and answering questions about the jobs of their family members.

Talk About Jobs

Listening

A • Have students look at and describe each person. For example: *He has short brown hair,* etc. Tell them to guess each person's job.

• Play the recording. Have students check their answers. 🔊 11

B • Direct students' attention to the Real Language box. Point out the questions and answers about age.

• Tell students they are going to hear the people talking again about their jobs.

• Play the recording one or more times and have students complete the chart. 🔊 11

• Have students compare answers with a partner.

• Check answers.

C • Present or review numbers in English. Tell students to listen as you read the numbers aloud.

• Read the numbers again and have students repeat after you.

• Divide the class into pairs and have them take turns reading the numbers in English.

D • Model the questions with a student. Have another student ask you the questions.

• Have students ask their classmates the questions and write down the answers.

• In small groups, have students draw graphs to show the range of ages in the class. Assign each group a different age category: students in the class, their parents, their grandparents.

• Have each group share their graph with the whole class.

B **GOAL 2:** Talk About Jobs

▲ Michelle

▲ Carlos

▲ Salim

Real Language

To ask about someone's age, we say: *How old is he/she?* We answer like this: *She's/He's 28 years old.*

Listening

A 🔊 11 Look at the pictures. Guess each person's age and job. Listen and check your guesses.

B 🔊 11 Listen again. Fill in the blanks in the chart.

	Michelle	Carlos	Salim
How old is he/she?	35	43	34
What is his/her job?	artist	taxi driver	architect
Is his/her job interesting?	yes	no	yes

C 🔄 Work with a partner. Take turns reading the numbers in English.

Numbers	10 ten	20 twenty	30 thirty
1 one	11 eleven	21 twenty-one	40 forty
2 two	12 twelve	22 twenty-two	50 fifty
3 three	13 thirteen	23 twenty-three	60 sixty
4 four	14 fourteen	24 twenty-four	70 seventy
5 five	15 fifteen	25 twenty-five	80 eighty
6 six	16 sixteen	26 twenty-six	90 ninety
7 seven	17 seventeen	27 twenty-seven	100 one hundred
8 eight	18 eighteen	28 twenty-eight	101 one hundred
9 nine	19 nineteen	29 twenty-nine	and one

D 👥 Take a survey of your classmates. Ask these questions:

1. What is your name?
2. How old are you?
3. How old are your parents?
4. How old are your grandparents?

For Your Information: How old are you?

This can be a sensitive question in English-speaking cultures. Traditionally, women wanted to appear younger than they really were, and many women did not like to tell their age. This is slowly changing, but in general it's not polite for a young person to ask an older person's age in social conversation. You may need to explain this to your students if ages and age differences are commonly discussed in their culture.

Pronunciation: Numbers

A 🔊 **12** Listen and circle what you hear.

1. six   sixteen   (sixty)
2. four   (fourteen)   forty
3. three   thirteen   (thirty)
4. (seven)   seventeen   seventy
5. eight   (eighteen)   eighty

B 🔊 **13** Listen and write the numbers.

1. I have ____three____ brothers and ____two____ sisters.
2. Alan is ____sixteen____ and his grandfather is ____sixty____.
3. We have ____three____ children. Bae is ____fifteen____,
   Chin Ho is ____eleven____, and Dong-Min is ____five____.
4. There are ____twenty-seven____ students in the class.

C 🔁 Work with a partner. Take turns reading the sentences in **B**.

Pronunciation: Contractions with *be*

A 🔊 **14** Listen and circle what you hear.

1. **A:** Is Fatima an artist?   **B:** No, ((she isn't) | she's not) an artist. ((She's) | She is) a doctor.
2. **A:** Are Bill and Jane married?   **B:** No, ((they aren't) | they're not) married. ((They're) | They are) single.
3. **A:** Look! A leopard!   **B:** ((It's) | It is) a lion. ((It isn't) | It's not) a leopard.
4. **A:** Are they teachers?   **B:** No, (they aren't | (they're not)). (They're | (They are)) students!

B 🔁 Listen again. Take turns practicing the conversations in **A** with a partner.

Communication

A 🔷 Read the questions and answer them for yourself. Use a dictionary if you need to. Then ask two classmates the questions. Write their answers.

Questions	Me	Classmate 1	Classmate 2
What is your name?			
How old are you?			
What is your job?			
Is it interesting?			

B 🔁 GOAL CHECK ✓ **Talk about jobs**

Tell a partner about the people you interviewed.

▲ He's a photographer. Is his job interesting?

Ivan is 27 years old and he's a chef.

His job is interesting.

Pronunciation: Numbers

A • Tell students to listen to the recording and circle the number they hear.
• Play the recording one or more times. 🔊 **12**
• Have students compare answers with a partner.
• Check answers.

B • Have students read the sentences as they listen and write the numbers. 🔊 **13**
• Have students compare answers with a partner.
• Play the recording again.
• Check answers.

C • Divide the class into pairs and have students take turns reading the sentences in **B** to each other.

Pronunciation: Contractions with *be*

A • Have students read the conversations as they listen and circle what they hear. 🔊 **14**
• Have students compare answers with a partner.
• Play the recording again.
• Check answers.

B • Divide the class into pairs and have students take turns practicing the conversations in **A.**

Communication

A • Have students work individually to complete the column for *Me.*
• Have students stand up with their books and pens, and walk around the class to talk to two classmates.

B 🔁 GOAL CHECK ✓
• Divide the class into pairs and have them talk about what they learned about their classmates.

Expansion Activity

Have each student make up a new identity with a new name and job (give help as needed with names of jobs). Then have them draw a chart on a piece of paper like in **Communication A** and repeat the steps of the activity to talk about their "new" name and job.

Talk About Countries

Language Expansion

- Introduce the words *country, city,* and *capital* by giving examples.
- Pronounce the names of the countries and cities on the map and have students repeat them.
- Direct students' attention to the Word Focus box. Point out that we need to use *the* with these two countries.
- Present the names of neighboring countries and countries that are currently in the news. Write them on the board.
- Go over the words for climate. Ask, *Is our country/city wet/hot/cold/ dry?* Elicit, *Yes, it is./No, it isn't.*

A • Have students work individually to guess the name of each country.
- Have students compare answers with a partner.
- Check answers.

Grammar

- Present the information in the box. Introduce the term *adjective* and elicit examples the students have learned: *old/young, interesting/ boring, hot/cold,* and so forth. Point out the placement of the adjective before the noun.

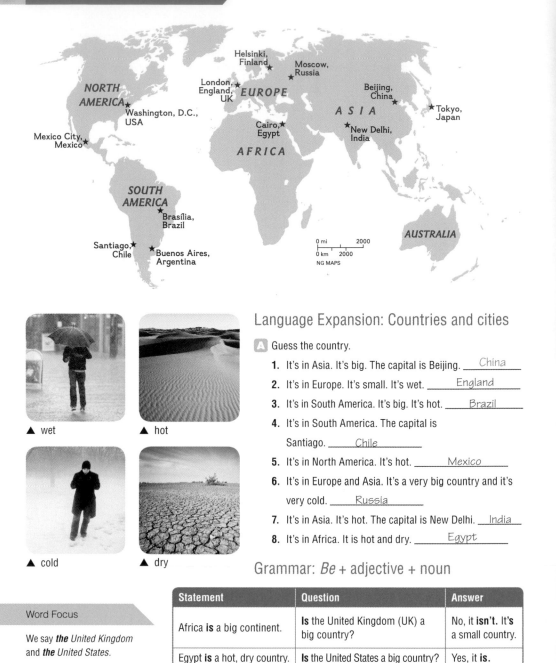

C **GOAL 3:** Talk About Countries

▲ wet

▲ hot

▲ cold

▲ dry

Word Focus

We say **the** *United Kingdom* and **the** *United States.*

Language Expansion: Countries and cities

A Guess the country.

1. It's in Asia. It's big. The capital is Beijing. ____China____
2. It's in Europe. It's small. It's wet. ____England____
3. It's in South America. It's big. It's hot. ____Brazil____
4. It's in South America. The capital is Santiago. ____Chile____
5. It's in North America. It's hot. ____Mexico____
6. It's in Europe and Asia. It's a very big country and it's very cold. ____Russia____
7. It's in Asia. It's hot. The capital is New Delhi. __India__
8. It's in Africa. It is hot and dry. ____Egypt____

Grammar: *Be* + adjective + noun

Statement	Question	Answer
Africa **is** a big continent.	**Is** the United Kingdom (UK) a big country?	No, it **isn't.** It**'s** a small country.
Egypt **is** a hot, dry country.	**Is** the United States a big country?	Yes, it **is.**

Word Bank: Countries

Africa: Kenya, Morocco, Nigeria, South Africa
Asia: India, Indonesia, the Philippines, Thailand
Europe: France, Germany, Italy, Spain
Central America: El Salvador, Guatemala, Honduras, Nicaragua
North America: Canada
South America: Colombia, Ecuador, Peru, Venezuela

Grammar:
Be + adjective + noun

In contrast to some other languages, English requires a verb (such as *be*) to be used with adjectives and adjective + noun. Emphasize to your students that every sentence in English needs a verb, and *be* is a verb.

▲ Cairo is the capital of Egypt.

A Unscramble the sentences and questions.

1. China Is a country? big   *Is China a big country?*

2. big The is a country. United States   *The United States is a big country.*

3. is a Russia country. cold   *Russia is a cold country.*

4. Is hot Egypt a country?   *Is Egypt a hot country?*

5. country? small Japan Is a   *Is Japan a small country?*

B Answer the questions.

1. Is Mexico a cold country?   *No, it isn't. It's a hot country.*

2. Is Chile a big country?   *Yes, it is.*

3. Is Japan a hot country?   *No, it isn't. It's a cold country.*

4. Is the UK a small country?   *Yes, it is.*

5. Is Egypt a wet country?   *No, it isn't. It's a dry country.*

Conversation

A 🔊 15 Listen to the conversation. Where is Mohamed from? *Cairo, Egypt*

Chris:	Where do you come from, <u>Mohamed</u>?		**Chris:**	So, tell me about <u>Egypt, Mohamed</u>.
Mohamed:	I'm from <u>Cairo</u>.		**Mohamed:**	Well, it's in <u>Africa—North Africa</u>.
Chris:	<u>Cairo</u> is in <u>Egypt</u>, right?		**Chris:**	Is it a <u>hot</u> country?
Mohamed:	Yes.		**Mohamed:**	Yes, it's <u>very hot</u>.

B 🔄 Practice the conversation with a partner. Switch roles and practice it again.

C 🔄 Change the underlined words and make a new conversation.

D 🔄 **GOAL CHECK** ✔ **Talk about countries**

Talk to a partner. Choose a country. Write a description of the country. Read it to the class. The class has to guess the country.

Jobs Around the World   **21**

A • Have students work individually to write the sentences and questions.
• Have students compare answers with a partner.
• Check answers.

B • Have students work individually to write the answers.
• Have students practice asking and answering the questions with a partner.
• Check answers. Students may have different opinions about answers depending on which country they are from. Discuss any differences.

Conversation

A • Have students listen to the conversation to answer the question.
• Play the recording. 🔊 15
• Check answers.

B • Play or read the conversation again for the class to repeat.
• Practice the conversation with the class in chorus.
• Have students practice the conversation with a partner and then switch roles and practice it again.

C • Have students work with the same partner to make a new conversation.
• Call on several pairs to present their conversation to the class.

D 🔄 **GOAL CHECK** ✔

• Write a short description of a country on the board and have students guess the country.
• Have students work with a partner and choose a country and write a description.
• Have students read their descriptions to the class for the class to guess the country. In large classes, this can be done in small groups.

Expansion Activity

Have students research a country in a different region of the world than the one in which they live. Have them find out about the country's size, climate, and capital city. Divide the class into small groups and have students present their information to their group.

Compare Jobs in Different Countries

Reading

A • Have students look at the pictures and describe what they see.

• Have students say where they think the farmers are from.

B • Have students read the article to complete the sentences. Tell them to circle any words in the article that they don't understand.

• Have students compare answers with a partner.

• Check answers.

• Go over the article with the class, answering questions from the students about vocabulary.

C • Have students work individually to answer the questions, giving short answers.

• Have students compare answers with a partner.

• Check answers.

Reading

A Look at the pictures. These people are farmers. Where do you think they come from?

B Read and complete the sentences.

1. Sofia and Yaroslaw are from _____Poland_____.

2. They are _____farmers_____.

3. Their potatoes go to countries like _____Germany_____ and _____England_____.

4. Jose is from _____Mexico_____.

5. He grows _____maize_____ and _____beans_____.

6. He is _____married_____ with three _____(small) children_____.

C Answer the questions.

1. Do Sofia and Yaroslaw come from Peru?
   No, they don't. (They come from Poland.)

2. Is it hot in Poland in the summer?
   No, it isn't. (It's cool and wet.)

3. Is their farm big?
   Yes, it is. (It is 55 hectares.)

4. Is Jose married?
   Yes, he is.

5. Is he a potato farmer?
   No, he isn't. (He is a maize farmer.)

6. Is it hot in Mexico in the summer?
   Yes, it is.

22   Unit 2

DIFFERENT FARMERS

Sofia is from Poland and she and her husband, Yaroslaw, are potato farmers. They have a big farm of about 55 hectares. The weather in Poland is good for potatoes because it is cool and wet in the summer. People in Poland eat a lot of potatoes. Some of the potatoes are for their family but they sell some of their potatoes to other countries, like Germany and England.

For Your Information: Poland and Mexico

Poland is a republic in Central Europe. It joined the European Union in 2004. In the north, the country has low plains with many small lakes. This geography makes good farmland. The only mountains are the Carpathians on the southern border. Mining is also important in Poland; there are many mineral resources, including iron, copper, and rock salt. There is even an old salt mine with a complete town inside. The mine no longer produces salt, but the underground town is a tourist attraction.

Mexico is in North America. It is a republic of federated states with 31 states and a Federal District, where Mexico City, the capital, is located. Mexico is very diverse in geography, climate, and plant and animal species. There are high mountains and canyons in the center of the country, large deserts in the north, and rain forests in the south. This diversity results in a large variety of crops from tomatoes to sugar cane to coffee. Mining, manufacturing, and tourism are also important industries.

Jose is also a farmer and he comes from Yucatan in Mexico. He is twenty-four years old and he is married with three small children. He is not a potato farmer. He is a maize farmer, and he also grows beans. The summer in Mexico is very hot and wet, and this is good for maize and beans. His wife makes *tortillas* from the maize and their children love tortillas with beans.

Jobs Around the World 23

For Your Information: Farming
The methods used for farming differ greatly from culture to culture, but farming and agriculture provide most of the world's food and fabrics. Before learning how to farm, most people spent their lives looking for food. They hunted and gathered wild plants. About 11,500 years ago, people learned how to grow crops and stay in one place, and by 2,000 years ago, the majority of humanity depended on farming. This led to the first permanent human settlements and civilizations.

Compare Jobs in Different Countries

Communication

A • Have students name two or three jobs. Write them on the board as a list. Then tell students to continue the list in their notebooks.

B • Have students compare their lists with a partner and identify three jobs which they think are interesting, and three they think are boring.

C • Tell students to look at the pictures and discuss the questions with their partner.

• Compare answers with the whole class.

Writing

A • Call on students to read the paragraph about Aapti.

• Have students work individually to complete a paragraph about Henry. Tell them to use the paragraph about Aapti as a model.

• Tell students to exchange papers with a partner. Ask them to mark corrections and suggestions for improvements on their partner's paper.

• If desired, have students rewrite their papers, to be collected for marking.

B 🔁 **GOAL CHECK** ✔

• Have students work in pairs to talk about farmers in their country.

Writing Tip

Editing and rewriting written work is an important stage of the writing process. Having students edit their own work, or peer edit work like that in **Writing A,** helps them notice their own mistakes and self-correct. Self-correction is often more beneficial to students' learning than teacher correction. By working out the correct language for themselves, they are more likely to remember it.

D **GOAL 4:** Compare Jobs in Different Countries

▲ Aapti

▲ Henry

Aapti is from Nepal. She is a farmer, but her farm is very small. She grows rice. Her rice does not go to other countries. It is for her family.

Communication

A In your notebook, make a list of jobs you know.

B 🔁 Compare your list with a partner. Name three jobs that are interesting. Name three jobs that are boring.

C 🔁 Look at the pictures. Discuss the following questions with a partner.

1. Where do you think these people are from?
2. What do they do?
3. Are they old or young?
4. Are their jobs interesting?

Writing

A Read about Aapti. Write a similar paragraph about Henry. Use these words: United States, big, wheat, Asia.

_____

_____

_____

_____

_____

B 🔁 **GOAL CHECK** ✔ Compare jobs in different countries

Talk to a partner about farmers in your country. What do they grow? What is the weather like? Are their jobs interesting or boring?

For Your Information: Icelandic puffins

One of the world's largest colonies of puffins lives in Iceland. Of the 8 to 10 million puffins that live there, as many as 3 million breed there.

The Westmann Islands in Iceland are an important breeding site. Puffins are allowed to be harvested, but they are also saved. Puffins have been an important source of food for people living on the islands. However, Icelanders have been careful not to decimate the population. In fact, a "Puffin Patrol" helps pufflings (baby puffins) get to sea when they get lost.

In the early 1900s, the puffin was nearly made extinct in the Westmann Islands because of harvesting. Besides being hunted for food, they were also hunted for their down, which was exported. A 30-year ban was placed and it was only lifted once the puffin colonies recuperated. Icelanders are very protective of their puffin colonies.

Video Journal:
A Job for Children

Before You Watch

A • Divide the class into pairs and have them answer the questions.

• Compare answers with the class.

While You Watch

A • Tell students they are going to watch a video about a job children do. Have students read the sentences. Tell them to watch the video and answer *true* or *false*.

• Play the video.

• Have students compare answers with a partner.

• Check answers.

B • Have students read the sentences. Tell them to complete them with words or phrases from the box as they watch.

• Play the video.

• Have students compare answers with a partner.

• Check answers.

After You Watch

A • Elicit information about what the puffin patrol does. Ask students to refer to the pictures for their ideas.

• Divide the class into pairs and have them take turns describing the job of the puffin patrol.

Before You Watch

A ⟳ Work with a partner. Look at the pictures. Answer these questions.

1. What do these children do?
   They rescue puffins.
2. Is their job interesting?
   Yes, it is.

While You Watch

A ▶ Watch the video. Circle **T** for *true* and **F** for *false*.

1. Puffin patrols look for bird nests.   T   (F)
2. There are puffin nests in the cliffs.   (T)   F
3. All the puffins fly out to sea.   T   (F)
4. Some puffins get lost in town.   (T)   F
5. Puffin patrols rescue pufflings.   (T)   F

B ▶ Complete the sentences with the words or phrases in the box. Watch the video again to check your answers.

| look for   leave   throw   get lost |

1. Some puffins _get lost_ in town.
2. The pufflings _leave_ the cliffs.
3. The children _throw_ the pufflings out to sea.
4. The puffin patrols _look for_ the lost pufflings in parking lots.

After You Watch

A ⟳ Work with a partner. Take turns describing the job of the puffin patrols.

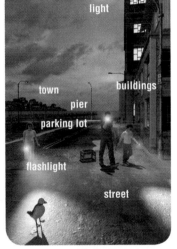

▲ A puffin patrol looks for and rescues lost pufflings.

Jobs Around the World   25

Teacher Tip: Starting and ending group and pair work

To make group and pair work go smoothly, it's helpful to use clear signals for beginning and ending the task. Some ideas:

• Write starting and ending times on the board (Group work starts: 10:15. Group work ends: 10:25.)

• Tell your students that group work ends when you clap your hands three times.

• Train your students so that when they see you raise your hand, they will also raise their hands and stop talking. The room will fall silent without you interrupting.

Houses and Apartments

Houses and Apartments

About the Photo

This photo shows part of Palm Jumeirah, an artificial island in the shape of a palm tree off the coast of Dubai. It is the largest man-made island in the world. The island is connected to the mainland by a 300-meter (985 ft) bridge. The buildings shown in the photo are on the fronds of the palm tree. Palm Jumeirah has hotels, restaurants, and shopping areas, and is a big tourist attraction, but there are also houses and apartments where people live. Palm Jumeirah is the first of three planned island resorts in Dubai.

- Introduce the theme of the unit. Ask students, *Do you have a house? Do you have an apartment?*

- Direct students' attention to the picture. Have students say how the houses are similar to or different from houses in their country.

- Have students discuss the questions with a partner.

- Have several pairs share their answers with the class.

- Go over the Unit Goals with the class, explaining as necessary.

- For each goal, elicit any words students already know and write them on the board.

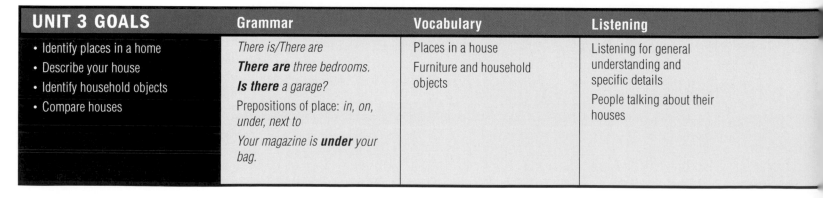

The "fronds" of the $14-billion Palm Jumeirah—the first of three planned resort islands in Dubai, United Arab Emirates—jut into the Persian Gulf.

26

UNIT 3 GOALS	Grammar	Vocabulary	Listening
• Identify places in a home • Describe your house • Identify household objects • Compare houses	*There is/There are* **There are** *three bedrooms.* **Is there** *a garage?* Prepositions of place: *in, on, under, next to* *Your magazine is* **under** *your bag.*	Places in a house Furniture and household objects	Listening for general understanding and specific details People talking about their houses

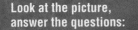

Unit Theme Overview

• The houses and apartments we live in are an expression of our culture and our identity, but they also show many similarities because of the shared human experience around the world. In this unit, students learn to talk about the common features of houses and apartments and also examine what makes each home unique. They begin by learning the names of rooms and parts of a house/apartment and practice describing their own and other houses. They learn vocabulary for furniture and common household appliances and talk about where these things are located. Finally, they learn about a new idea by TED speaker Kent Larson for housing people in growing cities.

UNIT 3 GOALS

1. Identify places in a home

2. Describe your house

3. Identify household objects

4. Compare houses

27

Speaking	Reading	Writing	Video Journal
Describing your house Compare homes **Pronunciation:** Final -s	**TED Talks:** "Kent Larson: Brilliant Designs to Fit More People in Every City"	Writing descriptions of houses Writing strategy: topic sentences	**National Geographic:** "A Very Special Village"

Identify Places in a Home

Vocabulary

A • Have students look at the picture. Go over the names of the areas of the house, and pronounce them for students to repeat. Ask students which rooms are in their house or apartment.

• Have students work individually to label the rooms in the apartment.

• Have students compare answers with a partner.

• Check answers.

B • Have students work individually to look at the picture and complete the sentences using words from the box.

• Have students compare answers with a partner.

• Check answers.

Grammar

• Introduce the structure. Say, *What's in our classroom? There is a teacher/window/clock*, and so forth. (Point to the items.) *There are ten desks/two computers*, and so forth. Elicit more answers from the class.

• Go over the information on how to make questions and short answers in the boxes.

• Point out that regular nouns can be made plural by adding *-s* or *-es*.

• Have students give examples of more plural objects in the classroom. Write them on the board.

A | **GOAL 1:** Identify Places in a Home

Vocabulary

A Label the rooms in the floor plan of the apartment.

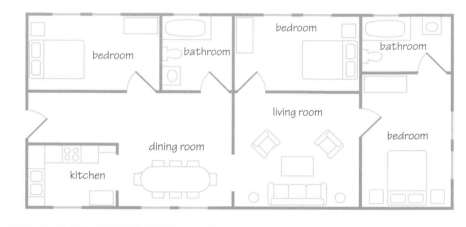

B Complete the sentences about the house in the picture. Use the words in the box.

> garage   downstairs   swimming pool   bedroom

1. The kitchen is ___downstairs___.
2. The ___swimming pool___ is in the backyard.
3. The ___bedroom___ is upstairs.
4. The car is in the ___garage___.

Grammar: *There is / There are*

Statement	Questions	Answers
There is a garage.	**Is there** a closet?	Yes, **there is.** No, **there isn't.**
There are three bedrooms upstairs.	**Are there** two bathrooms?	Yes, **there are.** No, **there aren't.**

*The contraction of *there is* = *there's.*

Singular nouns	Plural nouns
1 house 1 bedroom	2 houses 2 bedrooms

*Add an *-s* at the end of the word to make it plural.

28   Unit 3

Word Bank: House/Apartment areas

attic	garage
balcony	hall
basement	home office
courtyard	pantry
driveway	patio
family room	utility room

Grammar: *There is/There are*

There is/There are is used to talk about the existence of items in a particular place. These sentences must include an indication of quantity (*There are ten/many/some books on the table*) and a reference (explicit or understood) to a place. *There is/There are* is not used with proper nouns.

A Complete the sentences with the correct form: *there is* or *there are*.

1. _____There is_____ a big kitchen.
2. _____There are_____ three bathrooms.
3. _____Is there_____ a yard?
4. Are there stairs? Yes, _____there are_____.
5. Is there a garage? No, _____there isn't_____.

B Unscramble the sentences and questions.

1. a is big There garage.   There is a big garage.
2. isn't There closet. a   There isn't a closet.
3. a swimming Is there pool?   Is there a swimming pool?
4. there two Are bathrooms?   Are there two bathrooms?
5. bedrooms. are There two   There are two bedrooms.

C Write questions to ask about somebody's house. Use these words.

1. bathroom/upstairs
   Is there a bathroom upstairs?

2. swimming pool/backyard
   Is there a swimming pool in the backyard?

3. stairs/your house
   Are there stairs in your house?

4. garden/front yard
   Is there a garden in the front yard?

5. three bedrooms/your house
   Are there three bedrooms in your house?

6. closet/bedroom
   Is there a closet in the bedroom?

D 🔁 Ask your partner the questions in exercise **C**. Switch roles.

Conversation

A 🔊 16 Listen to the conversation. Is there a garage? Yes

Realtor: What about this <u>apartment</u>?
Client: Is it a big <u>apartment</u>?
Realtor: Yes. There <u>are three bedrooms</u>.
Client: And bathrooms?

Realtor: There is just one bathroom.
Client: Is there a <u>garden</u>?
Realtor: No, there isn't. But there's a <u>garage</u>.

B 🔁 Practice the conversation with a partner. Switch roles and practice it again.

C 🔁 Change the underlined words and make a new conversation.

D 🔁 **GOAL CHECK** ✔ **Identify places in a home**

Work with a partner. Draw a floor plan of your own home. Tell your partner about your home.

Real Language

What about can be used as a useful and simple way to ask for someone's opinion.

Houses and Apartments   29

A • Have students work individually to complete the sentences.
• Have students compare answers with a partner.
• Check answers.

B • Have students work individually to write the sentences.
• Have students compare answers with a partner.
• Check answers.

C • Have students write the questions.
• Check answers.

D • Ask a student the first and second questions, then have him or her ask you the questions.
• Have students ask and answer the questions with a partner.

Conversation

A • Tell students to listen to the conversation between a realtor and client and then answer the question. If necessary, explain that a *realtor* is a person who sells houses and apartments.
• Play the recording. 🔊 16
• Check answers.

B • Play or read the conversation again for the class to repeat.
• Direct students' attention to the Real Language box.
• Practice the conversation with the class in chorus.
• Have students practice the conversation with a partner and then switch roles and practice it again.

C • Have students work with the same partner to make a new conversation.
• Call on several pairs to present their conversation to the class.

D 🔁 **GOAL CHECK** ✔

• Have students draw a floor plan of their home.
• Divide the class into pairs and have students take turns describing their floor plan to their partner.

Grammar Practice: *There is/There are*

Have students work with a different partner to ask and answer questions about their houses or apartments. Model the activity for students: Ask, *Is there a living room in your apartment?* (*Yes, there is./No, there isn't.*) Call on students to tell the class one thing they learned about their partner's house or apartment.

Describe Your House

Listening

Listening

A 🔊 17 Guess how many bedrooms there are in these houses. Listen and check your guess. Then write the person's name for each house.

1. _____3; Joe_____   2. _____2; Heidi_____

3. _1 (It is the living room, too.); Li_   4. _____7; Ali_____

A • Have students look at each picture and describe each house and its location. Write their ideas on the board. For example: *trees, garden, snow, lights*, etc. Provide new vocabulary as necessary.

• Have students write down how many rooms they think each house has.

• Play the recording. Have students listen and check their guesses. 🔊 17

• Check answers.

B • Have students read the descriptions. Have them match any they think they already know.

• Have students listen again and check or complete their answers. 🔊 17

• Have students compare answers with a partner.

• Check answers.

C • Have students read the sentences. Have them answer *true* or *false* for any they think they already know.

• Have students listen again and check or complete their answers. 🔊 17

• Check answers.

• Have students say which house they like best and why.

B 🔊 17 Listen again. Match the house and the description.

1. Heidi's home ___d___   **a.** big, no garden

2. Joe's home ___c___   **b.** not big, one bedroom

3. Ali's home ___a___   **c.** big, garden

4. Li's home ___b___   **d.** not big, two bedrooms

C 🔊 17 Listen again. Circle **T** for *true* and **F** for *false*.

1. It is cold in Heidi's house.   T (F)

2. There are three bathrooms in Joe's house.   (T) F

3. There is a dining room in Li's apartment.   T (F)

4. There are six bedrooms in Ali's house.   T (F)

30 Unit 3

For Your Information: How many bedrooms?

In some countries, houses do not have bedrooms—rooms that are used only for sleeping. For example, in a traditional Korean house, people sleep on mats that are put away in the closet during the day. Floor cushions and low tables are brought out, and the "bedroom" becomes a "living room."

Pronunciation: Final -s

A 🔊 **18** Listen and check the correct column.

	Ends in /s/ sound	Ends in /z/ sound	Ends in /iz/ sound
gardens		✓	
apartments	✓		
garages			✓
bathrooms		✓	
kitchens		✓	
houses			✓
closets	✓		

B 🔊 **18** Listen again and repeat the words.

Communication

A 🔄 Work with a partner. Take turns describing these houses. Use your imagination.

There is one bedroom in this house.

B  **GOAL CHECK** ✓ **Describe your house**

Describe your house to the class.

Houses and Apartments **31**

Pronunciation

- Remind students that in English, plural nouns are formed by adding -s or -es at the end (with a few exceptions). Tell them that the -s has different pronunciations.

A • Go over the three different sounds.
- Write the three sounds on the board in columns. Remind students that they are *sounds,* not letters. Say *homes,* and have students tell you which sound it is. Write it in the correct column.
- Have students listen to the recording and work individually to mark the correct columns.
- Play the recording several times. 🔊 **18**
- Have students compare answers with a partner.
- Check answers.

B • Play the recording again one or more times for students to repeat the words. 🔊 **18**

Communication

A • Divide the class into pairs and have each student describe one of the houses. Tell them to use their own ideas about what is inside each house.
- Call on student pairs to share one sentence with the class.

B 🔗 **GOAL CHECK** ✓
- Tell students they are going to describe their house or apartment to the class. Give them a minute to think about what they will say. Have them write down key words, but not full sentences.
- Call on each student to describe his or her house to the class. For larger classes, divide students into groups of four or five and have them tell their group about their house.

Speaking Tip

Having students think about what they want to say before they do a speaking activity and write down key words and phrases (not whole sentences), as in **Communication A** above, helps them participate more effectively and, therefore, be more successful. If students are more successful with in-class speaking activities, this will help them become more confident and fluent when speaking in English both in and out of class.

Expansion Activity

Have students work with a partner to choose a famous person and imagine a description of his or her house. Walk around giving students help as needed. When all student pairs are ready, have them present their descriptions to the class: *My name is Bill Gates. In my house, there are . . .*

Identify Household Objects

Language Expansion

- Write the word *furniture* on the board. Elicit words students already know by asking, for example, *What is there in your living room?* Write their answers on the board.

- Go over the names of the objects in the pictures. Pronounce them for students to repeat.

A • Have students work individually to list the furniture and household objects in the chart. Explain that for some objects, more than one place may be correct.

- Have students compare their chart with a partner.

- Compare answers with the class, and draw a chart on the board.

Grammar

A • Have students look at the pictures and introduce the prepositions of place. Demonstrate using objects in the classroom.

- Have students give examples. Ask, for example, *Where is your cell phone? Where are your books?*, etc.

C **GOAL 3:** Identify Household Objects

Language Expansion: Furniture and household objects

▲ chair   ▲ armchair   ▲ table   ▲ microwave

▲ stove   ▲ bookcase   ▲ coffee table   ▲ lamp   ▲ refrigerator

▲ TV   ▲ sofa   ▲ bed

A In which rooms do you usually find the furniture and household objects above?

Kitchen	Dining room	Living room	Bedroom
stove refrigerator, microwave, table, chair	table, chair	sofa, armchair, coffee table, bookcase, lamp, TV	bed, bookcase, lamp, TV

Grammar: Prepositions of place

A Where is the computer?

▲ in   ▲ on   ▲ under   ▲ next to

32   Unit 3

Word Bank: Household items

bathtub	dresser	rug
bureau	floor	shower
carpet	mirror	sink
ceiling	night/bedside table	toilet
desk	picture	window
door	poster	

B Look at the pictures. Complete the sentences with *in, on, under,* or *next to*.

1. There's a TV ____in____ the bedroom.
2. There's a boy ____in____ the swimming pool.
3. There are four books ____on____ the table.
4. The stove is ___next to___ the refrigerator.
5. The dog is ___under___ the table.

C 🔄 What can you see in the pictures? Take turns describing them.

> There is a sofa and a coffee table.

Conversation

A 🔊 **19** Listen to the conversation. Where is Tracey's magazine? *It is under her bag.*

Tracey: Where is my <u>magazine</u>?
Kevin: Is it in the <u>bedroom</u>?
Tracey: No, it isn't. And it's not on the <u>kitchen table</u>.
Kevin: Here it is! It's under your <u>bag</u>.

B 🔄 Practice the conversation with a partner. Switch roles and practice it again.

C 🔄 Change the underlined words and make a new conversation that is true for you.

D 🔄 **GOAL CHECK** ✓ **Identify household objects**

Work with a partner. Take turns describing a room in your house.

Grammar: Prepositions of place

Prepositions are words that express relationships between two things. These can be relationships of time (*I work on Saturday.*), place (*The book is on the table.*), or abstract relationships (*I read an article on Japan.*).

Grammar Practice: Prepositions of place

Have students demonstrate sentences you say with prepositions of place: *The pen is on the book/ in the book/next to the book/under the book.* Use objects that all students have with them, such as their textbook, dictionary, wallet, and so forth. Then divide the class into pairs or groups and have them take turns saying sentences for the other students to demonstrate.

B • Have students work individually to fill in the prepositions.
• Have students compare answers with a partner.
• Check answers.

C • Divide the class into pairs and have them make as many sentences as possible about each picture.
• Call on each pair to share a sentence with the class. Write their sentences on the board.

Conversation

A • Have students close their books. Write the question on the board: *Where is Tracey's magazine?*
• Tell students they are going to listen to a conversation to answer the question on the board.
• Play the recording. 🔊 **19**
• Check answers.

B • Play or read the conversation again for the class to repeat.
• Practice the conversation with the class in chorus.
• Have students practice the conversation with a partner and then switch roles and practice it again.

C • Have students work with the same partner to make a new conversation.
• Call on student pairs to present their conversation to the class.

D 🔄 **GOAL CHECK** ✓

• Have students work with a partner to describe one room in their house or apartment.
• Call on students to tell the class one interesting thing they heard about their partner's room.

Compare Houses
Reading

A • Have students look at the inset picture of the city and describe what they see.

• Have students read the directions and the statements. Have them answer *true* or *false* for each statement.

• Have students compare answers with a partner.

• Check answers.

B • Divide the class into pairs and have students think of three cities in the world with urban sprawl. Give examples as necessary.

• Have them think of large cities in their country with urban sprawl and describe them. They should also describe typical homes in that city.

• Have several pairs share their ideas with the class.

C • Have students read the article and the statements. Point out the words in the Word Bank.

• Have students correct the statements.

• Have students compare answers with a partner.

• Check answers.

D | **GOAL 4:** Compare Houses

Reading

A Look at the picture and read the caption on page 35. What do you know about urban sprawl? Mark each statement true or false. Write *T* or *F*.

1. Urban sprawl = more and more people in the same space. __T__

2. Urban sprawl is a problem in countries like China. __T__

3. People are moving to the **countryside** to find jobs. __F__

4. Cities can fit more people only by growing larger in size. __T__

B ⚡ Are there large cities in your country? With a partner, describe those cities. What is a typical home like there?

> **Hong Kong is a city with a lot of people.**

> **The apartments are very small!**

C Read the article. Correct the false information.

model: Kent Larson is an ~~engineer.~~ *architect*

1. Cities will need more ~~jobs.~~ *small apartments*
2. Many people are moving to ~~the countryside.~~ *cities*
3. Small apartments are ~~expensive~~, but people don't like them. *affordable*
4. Kent Larson designs a new type of ~~house.~~ *apartment*
5. He uses ~~furniture~~ and design to solve a problem. *technology*

WORD BANK
affordable $
comfortable nice to live in
country(side) not a city
expensive $$$$
home where you live; a house or apartment
solve a problem fix something, make it better

Kent Larson Architect

BRILLIANT DESIGNS TO FIT MORE PEOPLE IN EVERY CITY

The following article is about Kent Larson. After Unit 3, you'll have the opportunity to watch some of Larson's TED Talk and learn more about his idea worth spreading.

This is Kent Larson. He is an architect. He wants to **solve a problem.** What problem? The world's population is growing, and more people are moving to cities. Where will all these people live?

These people all need houses or apartments. A city with many small apartments can fit more people than a city with large apartments or houses. Small apartments are **affordable** and use less energy. However, many people do not want to live in small **homes.** They want separate rooms in their homes for many different activities. This is a problem.

Kent Larson has an idea to solve this problem . . . a way to design homes in cities where people live **comfortably** in small spaces. He wants to use design and technology to make an entirely new type of apartment.

For Your Information: Kent Larson

Kent Larson works for the Massachusetts Institute of Technology (MIT) as director of the House_n research consortium and the Living Labs initiative in the School of Architecture and Planning. He is also the current director of the MIT Media Lab's Changing Places research project. Before joining MIT, Larson worked for many years as an architect in New York. He has also published books and articles on architecture. Larson is an architect who is looking toward the future and trying to find ways to solve the housing issues which are a consequence of cities becoming more and more crowded. He believes that we have to design cities and housing units very differently and make use of technology to improve city living. Population growth and its subsequent effect on how and where we live is a key issue in all our lives, so we need to learn from ideas such as Larson's and think about ways to live that are both energy efficient and comfortable.

Urban sprawl can happen when many people move to a city in a short time.

" More than half (50+%) the people in the world now live in cities, and that will just continue to escalate (↗)."

– Kent Larson

35

Expansion

After reading the article, have students find out more about Kent Larson and his work by looking at the TED blog post about his team and some of their research here:

blog.ted.com/2012/09/13/from-folding-cars-to-robotic-walls-5-innovations-to-make-future-cities-far-more-livable/

Reading Tip

Although students will not read out loud very often in the real world, it can be a useful way to go over new material at this level. Pick on students to each read one sentence of the article and go through it as a class. Students will understand the article better and you can discuss key words and ideas together.

After Reading

Have students write about an imaginary house that they would like to live in. Have them think about how their house can solve the problems of urban sprawl and overpopulation. Then have them read their work to a small group or to the class.

Compare Houses

Writing

A • Have students look at the picture and describe the kinds of buildings they see.

• Have students work individually to complete the paragraph about the house plan.

• Have students compare answers with a partner.

• Check answers.

B • Direct students' attention to the Writing Strategy. Explain that the topic is the main idea of a paragraph.

• Have students underline the topic sentence in the paragraph in **A** (*This is a plan of a house.*).

C • Have students draw a plan and write a paragraph about their own house or apartment, following the model in **A.** Remind students to include a clear topic sentence and underline it.

• Have students exchange papers with a partner. Ask students to mark corrections and suggestions for improvements on their partner's paper.

Communication

A • Write the name of a local city on the board and elicit the names of different neighborhoods. Ask, *Which neighborhoods have old buildings and which have modern buildings?*

• Divide the class into pairs and have students identify a city with urban sprawl.

• Have pairs identify which neighborhoods in the city they chose have old, traditional buildings and which ones have new, modern buildings.

B 🔁 | **GOAL CHECK** ✔

• With the same partner, have students compare the houses in the different neighborhoods.

D **GOAL 4:** Compare Houses

There are 24 million people in Shanghai now. In 2020, there will be 26.5 million people living there.

Writing

A Look at this plan of a house. Complete the paragraph.

This is a plan of a house. There is a small kitchen. In the kitchen, there is a _____*stove*_____ and a refrigerator. The kitchen is next to the _____*dining*_____ room. In the dining room there is a table with eight chairs. The living room is _____*next to*_____ the dining room. There is a sofa and two armchairs in the living room. There are three _____*bedrooms*_____ in the house—one big bedroom and two small bedrooms.

B Read the Writing Strategy. Underline the topic sentence in the paragraph in exercise **A.**

C Draw a plan of your house. Then write a paragraph about your house. Underline the topic sentence.

> **Writing Strategy**
>
> A topic sentence tells the topic, or main idea, of a reading. It is usually near the beginning. Use a topic sentence to help your reader understand what you are writing about.

Communication

A 🔁 In pairs, pick a growing city that you know. Which neighborhoods are traditional? Which neighborhoods are new?

B 🔁 | **GOAL CHECK** ✔ **Compare houses**

Work with a partner. Take turns comparing the homes in two of the neighborhoods you picked.

> There are houses with gardens in Coyoacán.

> Not in Santa Fe!

36 Unit 3

VIDEO JOURNAL: *A Very Special Village* **E**

Before You Watch

A Complete the video summary. Use the words in the box.

| fishermen | artists |
| village | paint | Sea | art |

Video summary

Camogli is a small town, or _____village_____, in Italy. Camogli is next to the Mediterranean _____Sea_____. Many people in Camogli are _____fishermen_____. Their job is to catch fish. There are also _____artists_____ in Camogli. They _____paint_____ houses and buildings. Their _____art_____ is called *trompe l'oeil*. It is very special. The paintings are very realistic. They make things look real, but they are not.

While You Watch

A ▶ Watch the video. Match the parts of the sentences.

1. Artists use *trompe l'oeil* to make __c__
2. People like to paint their houses __e__
3. The fishermen painted their houses __a__
4. Raffaella and Carlo are __b__
5. You can see the houses of Camogli __d__

a. with bright colors.
b. artists.
c. things look real.
d. from the sea.
e. with *trompe l'oeil* art.

B ▶ Watch the video again. Circle **T** for *true* and **F** for *false*.

1. Camogli is a large city. T (F)
2. In Camogli, people paint their houses in bright colors. (T) F
3. The houses in Camogli are very special. (T) F
4. All the artists in Italy use the *trompe l'oeil* technique. T (F)
5. Only fishermen paint their houses with *trompe l'oeil* art. T (F)

> I want to add two balconies.

After You Watch

A ⚡ Work with a partner. Take turns describing the changes you would make to your house with *trompe l'oeil*.

Houses and Apartments 37

Video Journal: *A Very Special Village*

Before You Watch

A • Have students look at the picture and describe what they see.
• Have students work individually to complete the video summary using the words in the box.
• Have students compare answers with a partner.
• Check answers.

While You Watch

A • Have students read the sentence parts.
• Tell students to watch the video and match the sentence parts.
• Play the video.
• Have students compare answers with a partner.
• Check answers.

B • Have the students read the statements. Tell students to watch the video again and answer *true* or *false*.
• Play the video.
• Have students compare answers with a partner.
• Check answers.

After You Watch

A • Divide the class into pairs. Have them take turns describing what things they would add to their house with *trompe l'oeil*.
• Compare answers with the class.

For Your Information: *Trompe l'oeil*

Trompe l'oeil is an art technique which means "trick the eye" in French. It depicts realistic imagery that seems to be in three dimensions. It creates an optical illusion when viewed. This technique has been used by artists since the ancient Greeks. It has often been used in murals. Renaissance painters used it in ceiling paintings.

Teacher Tip: Encouraging use of English

A common challenge in monolingual classes is motivating students to use only English in group work. Here are some approaches to consider:

• Explain the rationale for using only English. Tell students, *We learn to speak English by speaking English.*
• Establish a clear policy. For example, *It's OK to ask questions in (native language), but for all other things we use only English.*
• Use English for instructions and classroom management.

Brilliant Designs to Fit More People in Every City

Before You Watch

- Have students look at the pictures and captions on page 39. Ask, *What problem does Kent Larson want to solve? How does he want to solve it?*

A
- Have students look at the functions and spaces and match them.
- Have them compare answers with a partner.
- Check answers.
- Point out the information in the Word Focus box.

B
- Have students read the sentences and match the bold words to their meanings.
- Have them compare answers with a partner.
- Check answers.

C
- Have students read the directions and predict what they're going to hear about in the talk.
- Have them compare answers with a partner.
- Check answers.

While You Watch

A
- Have students read the list of items. Tell them to check what they see as they watch the talk.
- Have them compare answers with a partner.
- Check answers.

Kent Larson Architect
BRILLIANT DESIGNS TO FIT MORE PEOPLE IN EVERY CITY

Before You Watch

A Do you know what these words mean? Match each space (place) to its function (use).

Functions

guest	dance	exercise
work	hang out, relax	

Spaces

1. Office

work

2. Studio

dance

3. Living room

hang out, relax

4. Gym

exercise

5. Guest bedroom

guest

> **WORD FOCUS**
> A *studio* is also: a space for art; an apartment with only one room.
>
> A *wall* separates one room from another room. For example, there is a wall between this classroom and the classroom next door.

Kent Larson's idea worth spreading is that cities are all about people, not cars, and their design should reflect that more clearly. Watch Larson's full TED Talk on TED.com.

B Match the word in **bold** to its meaning.

a. change	d. go from one place to another
b. build, grow	
c. move parts of something to make it bigger/smaller	e. area

1. Janet **moves** from an apartment to a new house. ___d___

2. I **develop** my English skills in class. ___b___

3. There is **space** for four people in my car. ___e___

4. **Fold** your paper and give it to a partner. **Unfold** the paper your partner gives you. ___c___

5. In Rome, Americans **convert** their dollars ($) to euros (€). ___a___

C You are going to watch a TED Talk about a new way to design a house. Look at the pictures and the quotes on the next page. What do you think you will see? 1 and 2

1. A gym that converts into a dining room.

2. An apartment with walls that move.

3. A family that lives in a big space.

While You Watch

A Watch the video. Check what you see.

✓ an architect	✓ a bedroom
✓ a kitchen	✓ a dining room
✓ an office	✓ a garden
___ a doctor	✓ a gym
___ a garage	___ a swimming pool

38

Working with authentic spoken language

Activating prior knowledge of a subject is an important strategy to help students be effective listeners. Having students do pre-listening tasks activates knowledge and ideas they already have about the topic. They can then use this knowledge to help them understand when they listen and watch. These activities also help provide students with any necessary knowledge they may be lacking, so they can understand what they are going to hear. Finally, the activities provide a bridge between what the students already know and the new information, which helps them process what they hear and see.

> "We can make a very small apartment that functions as if it's twice (2x) as big."
>
> — Kent Larson

There are not a lot of jobs in the countryside; most jobs are in the city. Families live in small apartments.

One architect, Kent Larson, has an idea for how to make a great home in a small space.

"The most interesting implementation (use)… is when you can begin to have robotic walls."

USING VISUAL CUES

Understanding every word is not important. Look at the images and the words in the video to help you understand the main idea. You can understand the main idea even when you don't know many of the words you hear.

39

Teacher Tip: Visual Cues

Point out the *Using Visual Cues* box. Remind students that when watching a video, they may not understand every single word. The most important thing is to be able to understand the main themes being discussed. When using relevant, real-world content like TED Talks, visual cues can often be utilized for further understanding of the concepts. For example, the animations of the room changing that Larson uses.

After You Watch

A • Have students read the sentences. Tell them to circle the correct words as they watch the talk.

• Have them compare answers with a partner.

• Check answers.

B • Have students read the causes and effects and match them.

• Have them compare answers with a partner.

• Check answers.

TEDTALKS

Kent Larson Architect
BRILLIANT DESIGNS TO FIT MORE PEOPLE IN EVERY CITY

In the next 15 years, 90% of population growth will be in cities.

After You Watch

A Watch the TED Talk again. Circle the word you hear.

1. Many cities do not have a lot of ((space) | home) for housing.

2. Your space can (develop | (convert)) from an exercise to a work place.

3. You have ((guests) | walls) over, you have two guest rooms that are developed.

4. You have a dinner party: the table ((folds) | converts) out to fit sixteen people.

5. I think you have to build dumb (studios | (homes)) and put smart stuff in them.

B Match the cause and effect, based on the video.

Cause

1. _d_ There are not many jobs in the countryside. There are jobs in the cities.

2. _a_ There is not a lot of space for housing in the cities.

3. _b_ A wall moves.

4. _c_ An engineer wants to exercise and work at home.

Effect

a. Families live in small spaces.

b. The space changes from a dining space to a guest bedroom

c. In his apartment, the gym converts into an office.

d. Families move to the cities.

40

C Correct the false information in each statement.

model: In the countryside, houses are often small. *big*

1. There are many jobs in the ~~countryside.~~ *city*

2. Many people move to the cities to live in ~~big houses.~~ *small apartments*

3. In the city, many houses ~~have~~ a garden or backyard. *don't have*

4. Kent Larson is ~~a teacher.~~ *an architect*

5. In the apartment, the gym converts into ~~a dining space.~~ *an office*

6. To hang out, the walls unfold to make a ~~kitchen.~~ *living room*

7. The space to practice dance (or art, or music) is the ~~guest bedroom.~~ *studio*

8. This apartment is good in cities in places like ~~Antarctica.~~
    Answers will vary. Sample answers: the United States/China/Mexico/Brazil

Project

Kent Larson wants to change the way we live in cities. Use his ideas to design a new home. Follow these steps.

A Interview your partner. Learn about his or her family and what types of spaces they need in their home. Ask these questions.

1. How many people do you live with?

2. Who are they?

3. How old are people?

4. Do you have family that visits? (grandparents, aunts, uncles)

5. What do they do when they visit? (stay a few days, come for dinner)

6. What do the people in your family do? Are they students, athletes, business people, etc?

B Now draw the apartment. You can draw two or three versions to show how the walls convert the space. Label the spaces with the function.

C Show your design to your partner. Explain the function of each space. Does your partner like the design? Does he or she have ideas for improvements?

Challenge! What does Larson think we need to change about transportation in cities? Watch his full talk at TED.com and choose the best answer.

- Save space
- Improve transportation
- (• Share resources)
- Use advanced technology

41

C • Have students read the statements and correct them. Point out the model.
- Have them compare answers with a partner.
- Check answers.

Project
- Have students read the instructions.

A • Have students read the questions. Divide the class into pairs and have students ask each other the questions.

B • Have students use the information from the interview and draw an apartment plan for their partner. Remind them of the uses and functions in **Before You Watch A** on page 38.

C • Have students show and explain their apartment designs to their partner. Encourage them to ask each other questions and make suggestions for improvements.
- Have several students share their designs with the class and explain the reasons for the design. In large classes, this can be done in small groups.

Challenge
- Have students watch more of the TED talk outside of class at TED.com to answer the question, *What does Larson think we need to change about transportation in cities?* Have them answer the question and share what else they learned with their classmates.

Extension
Have students watch the beginning of Larson's full TED Talk. Ask students to take notes on what he says about cities in the past vs. modern cities. Tell students to pick a major difference and add their own ideas and do research on that one issue. Then, have students make a presentation about how things have changed and what they think will happen in the future. For example, in the past people rode horses, now they drive cars, in the future they might use driverless cars.

Possessions

About the Photo

This photo shows a woman in her backyard in Canelli, Italy. She is looking at a sculpture she has of a swordfish. This sculpture is important to her; it is something she considers a special possession. She is a fish enthusiast and received the sculpture as a gift after hosting an aquarium exhibition in her town. People around the world consider different things important and for different reasons, but we all have special possessions.

- Direct students' attention to the photo. Have students describe what they see.
- Introduce the term *possessions*—things that we own.
- Have students work with a partner to discuss the questions.
- Compare answers with the class.
- Go over the Unit Goals with the class, explaining as necessary.
- For each goal, elicit any words students already know and write them on the board. For example, have them name some of their possessions, list the kind of things they give/have received as presents, etc.

Possessions

A woman in Italy inspects a plastic fish head that she received as a gift from her town.

42

UNIT 4 GOALS	Grammar	Vocabulary	Listening
• Identify personal possessions • Talk about other people's possessions • Buy a present • Talk about special possessions	Demonstrative adjectives *Are **these** your books?* ***That** is not your bag.* Possessive nouns *It's **Jim's** bag.* Have *She **has** a camcorder.*	Personal possessions Electronic products	Listening for specific information People proving ownership

Look at the photo, answer the questions:

1 Have you ever received a gift? **2** What is your favorite personal possession?

Unit Theme Overview

- However young or old we are, or rich or poor, we all have certain possessions that mean a lot to us—either because they are important in our daily lives for their usefulness or because they hold important meanings. In this unit, students look at both kinds of possessions, the useful and the personally significant, and examine them in a more global context. Students begin by learning the names of objects that are used in daily life. They talk about common electronic products and discuss buying a present for someone. Finally, they learn about possessions that have special meaning to people in different cultures and talk about their own important possessions.

UNIT 4 GOALS

1. Identify personal possessions

2. Talk about other people's possessions

3. Buy a present

4. Talk about special possessions

43

Speaking	Reading	Writing	Video Journal
Talking about the personal possessions of others	**National Geographic:** "Jewelry"	Summarizing a class survey	**National Geographic:** "Uncovering the Past"
Describing possessions			
Pronunciation: /i/ and /ɪ/ sounds			

Identify Personal Possessions

Vocabulary

A • Pronounce the words in the box for students to repeat.

• Have students complete the captions for the pictures.

• Check answers.

B • Divide the class into pairs. Assign each student a role, student A or student B, and tell them to look at their picture. Model the example with a student.

• Havc students talk to their partner about differences in the pictures.

• Compare answers with the class.

A GOAL 1: Identify Personal Possessions

Vocabulary

A Complete the names of the objects in the pictures. Use the words in the box.

| book | pen | watch | bag | glasses | backpack |
| wallet | ring | keys | necklace | dictionary | notebook |

▲ 1. b o o k ▲ 2. n o t e b o o k ▲ 3. d i c t i o n a r y ▲ 4. b a g

▲ 5. p e n ▲ 6. w a t c h ▲ 7. b a c k p a c k ▲ 8. w a l l e t

▲ 9. r i n g ▲ 10. n e c k l a c e ▲ 11. g l a s s e s ▲ 12. k e y s

> There are glasses in my picture.

> There are no glasses in my picture, but there's a cell phone.

B Take turns. Find the differences between the two pictures.

Student A **Student B**

44 Unit 4

Word Bank: Possessions

address book	ID card
appointment book	key ring (car key/house key)
bracelet	money
business card	pencil phone
driver's license	tablet
earrings	

Grammar: Demonstrative adjectives

	Singular	Plural
Near ☞	**This** is your bag.	Are **these** your books?
Far ☞	**That** is not your bag.	**Those** are not my pens.

A Match the questions and the answers. There can be more than one correct answer.

Question

1. Is this your pen? _b/c_
2. Are those your keys? _a/d_
3. Are these your glasses? _a/d_
4. Is that your dictionary? _b/c_

Answer

a. Yes, they are.
b. No, it isn't.
c. Yes, it is.
d. No, they aren't.

B Look at the pictures. Use the cues to write questions.

1. (far) _Are those your glasses?_
2. (far) _Is that your book?_
3. (near) _Is this your house?_
4. (near) _Are these your dogs?_
5. (far) _Is that your book bag?_

Conversation

A 🔊 **20** Listen to the conversation. What is in the bag? _a book, a dictionary, a pen, and a bracelet_

Andrea: Where's my bag?
Jennifer: Is *this* it?
Andrea: No, my bag is black.
Jennifer: Well, is *that* it? It's black.
Andrea: Is there <u>a bracelet</u> in it?
Jennifer: Let me see. There's <u>a book, a dictionary, a pen, . . . a bracelet</u>!
Andrea: Great! That's my bag. Thanks!

B 🔁 Practice the conversation with a partner. Switch roles and practice it again.

C 🔁 Change the underlined words and make a new conversation.

D 🔁 **GOAL CHECK** ✔ Identify personal possessions

Tell a partner what is in your bag.

1.

2.

3.

4.

5.

Possessions **45**

Grammar: Demonstrative pronouns

In English, *this* and *these* refer to things close to the speaker, while *that* and *those* refer to things far from the speaker. This pattern can cause difficulty for students whose language makes different types of divisions, such as near the speaker versus near the listener, or three different degrees of distance rather than two. When teaching *this* and *these*, point out that there are two pronunciation differences. *This* /ðɪs/ has a lower vowel and a different ending sound than *these* /ðiz/.

Grammar Practice: Possessive nouns

Have each student come up and put one of their possessions on your desk, such as a key, ring, or watch. Hold each one up and ask the class, *What's this?/What are these?* Have students answer, *That's Aisha's dictionary./Those are Toshi's keys.* Give each possession back to its owner as it is identified.

Grammar

- Introduce the demonstrative adjectives using objects in the classroom.
- Go over the demonstrative adjectives in the chart.

A • Have students work individually to match the columns.
- Have students compare answers with a partner.
- Check answers.

B • Have students work individually to write questions about the possessions in the pictures.
- Have students compare answers with a partner.
- Check answers.

Conversation

A • Have students close their books. Write the question on the board: *What is in the bag?*
- Play the recording. 🔊 **20**
- Check answers.

B • Play or read the conversation again for the class to repeat.
- Practice the conversation with the class in chorus.
- Have students practice the conversation with a partner and then switch roles and practice it again.

C • Have students work with the same partner to make a new conversation.
- Call on student pairs to present their conversation to the class.

D 🔁 **GOAL CHECK** ✔

- Have students work with a partner to talk about what's in their bag.
- Call on students to tell the class what's in their bag and discuss any interesting/unusual answers.

Talk About Other People's Possessions

Grammar

- Introduce possessive nouns, using objects in the classroom. Elicit more examples from the class.
- Go over the example in the chart and point out the use of *-'s* to show possession.

Listening

A
- Direct students' attention to the picture. Ask where the people are.
- Tell students they are going to hear two people talking about what's in their bags. They should answer *true* or *false*. Have them read the sentences.
- Play the recording one or more times. 🔊 21
- Check answers.

B
- Tell students to listen again and answer the questions.
- Have students compare answers with a partner.
- Play the recording one or more times. 🔊 21
- Check answers.

C
- With the class, make a list on the board of what Jill and Lee have in their bags.
- Divide the class into pairs and have them ask and answer the questions.

Pronunciation

- Explain to the class that in English, the words *ship* and *sheep* have two different sounds. Pronounce them for the class. Tell them that the sound in *sheep* is called long /i/ and the sound in *ship* is called short /ɪ/.

A
- Tell students to listen to the recording and mark with a check the sound they hear. Play the recording several times. 🔊 22
- Have students compare answers with a partner.
- Check answers.

B   GOAL 2: Talk About Other People's Possessions

Grammar: Possessive nouns

Singular nouns	Plural nouns
Jim's bag Ross's father the student's homework (one student)	the students' homework (more than one student)

Listening

A 🔊 **21** Listen to Jill, then Lee. Circle **T** for *true* and **F** for *false*.

1. There is a cell phone in Jill's bag.   T   (F)
2. There is a dictionary in Jill's bag.   (T)   F
3. There is a cell phone in Lee's bag.   (T)   F
4. There is a notebook in Lee's bag.   T   (F)

B 🔊 **21** Listen again. Answer the questions.

1. What does Jill have in her bag that Lee doesn't have in his bag?
   a notebook, a dictionary, and a *World English* book

2. What does Jill have in her bag that Lee has in his bag?
   a wallet

3. What does Lee have in his bag that Jill doesn't have in her bag?
   a cell phone

C 🔄 Work with a partner. Take turns. Ask and answer the questions.

1. What does Jill have in her bag that you don't have in your bag?
2. What does Jill have in her bag that you have in your bag?
3. What does Lee have in his bag that you don't have in your bag?
4. What does Lee have in his bag that you have in your bag?

Pronunciation: /i/ and /ɪ/ sounds

A 🔊 **22** Listen and check the boxes. Listen again and repeat the words.

	/i/ sound	/ɪ/ sound
this		✓
these	✓	
heat	✓	
hit		✓
his		✓
he's	✓	
sheep	✓	
ship		✓

46   Unit 4

For Your Information:
Security checks

Common sites for security checks include airports, train stations, government buildings, museums, schools, and sports facilities.

ship

Sounds in English can be written in different ways.			
/ɪ/ sound		/i/ sound	
Written	**Example**	**Written**	**Example**
i	k<u>i</u>tchen	e	b<u>e</u>
e	pr<u>e</u>tty	ee	sh<u>ee</u>p
ui	g<u>ui</u>tar	ea	t<u>ea</u>cher
		eo	p<u>eo</u>ple

sheep

B 🔊 **23** Listen and circle the word that you hear.

1. ship | (sheep)
2. it | (eat)
3. (this) | these
4. sit | (seat)
5. (live) | leave

Communication

A 🔀 Complete the following steps.

1. Write the name of an object on a small piece of paper. Give the paper to your teacher.

2. Your teacher mixes the papers and gives you someone else's paper.

3. Ask questions to find the owner.

B 🔁 **GOAL CHECK** ✓ **Talk about other people's possessions**

Ask a partner about what is in his or her bag. Share the information with the class.

> Excuse me, is this your watch?

> No, it isn't. I think it's Ling's.

> Yes, it is. Thanks a lot!

> Is there a pencil in your bag?

Possessions **47**

Buy a Present

Language Expansion

A • Introduce the items on the Web page. Ask which ones students can name.

• Pronounce the items in the box for students to repeat. Then have students work individually to label the items on the page.

• Have students compare answers with a partner.

• Check answers.

B • Have students work individually to complete the sentences.

• Have students compare answers with a partner.

• Check answers.

C • Write on the board *Wish List*. Elicit from students what it is, and write some items under it that students suggest.

• Tell students they have $2,000 to spend on items from the Web page. Have them write their wish lists.

• Have students share their lists with partners.

• Call on two or three students to share their lists with the whole class and write the lists on the board.

C GOAL 3: Buy a Present

Language Expansion: Electronic products

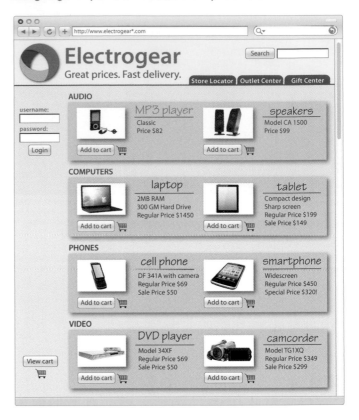

A Label the items on the Web page. Use the words in the box.

> camcorder   cell phone   tablet   speakers
> laptop   DVD player   smartphone   ~~MP3 player~~

B Read the Web page. Complete the sentences.

1. The camcorder is in the _____video_____ section.
2. The _cell phone_ and the _smartphone_ are in the phones section.
3. The tablet is in the _computer_ section.
4. The MP3 player is in the _____audio_____ section.

C Write a wish list of the things you would like to have. You have $2,000 to spend.

Word Bank: Electronics

desktop computer	keyboard
digital camera	memory card
earphones	printer
flash drive	router
GPS	screen
headphones	server
	wireless

Grammar: *Have*

Have is both a lexical verb (a verb for an action, event, or state) and an auxiliary verb. In this unit, it is taught in its basic lexical meaning: to express possession.

Grammar: *Have*

Statements	Negative
I/You/We/They **have** a laptop.	I/You/We/They **don't have** a CD player.
He/She **has** a camcorder.	He/She **doesn't have** a DVD player.
Yes/No questions	**Short answers**
Do I/you/we/they **have** an MP3 player?	Yes, I/you/we/they **do.** No, I/you/we/they **don't.**
Does he/she **have** a cell phone?	Yes, he/she **does.** No, he/she **doesn't.**

A Complete the sentences with *have* or *has*.

1. Jim _____*has*_____ a new laptop.
2. Do you _____*have*_____ a laptop?
3. I don't _____*have*_____ a cell phone.

4. Does Chen _____*have*_____ a tablet?
5. Sofia _____*has*_____ a smartphone.

B Write questions with *have* and complete the answer.

1. you | cell phone? ___*Do you have a cell phone?*___ Yes, ___*I do.*___
2. Alison | big house? *Does Alison have a big house?* Yes, *she does.*
3. you | my keys? *Do you have my keys?* No, *I don't.*
4. Aki | a laptop? *Does Aki have a laptop?* Yes, *she does.*
5. Mario and Dan | an apartment? *Do Mario and Dan have an apartment?* No, *they don't.*

Conversation

A 🔊 24 Sun-Hee and Hana are buying a present for Sun-Hee's brother. Listen to the conversation. What do they buy? *a smartphone*

Sun-Hee: Look at these new products!
Hana: Wow, these <u>cameras</u> look cool. And cheap!
Sun-Hee: My brother already has a good <u>camera</u>.
Hana: Does he have <u>a smartphone</u>?
Sun-Hee: No, he doesn't. Let's get <u>a smartphone</u>!

B 🔁 Practice the conversation with a partner. Switch roles and practice it again.

C 🔁 Change the underlined words and make a new conversation.

D 🔁 **GOAL CHECK** ✔ **Buy a present**

Work with a partner. Practice buying a present for a friend. Use the conversation and the Web site on page 48 for ideas.

▲ Most smartphones have cameras.

> **Real Language**
>
> We use *Wow!* and *Cool!* to show interest and excitement. Both are informal.

Grammar

- Say, *I have a cellphone.* Elicit more examples from students. Ask, *Do you have a smartphone?* Model, *Yes, I do./No, I don't.* Encourage students to answer your questions.

- Go over the information in the box. Focus students' attention on the negative and question forms, point out *don't/doesn't* and *do/does.*

- Elicit more examples from students.

A • Have students work individually to complete the sentences.
- Have students compare answers with a partner.
- Check answers.

B • Have students work individually to write the questions.
- Have students compare answers with a partner.
- Check answers.

Conversation

A • Have students close their books. Write the question on the board: *What do they buy?*
- Play the recording. 🔊 24
- Check answers.

B • Play or read the conversation again for the class to repeat. Direct students' attention on the information in the Real Language box.
- Practice the conversation with the class in chorus.
- Have students practice the conversation with a partner and then switch roles and practice it again.

C • Have students work with the same partner to make a new conversation.
- Call on student pairs to present their conversation to the class.

D 🔁 **GOAL CHECK** ✔

- Match students with a partner. Have them choose a friend to buy a present for and then role-play a conversation.
- Call on student pairs to present their conversation to the class.

Grammar Practice: *Have*

Have students list the items pictured in **Vocabulary A** on page 44 on a sheet of paper. Encourage them to add more ideas of their own. Then divide the class into pairs and have them interview each other to find out which items their partner has (*Do you have a cell phone? Yes, I do./No, I don't.*). Tell them to write down their partner's answers. Then have them change partners and tell them what they found out about their first partner (*She has an MP3 player. She doesn't have a smartphone.*).

Talk About Special Possessions

Reading

- Introduce the topic of the reading. Talk briefly about jewelry, giving examples that students are wearing. *(Mari has a ring. Estela has earrings.)*

A • Have students write a list of their own jewelry or someone in their family's.

- Have students share their lists with a partner.

- Have several students share their lists and write a list of different items of jewelry on the board.

B • Have students read the article to answer *true* or *false*. Tell them to circle any words they don't understand.

- Have students compare answers with a partner.

- Check answers.

- Go over the article with the class, and answer any questions from the students about vocabulary.

C • Have students read the article again to find the information.

- Have students compare answers with a partner.

- Check answers.

D   GOAL 4: Talk About Special Possessions

Reading

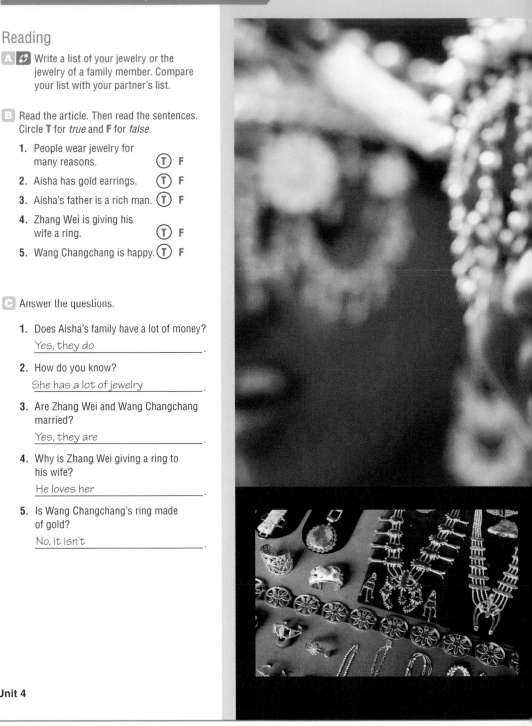

A ⚡ Write a list of your jewelry or the jewelry of a family member. Compare your list with your partner's list.

B Read the article. Then read the sentences. Circle **T** for *true* and **F** for *false*.

1. People wear jewelry for many reasons.   (T) F
2. Aisha has gold earrings.   (T) F
3. Aisha's father is a rich man.   (T) F
4. Zhang Wei is giving his wife a ring.   (T) F
5. Wang Changchang is happy.   (T) F

C Answer the questions.

1. Does Aisha's family have a lot of money?
   Yes, they do .

2. How do you know?
   She has a lot of jewelry .

3. Are Zhang Wei and Wang Changchang married?
   Yes, they are .

4. Why is Zhang Wei giving a ring to his wife?
   He loves her .

5. Is Wang Changchang's ring made of gold?
   No, it isn't .

50   Unit 4

Reading Tip

Remind students that they don't need to know all the words in a text in order to understand it, and that they can guess the meaning of new words. Encourage them to read a text quickly at first, just focusing on main ideas and underlining words they don't know. Help them use the context to guess the meaning of these new words. Often, they can work out the meaning from the rest of the sentence or the main idea of the paragraph.

For Your Information

Djibouti is a small country with a population of only 800,000 people. It is located on the Red Sea in the Horn of Africa. Most of its people live in Djibouti City, the capital, which is a free-trade port. The rest of the people are nomadic herders. For special occasions, some women wear intricate face jewelry and headdresses.

JEWELRY

In every country, people have jewelry. But why is jewelry important to people? Well, it is beautiful, but there are other reasons. Two of the most popular reasons are to say, "I am rich," or to say, "I love you."

This is Aisha, and she comes from Djibouti. She is from an important family, and her father has a lot of money—he is wealthy. Aisha has a lot of jewelry, and it is made of gold. She has gold earrings, gold necklaces, and also gold jewelry that goes over her face. We can see she comes from a rich family because she has a lot of jewelry.

Zhang Wei and his wife Wang Changchang are from Beijing, in China. Zhang Wei is giving his wife a beautiful silver ring. They are in love, and they are very happy. The ring is a sign of Zhang Wei's love for Wang Changchang.

Possessions 51

Expansion Activity

Have students discuss in groups a piece of jewelry that is important to them or someone in their family. Tell them to say what it is and why it is important.

After Reading

Talk with the class about different items of jewelry (rings, necklaces, earrings, etc.) and why people wear them. Which ones do students wear? Why?

Talk About Special Possessions

Communication

A • Have students complete the first column by writing a question of their own. Then complete the second column by writing *yes* or *no*.

• Have students move around the classroom and ask a classmate the questions.

Writing

A • Write on the board: *and, or, but*. Have a student give you information about someone in the class from their chart. Have students help you write sentences about that person using *and, or, but*.

• Have students read the Writing Strategy information.

• Have students write sentences about themselves and their classmates, referring back to the chart in **Communication A.**

• Ask students to exchange papers with a partner and mark corrections and suggestions for improvements on their partner's paper.

• If desired, have students rewrite their papers, to be collected for grading.

B 🔁 **GOAL CHECK** ✔

• Match students with a partner and have them talk about their special possessions.

• Compare answers with the class.

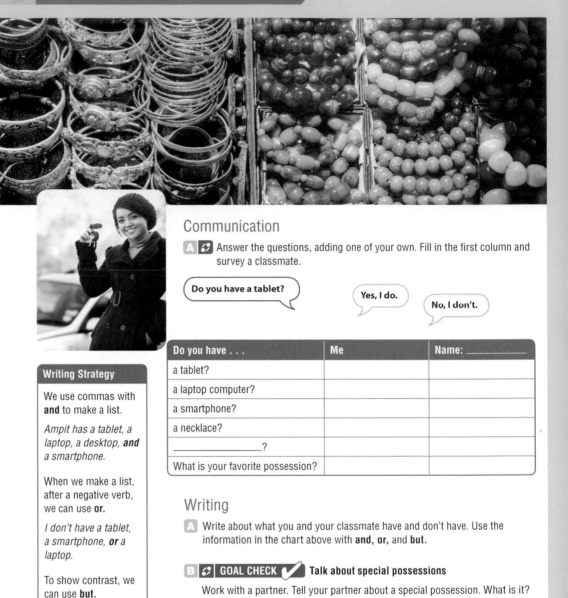

Communication

A 🔁 Answer the questions, adding one of your own. Fill in the first column and survey a classmate.

> **Do you have a tablet?**

> **Yes, I do.**

> **No, I don't.**

Do you have . . .	Me	Name: _____
a tablet?		
a laptop computer?		
a smartphone?		
a necklace?		
_____?		
What is your favorite possession?		

Writing Strategy

We use commas with **and** to make a list.

Ampit has a tablet, a laptop, a desktop, and a smartphone.

When we make a list, after a negative verb, we can use **or**.

I don't have a tablet, a smartphone, or a laptop.

To show contrast, we can use **but**.

I have a smartphone, but Isabelle doesn't.

Writing

A Write about what you and your classmate have and don't have. Use the information in the chart above with **and, or,** and **but**.

B 🔁 **GOAL CHECK** ✔ **Talk about special possessions**

Work with a partner. Tell your partner about a special possession. What is it? Where is it from? Is it old or new?

52 Unit 4

For Your Information: The Maya civilization

The Maya civilization flourished in Mexico and Central America from 2000 BCE to about 900 CE, and Mayan people still live in the same area. It was one of the most advanced civilizations of its time, with highly developed sciences and systems of writing and architecture that still amaze people in the 21st century. They raised food in irrigated fields connected by a system of canals and built very complex cities with palaces, temples, pyramids, astronomical observatories, and ball courts for sports.

VIDEO JOURNAL: *Uncovering the Past* **E**

▲ cave painting

Before You Watch

A 🔄 Work with a partner. Look at the pictures. Decide which of these things are interesting to archaeologists.

While You Watch

A ▶ Watch the video. Check the things that you saw.
jewelry, pot, plate, painting, skull

B ▶ Watch the video again and complete the sentences using the words in the box.

paintings	interesting
skulls	old slow

1. They are looking for
   _____*old*_____ things.

2. Archaeologists study human remains,
   like these _____*skulls*_____ .

3. It is _____*slow*_____ work.

4. Archaeologists also study
   _____*paintings*_____ in caves.

5. Sometimes the work is dangerous, but it is always
   _____*interesting*_____ .

After You Watch

A Match the tools to the job. There can be more than one correct answer.

Tools

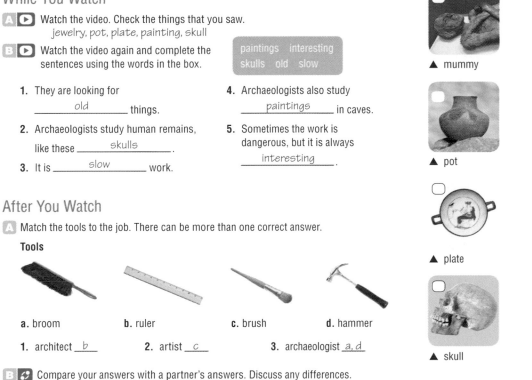

a. broom   b. ruler   c. brush   d. hammer

1. architect _b_   2. artist _c_   3. archaeologist _a, d_

B 🔄 Compare your answers with a partner's answers. Discuss any differences.

▲ jewelry

▲ mummy

▲ pot

▲ plate

▲ skull

Possessions **53**

Video Journal:
Uncovering the Past

Before You Watch

A • Introduce the idea of an archaeologist by directing students' attention to the pictures. Pronounce the vocabulary for the activity and have the class repeat it. Then have students work with a partner to discuss the things that interest archaeologists.

• Compare answers with the class.

While You Watch

A • Tell students they are going to watch a video about archaelogists. Tell them to watch the video and check the items in the pictures that are in the video.

• Play the video.

• Check answers.

B • Tell students to watch the video again and complete the sentences. Have the students read the statements.

• Play the video.

• Have students compare answers with a partner.

• Check answers.

After You Watch

A • Have students work individually to match the tools and jobs.

B • Divide the class into pairs and have them compare answers.

• Compare answers with the class.

Teacher Tip: Errors in spoken English

Giving immediate corrections to students during group and pair work is not usually effective because students are too involved in the activity and won't retain the information. Instead:

• Make notes on errors frequently heard during the activity, and give a mini-lesson after the activity contrasting the error and the correct form.

• Listen to different groups in rotation, write down important errors, and give the list to the group members to correct.

• Note sentences with errors during the activity and write them on the board. Together, the class identifies the errors and corrects them.

For all of these activities, it's best NOT to include the name of the student who made the error. Students generally recognize their own sentences even without names.

Daily Activities

About the Photo

This photo by Randy Olson shows people moving along train platforms during rush hour at Churchgate Railway Station in Mumbai. The station opened in 1855 to serve one line and is now the headquarters of the Western Line of the Mumbai Suburban Railway, which serves 3.5 million people a day.

This photo is part of National Geographic's series *Seven Billion,* which chronicles the skyrocketing global population and how it will affect people's lives. As resources and land become scarce, people will be forced to make decisions that will affect both daily and long-term activities.

- Direct students' attention to the photo. Have students describe what they see.

- Ask the class to tell you things they do every day. Help with vocabulary as needed. Compile a list on the board.

- Have students work with a partner to ask and answer the questions.

- Have several pairs share their answers with the class.

- Go over the Unit Goals with the class, explaining as necessary.

- For each goal, elicit any words students already know and write them on the board; for example, the daily activities from the second step above, jobs, work and school activities.

UNIT
5
Daily Activities

People move quickly along the platforms at the Churchgate Railway Station in Mumbai, India.

54

UNIT 5 GOALS	Grammar	Vocabulary	Listening
• Tell time • Talk about people's daily activities • Talk about what you do at work or school • Describe a dream job	Simple present tense—statements, negatives, and *What time . . . ?* questions Time expressions: *every, at, in, on* Simple present tense—questions and answers Adverbs of frequency: *always, sometimes, never*	Telling time Daily activities Work and school activities	Listening for general understanding and specific details Describing a photographer's work

Look at the photo, answer the questions:

1 Where do you go every day?   **2** What do you do every day?

Unit Theme Overview

- Around the world, many daily activities are nearly universal. We all get up, get dressed, prepare for the day, and start our day's work—at home or in an office, outdoors, or at school. At the end of the day, we eat dinner and relax, alone or with family and friends. In this unit, students acquire vocabulary for daily routines and learn to use the simple present tense to talk about them. They begin by learning to tell time in English and move on to talk about their usual activities at different times of the day. They ask and answer questions about their work activities. In the reading they learn about the life of TED speaker and National Geographic filmmaker Karen Bass, and in the video, they consider the daily lives of people with a very unique profession.

UNIT 5 GOALS

1. Tell time

2. Talk about people's daily activities

3. Talk about what you do at work or school

4. Describe a dream job

55

Speaking	Reading	Writing	Video Journal
Asking and answering questions about work activities **Pronunciation:** Falling intonation on statements and information questions	**TED Talks:** "Karen Bass: Unseen Footage, Untamed Nature"	Writing a job description	**National Geographic:** "Zoo Dentists"

Tell Time

Vocabulary

- Have students focus on the activities shown in the pictures.
- Direct students' attention to the sidebar. Review the ways of saying the time. Say the times for students to repeat.
- Point out that sometimes there are two different ways to say the time (*six thirty, half past six*). Review numbers 1 to 60 if necessary.
- Draw a clock face on the board and draw the hands in at various times. Ask, *What time is it?* and have the class tell you. Then have students come up to the board and draw in the hands and ask the class, *What time is it?*

A
- Have students write the times under the clocks.
- Have students compare answers with a partner.
- Check answers.

B
- Present the activities in the pictures. Read the phrases for students to repeat.
- Have students complete the sentences with times.
- Compare answers with the class.

Grammar

- Go over the chart with the class. Give/elicit more examples. First, talk about yourself (*I get up at seven o'clock.*). Have students tell what time they get up. Then introduce *-s* with *he* and *she*. Point out that some verbs take an *-es*. Ask the class about classmates, *What time does Ali get up? (He gets up at 8:00.).*
- Introduce negatives in a similar way.
- Present the questions with *What time . . . ,* and have students ask each other questions about the activities they learned in the Vocabulary section.

A | **GOAL 1:** Tell Time

Vocabulary

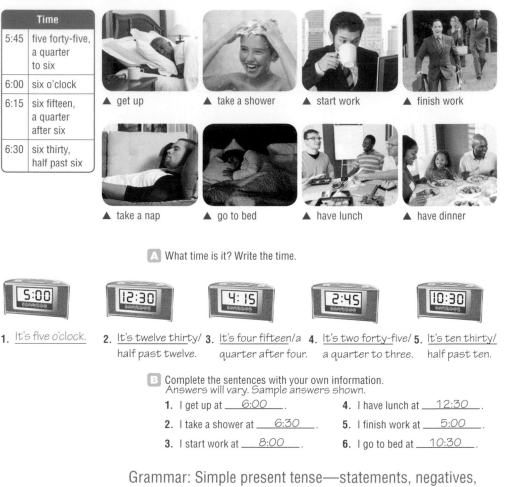

Time	
5:45	five forty-five, a quarter to six
6:00	six o'clock
6:15	six fifteen, a quarter after six
6:30	six thirty, half past six

▲ get up ▲ take a shower ▲ start work ▲ finish work

▲ take a nap ▲ go to bed ▲ have lunch ▲ have dinner

A What time is it? Write the time.

1. It's five o'clock.
2. It's twelve thirty/ half past twelve.
3. It's four fifteen/a quarter after four.
4. It's two forty-five/ a quarter to three.
5. It's ten thirty/ half past ten.

B Complete the sentences with your own information.
Answers will vary. Sample answers shown.

1. I get up at ___6:00___.
2. I take a shower at ___6:30___.
3. I start work at ___8:00___.
4. I have lunch at ___12:30___.
5. I finish work at ___5:00___.
6. I go to bed at ___10:30___.

Grammar: Simple present tense—statements, negatives, and *What time . . . ?* questions

Statement	Negative	What time . . . ?
I/You/We/They **get up** at seven o'clock.	I/You/We/They **don't go** to work on Saturdays.	**What time do** I/you/we/they **start** work?
He/She **gets up** at seven thirty.	He/She **doesn't go** to bed at nine thirty.	**What time does** he/she **start** work?

*The simple present tense is used for actions that we do every day.

Word Bank: Daily activities

clean the house

go to work

make/cook lunch/dinner

start/finish work/class

take a bath/shower

take care of my children/parents

take public transportation to work/school

Grammar: Simple present tense

The simple present tense is used to talk about regular and habitual events, as presented in this unit (*I start work at nine o'clock.*). It is also used for general statements (*I live in Caracas.*) and facts that are always true *(Water freezes at 32 degrees Fahrenheit/0 degrees Celsius.).*

Time expressions with the simple present tense	
every day/morning/afternoon/evening	**on** Sundays
at three o'clock	**at** night
in the morning/the afternoon/the evening	**on** weekdays/**on** weekends

A Complete the sentences. Use the verbs in parentheses.

1. Matt _____gets up_____ (get up) at eight o'clock on Mondays.

2. I _____start_____ (start) work at seven thirty in the evening.

3. We _____don't take_____ (not take) a nap in the afternoon.

4. Wendy and Kate _____don't have lunch_____ (not have lunch) on Thursdays.

5. Dae-Ho _____finishes_____ (finish) work at two o'clock every day.

6. Hussein _____takes_____ (take) a shower at night.

B Unscramble the sentences.

1. take a nap I in the afternoon.   I take a nap in the afternoon.

2. does not at eight o'clock. Helen start work   Helen does not start work at eight o'clock.

3. at one thirty. have lunch We   We have lunch at one thirty.

4. morning. I every take a shower   I take a shower every morning.

5. work finishes at five o'clock. Paul   Paul finishes work at five o'clock.

6. at night. starts work My father   My father starts work at night.

Conversation

A 🔊 25 Listen to the conversation. What time does Marco go to bed on weekdays? *about eleven o'clock*

Abel: What time do you get up?
Marco: I get up at seven thirty on weekdays.
Abel: And on the weekend?
Marco: I get up at about ten o'clock.
Abel: And what time do you go to bed?
Marco: On weekdays, at about eleven o'clock, but on the weekend . . . late!

B 🔄 Practice the conversation with a partner. Switch roles and practice it again.

C 🔄 Practice the conversation again. Use your own information.

D 🔄 **GOAL CHECK** ✔ **Tell time**

Work with a partner. Ask and answer time questions about a friend or relative.

> What time does your mother get up?

> She gets up at six thirty.

Daily Activities **57**

• Go over the time expressions used with the simple present tense. Ask, *What time do you get up on Sundays? What time do you have lunch on weekdays?*, etc.

A • Have students work individually to complete each sentence with the correct present tense form of each verb.

• Have students compare answers with a partner.

• Check answers.

B • Have students work individually to write the sentences.

• Have students compare answers with a partner.

• Check answers.

Conversation

A • Have students close their books. Write the question on the board: *What time does Marco go to bed on weekdays?*

• Play the recording. 🔊 25

• Check answers.

B • Play or read the conversation again for the class to repeat.

• Practice the conversation with the class in chorus.

• Have students practice the conversation with a partner and then switch roles and practice it again.

C • Have students work with the same partner to make a new conversation.

• Call on student pairs to present their conversation to the class.

D 🔄 **GOAL CHECK** ✔

• Divide the class into pairs and tell each student to choose a friend or family member to talk about. Have students ask and answer questions about the person's daily routine.

• Call on student pairs to present a question and answer to the class.

Grammar Practice: Simple present tense

Have students write as many sentences as they can about things they do regularly (*I take a shower in the morning. I eat lunch at work.*). Remind students to include times in some of their sentences.

Then match them with a partner and have them take turns reading their sentences. The listener should cross out any sentence that's the same on his or her own list and write down any sentence that's different. Then listeners should write sentences about the things their partner does that are different (*He goes to bed late.*).

Talk About People's Daily Activities

Listening

A • Tell students they are going to hear an interview with a man. Have them look at the pictures and try to guess the man's job.

• Direct students' attention to the first Word Focus box.

• Play the recording one or more times. 🔊 **26**

• Check answers.

B • Tell students to listen again to answer the questions.

• Play the recording one or more times. 🔊 **26**

• Have students compare their answers with a partner.

• Check answers.

C • Draw students' attention to the planner. Pronounce the days of the week for students to repeat.

• Point out the second Word Focus box. Help students understand the difference between the two expressions. Remind students that days of the week always start with a capital letter in English.

• Ask students what day of the week it is. With the class, elicit activities that students do on specific days of the week.

• Divide the class into pairs and have them take turns asking and answering questions about their daily activities. Remind them to say the day of the week and the time.

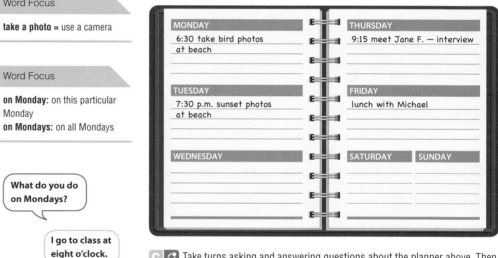

photographs by Joel Sartore

▲ Joel Sartore at work

Word Focus

take a photo = use a camera

Word Focus

on Monday: on this particular Monday
on Mondays: on all Mondays

> **What do you do on Mondays?**

> **I go to class at eight o'clock.**

Listening

A 🔊 **26** Look at the pictures. What is Joel's job? Listen to the interview and check your answer. *photographer*

B 🔊 **26** Listen again and answer the questions.

1. What is Joel's job? *photographer*

2. What time does he get up? *6:00 a.m.*

3. What time does he take a nap? *12:00 (noon)*

4. What time does he take photos? *in the evening/at 8:00 p.m.*

MONDAY		THURSDAY
6:30 take bird photos at beach		9:15 meet Jane F. — interview
TUESDAY		**FRIDAY**
7:30 p.m. sunset photos at beach		lunch with Michael
WEDNESDAY		**SATURDAY** **SUNDAY**

C 🔄 Take turns asking and answering questions about the planner above. Then ask and answer questions about what you do every day.

58 Unit 5

Word Bank: Days of the week

Sunday	Thursday
Monday	Friday
Tuesday	Saturday
Wednesday	

Note: The days of the week are always capitalized in a sentence.

For Your Information: Working hours

In the United States and Canada, the most typical hours for office workers are 9:00 a.m. to 5:00 p.m. Elementary, middle, and high schools normally have classes from about 8:00 a.m. to 3:00 p.m., although teachers stay at school much later than that. Universities have classes from about 7:30 a.m. until 9:00 p.m. If a factory operates with three shifts, these are typically 8:00 a.m. to 4:00 p.m. (first shift), 4:00 p.m. to midnight (second shift), and midnight to 8:00 a.m. (third shift—a slang expression for this is "graveyard shift" because everything is dark and quiet!).

Pronunciation: Falling intonation on statements and information questions

A 🔊 27 Listen and repeat.

1. What time do you get up? I get up at six o'clock.

2. What time do they have lunch? They have lunch at one thirty.

3. What time does Bill go to bed? He goes to bed at eleven o'clock.

B 🔄 Take turns reading the following questions and answers to a partner. Use falling intonation.

1. What time does Salma start work? She starts work at eight thirty.

2. What time do they get up? They get up at a quarter to seven.

3. What time do you finish work? I finish work at six o'clock.

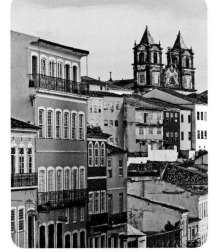

▲ In parts of Latin America, it is common for people to take an afternoon nap called a *siesta*.

Communication

A ♻ Follow these three steps.

1. Write two more questions.

2. Answer all the questions.

3. Ask two classmates the questions.

What time do you . . .	Me	Classmate 1	Classmate 2
1. get up?			
2. have breakfast?			
3. start work?			
4. _____			
5. _____			

B 🔄 **GOAL CHECK** ✓ **Talk about people's daily activities**

Tell a partner about your classmates' activities.

> **Alison gets up at eight o'clock.**

> **She has breakfast at nine thirty.**

Pronunciation

- Introduce the idea of intonation— the way our voices rise and fall when we speak. Demonstrate with your hand. Tell students that every language has its own special intonation. Explain that practicing intonation will make students' English sound more natural.

A
- Tell students to listen to the intonation in the sentences. Play the recording. Show the intonation pattern with your hand. 🔊 27
- Play the recording again several times for students to repeat.

B
- Read through the sentences with the class and have them mark the intonation by drawing arrows above the correct words.
- Have students practice reading the questions and answers with a partner. Walk around helping any pairs with difficulties.
- Call on student pairs to read a question and answer to the class.

Communication

A
- Have each student complete the chart with two more questions and then write their answers to all of the questions.
- Tell students to stand up with their book and pen and move around the room to ask two other classmates for information about their daily activities. Have them sit down when they are finished.

B 🔄 **GOAL CHECK** ✓

- Divide the class into pairs. Students should not be with someone they talked to in **A**.
- Have students tell their new partner what they learned about their classmates.
- With the class, discuss any interesting or surprising answers.

Expansion Activity

Talk with the class about people who work at night. Make a list of jobs that are done at night (for example, *police officer, taxi driver, doctor, nurse, singer, factory worker, bus driver, truck driver*, etc.). Choose several jobs and, with the class, discuss each person's daily schedule. For example, a nurse: *She starts work at eleven o'clock in the evening, she eats lunch at four o'clock in the morning.* Ask, *Is this a good job? Why or why not?*

Talk About What You Do at Work or School

Language Expansion

- Go over the activities in the pictures and say the expressions for students to repeat. Ask questions about each one, for example, *Who do you think he's talking to? Where do you think he's traveling to?,* etc.

- If your learners are younger, you may want to add or substitute more "student activities" from the list in the Word Bank box below.

A
- Have students work individually to complete the chart.
- Compare answers with the class.

B
- Have students work individually to list more things they do at work/school. Help with vocabulary as needed.
- Divide the class into pairs and have students take turns talking about their activities.
- Compare answers with the class.

Grammar

- Go over the information in the box. Ask students questions about everyday activities and elicit short answers. Help them form questions and ask other students.
- Introduce the adverbs of frequency.
- Elicit information from students about their activities. Ask them to use adverbs of frequency to describe their activities.

C   GOAL 3: Talk About What You Do at Work or School

Language Expansion: Work and school activities

▲ check e-mail

▲ meet clients

▲ go to meetings

▲ travel

▲ talk to people on the phone

▲ go to the bank

▲ make photocopies

▲ write reports

A Write the work and school activities in the correct columns for you.

Things I do every day	Things I do every week	Things I don't do
I check my e-mail.		

B 🔁 What other things do you do at work or school? Make a list. Then tell a partner.

Grammar: Simple present tense—questions and answers

Question	Short answer
Do I/you/we/they **meet** clients every day?	Yes, I/you/we/they **do.** No, I/you/we/they **don't.**
Does he/she **meet** clients every day?	Yes, he/she **does.** No, he/she **doesn't.**

Adverbs of frequency

I **always** check my e-mail.	100%
I **sometimes** meet clients.	50%
I **never** answer the phone.	0%

60   Unit 5

Word Bank:
Student activities

do homework	go to the library
do projects	take notes
do research	take a quiz/test
go to class	talk to teachers

For Your Information

Note: *E-mail* is used to refer to e-mail in general. The single form is used even when you are referring to more than one e-mail. For example: *I get so much e-mail every day. We use e-mail to communicate at work.*

We use the plural form, *e-mails,* when we are referring to specific e-mails, not e-mail in general. For example, *I need to send e-mails to my students. I sent three e-mails to Mr. Jones yesterday.* When spelling, you can also use *email,* with no hyphen. Both *e-mail* and *email* are correct spellings of the word.

Grammar: Adverbs of frequency

This lesson introduces *always, sometimes,* and *never.* Other common adverbs of frequency include *usually, often,* and *occasionally.* All of these adverbs precede the verb, except when the verb is *be.*

I <u>*never*</u> *get up early.*

I am <u>*never*</u> *on time for class.*

A Match the questions and the answers.

Questions

1. Do you meet clients every day? _c_
2. Does Ali make photocopies every day? _e_
3. Do Chris and Helen travel a lot? _a_
4. Does Hilary go to the bank every day? _b_
5. Do you go to meetings every day? _d_

Answers

a. Yes, they do.
b. No she doesn't. She goes every week.
c. No, I don't. I never meet clients.
d. Yes, I do. I always go to meetings.
e. Yes, he does.

▲ Singapore is a financial center in Southeast Asia.

B Write about your work or school. Complete the sentences using *always*, *sometimes*, or *never*.

1. I _____ check my e-mail at nine o'clock.
2. I _____ go to meetings on Mondays.
3. I _____ make photocopies.
4. I _____ go to the bank.
5. I _____ write reports.

C 🔁 Write three questions to ask your partner about what he or she does at work or school. Ask and answer questions with your partner.

Conversation

A 🔊 28 Listen to the conversation. What does Brenda do at work? *She checks (her boss's) e-mail, makes photocopies, goes to the bank, and travels.*

Yoshi: Tell me about your work.
Brenda: Well, I'm a personal assistant at a travel agency.
Yoshi: What do you do at work?
Brenda: Oh, I check my boss's e-mail. I make photocopies. I go to the bank. It's not very interesting.
Yoshi: Do you travel?
Brenda: Sometimes. I go to meetings with my boss, like to Rio and Singapore.
Yoshi: Not interesting? It sounds fantastic to me!

Word Focus

boss = your superior, the person at the top

B 🔁 Practice the conversation with a partner. Switch roles and practice it again.

C 🔁 Change the underlined words and make a new conversation.

Real Language

We can use *like* to give examples.

D 🔁 **GOAL CHECK** ✓ Talk about what you do at work or school

Talk to a partner about what you do at work or school.

Grammar Practice: Adverbs of frequency

Tell students to write a list of eight activities on a piece of paper (for example, *get up early, eat breakfast*, etc.). Have them write their names on the top of the paper. Collect the papers and redistribute one to each student. Next to each activity, students should write a true sentence about themselves for the activity, using an adverb of frequency where possible and adding any other information they want (for example, *eat breakfast: I never eat breakfast at home.*). Have them write their names. Collect the papers again, give them back to the original student, and have each student choose one interesting sentence from the paper to share with the class (*Joseph never eats breakfast at home.*).

A • Have students work individually to match the columns.
• Have students compare answers with a partner.
• Check answers.

B • Have students work individually to fill in the adverbs of frequency.
• Compare answers with the class.

C • Write on the board, *Do you go to meetings at work?* Have students suggest other questions and answer them using adverbs of frequency.
• Have students write three questions to ask their partner about what they do at work or school.
• Have students ask and answer the questions in pairs.
• Have several students share what their partner does at work or school.

Conversation

A • Have students close their books. Write the question on the board: *What does Brenda do at work?*
• Play the recording. 🔊 28
• Check answers.
• Point out the meaning of *boss* in the Word Focus box.
• Direct students' attention to the Real Language box. Point out that *like* is often used to give examples in informal conversations.

B • Play or read the conversation again for the class to repeat.
• Have students practice the conversation with a partner and then switch roles and practice it again.

C • Have students work with the same partner to make a new conversation.
• Call on student pairs to present their conversation to the class.

D 🔁 **GOAL CHECK** ✓

• Divide the class into pairs and have them take turns telling each other about their activities.

Describe a Dream Job

Reading

A • Elicit different jobs from students and write them on the board. Ask questions about some of the jobs, for example, *What does a teacher do? What are some of a teacher's daily activities?*

• Have students look at the jobs in the box and match them to the descriptions.

• Check answers.

B • Elicit ideas for dream jobs from students and write one or two on the board. Ask, *What makes this job an interesting job?*

• Have students think of a dream job and write down what the daily activities are for that job.

• Have students discuss their dream jobs with a partner. Remind them to explain what activities make it an interesting job.

• Have several students share their dream job and say what makes them more interesting than other jobs.

C • Have students read the article and answer the questions.

• Have students compare their answers with a partner.

• Check answers.

D **GOAL 4:** Describe a Dream Job

Reading

A What is the job? Match the job with the correct description.

student   pilot   photographer   teacher
explorer   filmmaker

1. I give students homework. _teacher_
2. I fly helicopters and planes. _pilot_
3. I make movies. _filmmaker_
4. I take pictures. _photographer_
5. I study and write reports. _student_
6. I travel to discover new things. _explorer_

B Describe a dream job to a partner. What daily activities make it more interesting than other jobs?

C Read the article. Circle the correct answer for each question.

1. What does Karen Bass do at work?
   (make films)   hunt wildlife

2. What does Karen film in the Altiplano?
   (the night sky)   bats

3. Why does Karen say she's lucky?
   (People everywhere see her work.)   She saves animals.

4. Who does Karen have meetings with?
   (scientists)   clients

5. Karen takes a helicopter to film grizzly bears high in the mountains. Why do the bears live there?
   (to hibernate)   to look for food

WORD BANK
behavior habits or routines
environment where you live
filmmaker someone who makes movies
hibernate winter sleep for animals
privileged lucky

 Ideas worth spreading

Karen Bass Filmmaker

UNSEEN FOOTAGE, UNTAMED NATURE

The following article is about Karen Bass. After Unit 6, you'll have the opportunity to watch some of Bass's TED Talk and learn more about her idea worth spreading.

Karen Bass is a **filmmaker.** She travels for work and makes films about wildlife. She tries to show animal **behavior** that most people never see.

Karen's job is not like most people's. When Karen wants to make a film, she starts by finding a new story to tell. Karen sometimes goes to meetings with scientists and experts, but she also travels to many places, such as the Altiplano in Bolivia, where she films the night sky. Karen's work for National Geographic's *Untamed Americas* shows a new species of bat in Ecuador. She works days, nights, weekends, and in hot and cold **environments.** The work is very hard, but Karen doesn't complain about it.

Karen also has a film about grizzly bears. The bears **hibernate** high in the mountains. Flying in a helicopter is the only way to get there. These amazing experiences make Karen like making films even more. Karen believes she's very lucky. She has a job that she loves and she gets to share something special with millions of people.

For Your Information: Karen Bass

Karen Bass is a natural history filmmaker from the UK. Bass is both a producer and a director and has made nature films for the BBC and National Geographic. She has traveled and filmed animals and the natural world in many different environments world-wide: erupting volcanoes in the Caribbean, rain forests in the Congo, deserts in Jordan, snow-capped mountains in the Andes, and the swamps of the Amazon. Her work includes the series *Andes to Amazon, Jungle, Wild Caribbean, Nature's Great Events,* and *Untamed Americas.* For Bass, one of the privileges of her job is that she can share what she observes in the wild with millions of people around the world, thus enabling them to witness amazing moments in nature, too, through her films. Understanding the natural world better is important for all of us, and Bass's work helps us do that.

"I'm a very lucky person. I've been **privileged** to see so much of our beautiful Earth and the people and creatures that live on it."

— Karen Bass

63

Describe a Dream Job

Writing

A
- Write on the board: *travel agent.* Ask, *What do you think a travel agent does?*
- Have students read the directions and the job description. Ask, *What are holidays? What are duties?* Explain as necessary.
- Have students complete the paragraph.
- Have students compare answers with a partner.
- Check answers.

B
- Have students read the directions and the three categories. Have them complete any information they can remember from the article.
- Have students read the article again and complete the information.
- Have students compare answers with a partner.
- Check answers.

C
- Have students read the directions. Remind them to use the job description in **A** as a guide.
- Have students write a job description for Karen Bass.

Communication

A
- Have students exchange job descriptions with a partner and identify any differences.
- Have students mark corrections and suggestions for improvements on their partner's paper.

B 🔁 **GOAL CHECK** ✔

- Have students read the directions and the list of jobs.
- Divide the class into pairs to talk about a job they would like to have. Remind them to include daily activities, working hours, and vacation days.
- Have several students tell the class about the job they want.

D GOAL 4: Describe a Dream Job

Karen travels to beautiful places for her work, like the Altiplano.

> **Job Description:**
> **Travel Agent**
>
> Working Hours:
> 9.00 a.m. to 5.00 p.m,
> Monday to Friday
>
> Holidays:
> Public holidays + 10 vacation days per year
>
> Duties:
> Answer the phone. Write e-mails. Plan flights and hotels. Send tickets to clients.

A Read the job description. Travel agents help people travel to beautiful places like the ones Karen works in. Complete the paragraph below with the missing information.

This is a job description for a ___travel agent___ . The job is very interesting! You work from ___9:00___ a.m. to ___5:00___ p.m. and never on the weekends. The duties are to answer the phone, write e-mails, plan flights and hotels, and send tickets to ___clients___ . The best thing about the job is the vacation days! You have ___10___ per year!

B Go back to the reading. Then complete the information about Karen Bass's job.

1. Job Description: _(wildlife) filmmaker_
2. Working Hours: _every day; Monday to Friday and the weekend_
3. Duties: _make films, film wildlife; travel; share information_

C Use the information from exercise **B**. Write a complete job description for Karen Bass in your notebook.

Communication

A 🔁 Share your description with a partner.

B 🔁 **GOAL CHECK** ✔ Describe a dream job

Tell your partner about a job you want to do. Use one from the list or choose your own.

– (wildlife) filmmaker   – helicopter pilot
– (wildlife) photographer   – scientist

64   Unit 5

Teacher Tip: Helping groups finish at the same time

A common situation in group work is that one group completes the task long before the others—or long after. Here are some approaches you can take with a group that finishes too quickly:

- Check to be sure they have understood the task and completed all parts correctly.
- Give them additional questions.
- Have the group prepare a written report of their ideas, answers, etc.

With a group that finishes too slowly:

- Tell them to omit parts of the task.
- Take over briefly as discussion leader to help them move along.
- Set a time limit. Tell them, *I'll ask for your answers in five minutes.*

Video Journal: *Zoo Dentists*

Before You Watch

A Read the Video Summary. Use the words in blue to label the pictures.

> Two dentists go to the San Francisco Zoo to treat animals. Their first patient is a sea lion named Artie. His teeth are fine. Then they examine an elephant named Sue. They check teeth in her mouth, and her tusks. Their last patient is a very difficult patient. Sandy is a black jaguar with a toothache. Her teeth are very bad and she needs surgery. The dentists have a very hard day.

1. black jaguar

2. elephant

3. sea lion

While You Watch

A ▶ Watch the video, and then complete the sentences. Use *always, sometimes,* or *never.*

1. Dr. Sarah de Sanz ___sometimes___ treats animal patients.
2. Dr. Brown's animal patients are ___sometimes___ dangerous.
3. Animals ___sometimes___ have dental problems.
4. Artie ___never___ brushes his teeth.
5. Humans and animals ___always___ need good teeth.

4. toothache

After You Watch

A Which of these people might work in a zoo? Check (✓) the box.

1. ☐ a chef
2. ☐ an engineer
3. ☐ an artist
4. ☐ a doctor
5. ☐ a teacher
6. ☐ a photographer

B 🔃 Form a group and compare answers. Be ready to explain your answers.

5. teeth

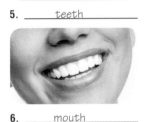

6. mouth

Daily Activities **65**

Video Journal: *Zoo Dentists*

Before You Watch

A • Write on the board: *dentist.* Ask, *What does a dentist do?*

• Point out the blue words in the Video Summary. Say them so students are familiar with the pronunciation.

• Have students read the video summary and label the pictures with the words in blue.

• Compare answers with the class.

While You Watch

A • Tell students to watch the video about a type of dentist and complete the sentences.

• Play the video.

• Have students compare answers with a partner. Play the video again as necessary.

• Check answers.

After You Watch

A • Have students read the jobs and decide which ones might be in a zoo.

• Tell them to make notes about the reasons for their choices. Provide a model on the board, for example: *an engineer – design cleaning system*

B • Divide the class into small groups (three or four students).

• Have students share and justify their decisions with their group.

• Have one person from each group report to the class the jobs their group discussed.

For Your Information: Root canal

The root canal is the space inside the root of a tooth. There can be one or two main canals in each root. This space is filled with a loose tissue called dental pulp. When an adult tooth has reached its final size and shape (about one to two years after eruption into the mouth), its original function as a connective tissue is over, and it becomes a sensory organ.

Root canal is a common term for a dental operation where the dental pulp is cleaned out and the space is disinfected and then filled.

Getting There

About the Photo

This photo by Sungjin Kim shows a busy Seoul intersection where the lights of the traffic have made a rainbow on the roads. The traffic is stopped at stoplights on all sides of the junction, and there is one solitary person in the middle. The photo seems to show how imposing all of the traffic in cities can be. Seoul is a sprawling city with a large population and consequent traffic and pollution issues, but city planners are now working hard to improvc transportation conditions in the city and implement greener transportation options.

- Direct students' attention to the photo. Have them describe what they see.
- With the class, list other methods of transportation, such as bicycle, boat, bus, taxi, subway, and so forth.
- Have students work with a partner to ask and answer the questions.
- Have several pairs share their answers with the class.
- Go over the Unit Goals with the class, explaining as necessary.
- For each goal, elicit any words students already know and write them on the board. For example, the transportation methods from the second step above, places you can visit on a tour, words for directions (*left, right, turn,* etc.)

Getting There

Traffic on Friday night in Seoul, South Korea, makes a colorful route.

66

UNIT 6 GOALS	Grammar	Vocabulary	Listening
• Ask for and give directions • Create and use a tour route • Describe transportation • Record a journey	Prepositions of place; Imperatives ***Turn*** left. The art gallery is **across from** the library. *Have to/Has to* She **has to** change buses.	Places downtown Directions Ground transportation	Listening for specific information Sight-seeing tour description

Unit Theme Overview

- Transportation is an increasingly important issue around the world, as people confront the impact of burning fossil fuels on the global climate. Furthermore, with the increasing price of gasoline, driving a car has become more expensive, and people in some countries are beginning to question the future of auto-based transportation systems—at the same time as more and more people in developing countries are finally able to afford their first car. One thing is certain: We will need to find better and more efficient ways to move greater numbers of people in the future.

- In this unit, students look at different ways of "getting there" and learn language they will need to get directions to the places they want to go. They begin by learning to ask for and give directions to common places needed by visitors to a city, and they practice describing more complicated routes. They consider different means of transportation to get to a destination. Finally, they learn to talk about a longer trip.

UNIT 6 GOALS

1. Ask for and give directions

2. Create and use a tour route

3. Describe transportation

4. Record a journey

Speaking	Reading	Writing	Video Journal
Ask for and give directions **Pronunciation:** *Yes/No* questions and short answers	**National Geographic:** "Journey to Antarctica"	Writing a travel itinerary	**National Geographic:** "Volcano Trek"

67

Ask for and Give Directions

Vocabulary

A • Introduce the vocabulary items in the box. For each item, ask a question to check understanding. For example, *What do you do at the tourist office?* Ask the class to give you examples and/or the location of these places in their city.

• Have students work with a partner to locate each place on the city map.

• Call on students to tell where each place is.

B • Go over the directions with the students and have them follow the arrow on the map.

C • Have students work individually to follow the directions on the map and write the correct places.

• Have students compare answers with a partner.

• Check answers.

• Direct students' attention to the Real Language box. Review the different ways to ask for directions.

A | **GOAL 1:** Ask for and Give Directions

tourist office	train station
supermarket	post office
restaurant	hotel
museum	park
bus station	art gallery
library	movie theater

Vocabulary

A ◆ Work with a partner. Locate the places on the map. Use the words in the box.

B Read the directions below and follow the red arrow.

> **There is a tourist office on Grand Street.**

Directions

You are in the tourist office. Go right and cross Lincoln Avenue. Walk two blocks to Long Avenue. Turn left and walk two blocks. Turn right and go into the museum.

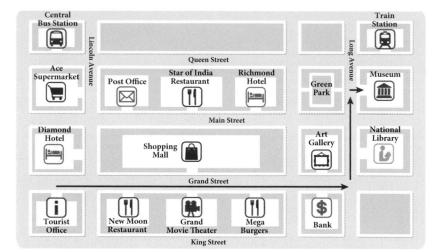

C Follow the directions and write the destination.

1. From the tourist office, turn right. At the corner of Lincoln Avenue and Grand Street, turn left. Walk one block up Lincoln Avenue. Turn right on Main Street, and walk one block. Cross the street. Turn right into _____ *the art gallery* _____ .

2. From Central Bus Station, turn left, then turn right on Lincoln Avenue. Walk one block to the corner of Lincoln Avenue and Main Street. Turn left on Main Street, and walk two blocks to the corner of Long Avenue and Main Street. Turn right, and on your left is the _____ *National Library* _____ .

3. From the front of the Diamond Hotel, turn right on Lincoln Avenue, turn left on Grand Street, and walk two blocks to the art gallery. To your right is the _____ *bank* _____ .

Word Bank: Places in cities

bus stop	newsstand
church	office building
city hall	parking garage
courthouse	parking lot
department store	subway station
drugstore	temple
mosque	traffic light

Grammar: Imperatives

The imperative is the base form of the verb. It is used for giving instructions and also for giving orders and commands. It is considered very direct and in polite conversation is softened with *please.*

Sit down. (direct command)

Please sit down. (polite request)

Grammar: Prepositions of place; Imperatives

Prepositions of place	
on the corner of	The Diamond Hotel is **on the corner of** Lincoln Avenue and Grand Street.
across from	The art gallery is **across from** the library.
between	There is a restaurant **between** the post office and the Richmond Hotel.

A Use the map on page 68, and write the affirmative or negative imperative.

Affirmative	Negative
Turn right.	**Don't turn** left.

*The imperative is used for giving instructions.

1. To get to the shopping mall from the Grand Movie Theater, ___cross___ (cross) Grand Street.

2. From the bus station, ___turn___ (turn) left to get to the tourist office.

3. From the bank, turn left, and ___walk___ (walk) one block to New Moon Restaurant.

B Use the map again, and write the correct prepositions.

1. The art gallery is ___on the corner of___ Long Avenue and Grand Street.

2. The museum is ___across from___ Green Park.

3. Grand Movie Theater is ___between___ Mega Burgers and New Moon Restaurant.

4. The post office is ___across from___ Ace Supermarket.

▲ Big Ben is across the river from the London Eye.

Conversation

A 🔊 29 Listen to the conversation. Where does the guest want to go? *to a supermarket*

Hotel Guest: Is there a <u>supermarket</u> near here?
Receptionist: There's one <u>on the corner of Lincoln Avenue and Main Street, across from the post office</u>.
Hotel Guest: How do I get there?
Receptionist: OK. <u>Leave the hotel and turn right. Walk one block, and cross Lincoln Avenue</u>.
Hotel Guest: Thank you very much.
Receptionist: You're welcome.

B 🔄 Practice the conversation with a partner. Switch roles and practice it again.

C 🔄 Change the underlined words and make a new conversation.

D 🔄 **GOAL CHECK** ✔ Ask for and give directions

Work with a partner. Take turns asking for and giving directions using the map on page 68. Then take turns giving directions to places in your town or around your school.

Grammar Practice: Imperatives

Simon Says is an old American children's game. Tell students they should listen and follow your directions, but only if you say *Simon says* first. Have the class stand up. Say, *Simon says, look at the window*. All should look at the window. *Simon says, close your book*. All should close their books. Say, *Pick up your bag*. They should **not** pick up their bags because you didn't say *Simon says*—anyone who does must sit down. Continue giving directions at a quick pace, using the vocabulary from the lesson and other items. Then ask students to come up to the front and give directions. The last student who is standing is the winner.

Grammar

- Go over the prepositions of place. Give/elicit more examples from the class, using places near the school.

- Go over the forms of the imperative. Explain that we use the imperative to tell people to do things. Point out to students that they should use *please* with imperatives to be more polite.

A • Have students complete the sentences with imperatives.
- Have students compare answers with a partner.
- Check answers.

B • Have students complete the sentences with prepositions.
- Have students compare answers with a partner.
- Check answers.

Conversation

A • Have students close their books. Write the question on the board: *Where does the guest want to go?*
- Play the recording. 🔊 29
- Check answer.

B • Play or read the conversation again for the class to repeat.
- Practice the conversation with the class in chorus.
- Have students practice the conversation with a partner and then switch roles and practice it again.

C • Have students work with the same partner to make a new conversation.
- Call on student pairs to present their conversation to the class.

D 🔄 **GOAL CHECK** ✔

- Divide the class into pairs. Review the questions in the Real Language box on page 68. Have students take turns asking for and giving directions to places in town.
- Call on student pairs to present a conversation to the class.

Create and Use a Tour Route

Listening

- Ask students about the most famous stores in their city and in other cities. Tell them they are going to hear about a walking tour of famous stores in New York City.

A • Have students look at the map. Read the names of the streets to them.

- Have students read the directions for each store. Tell them to write the numbers of the stores on the map.

- Have students compare answers with a partner.

- Check answers.

- Draw a map on the board and fill in the names.

B • Tell students to listen to the recording and mark the tour on the map with arrows.

- Play the recording one or more times. 🔊 30

- Have students compare answers with a partner.

- Check answers.

- Mark arrows on the map you have drawn on the board.

B | **GOAL 2:** Create and Use a Tour Route

▲ New York City, United States

Listening

A Write the numbers of the stores on the map.

1. **Bergdorf Goodman** is on Fifth Avenue between East 57th Street and East 58th Street.

2. **FAO Schwarz** is on the corner of East 58th Street and Fifth Avenue.

3. **Barneys New York** is on the corner of East 61st Street and Madison Avenue.

4. **Tiffany & Co.** is on East 57th Street and Fifth Avenue.

5. **Bloomingdale's** is on Lexington Avenue between East 59th Street and East 60th Street.

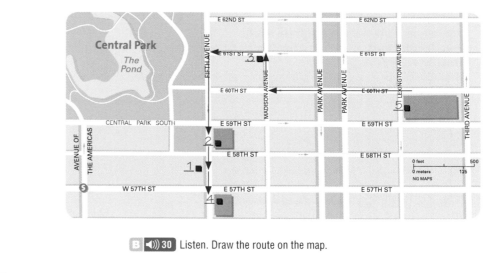

B 🔊 30 Listen. Draw the route on the map.

70 Unit 6

For Your Information: New York stores

Bergdorf Goodman is a luxury department store. It was the first store to sell fashionable women's clothing that was ready to wear (not made by a tailor), in 1914.

FAO Schwarz is a famous toy store that was founded in 1862. It is known for unusual and expensive toys.

Barneys New York is a luxury department store that began in 1923. It was one of the first stores to advertise on the radio.

Tiffany & Co. was founded in 1837 and sells diamonds, jewelry, and silverware. The company now has over 200 stores worldwide.

Bloomingdale's is a department store that began in 1861 when two brothers started selling women's clothing in a small shop.

Pronunciation: *Yes/No* questions and short answers

A 🔊 31 Listen and repeat.

1. Is there a movie theater near here? Yes, there is.

2. Is the bus station on York Street? No, it isn't.

3. Is Barneys on the corner of East 61st Street and Madison Avenue? Yes, it is.

B 🔁 With a partner, take turns reading the questions and answers.

A: Is there a hotel near here?

B: No, there isn't.

A: Is the library next to the museum?

B: Yes, it is.

A: Is there a tourist office in this town?

B: No, there isn't.

Communication

A 🔁 Use the map on page 70. Ask for and give these directions to a partner.

1. From Barneys New York to Tiffany & Co.

2. From Bergdorf Goodman to Barneys New York.

3. From Bergdorf Goodman to Bloomingdale's.

4. From Tiffany & Co. to Bloomingdale's.

B 🔁 In pairs, answer these questions about your town or city.

1. Is there a museum? What is it called? Where is it?

2. Is there a park? Where is it?

3. Are there good restaurants? Where are they?

4. What other places are interesting for tourists?

C 🔁 **GOAL CHECK** ✔ **Create and use a tour route**

With a partner, work together and write a tour route for your town.

▲ Rockefeller Center is between Fifth Avenue and the Avenue of the Americas.

Pronunciation

- Review the idea of intonation—the rise and fall of our voices while speaking. Remind students that practicing intonation will help make their English sound more natural.

A
- Tell students to listen to the intonation in the questions and answers.
- Play the recording. Use your hand to emphasize the rising and falling. 🔊 31
- Play the recording again several times for students to repeat.

B
- Read the questions and answers with the class. Have students mark the intonation with arrows.
- Divide the class into pairs and have them practice reading the questions and answers. Walk around helping with difficulties.
- Call on student pairs to read a question and answer to the class.

Communication

A
- Divide the class into pairs and have them take turns giving directions between the pairs of places listed.
- Ask student pairs to present directions to the class.

B
- Have student pairs take turns asking and answering the questions about their town or city.
- Call on students to read questions and present their partner's answers.

C 🔁 **GOAL CHECK** ✔

- Have students work in pairs to choose three or four interesting places in their city and prepare directions for a walking tour that connects them.
- Call on student pairs to present their tours to the class.

Expansion Activity

With the class, make a list of four or five places near the school. Have students work in pairs to practice giving directions to each place.

Describe Transportation

Language Expansion

- Ask students if they have ever been to an airport. How do people travel to and from the airport?

- Go over the information about traveling from the airport, and talk about different kinds of transportation. Are they fast or slow? Cheap or expensive?

A
- Have students work individually to complete the chart.
- Have students compare answers with a partner.
- Check answers.

B
- Direct students' attention to the question in the speech bubble. Ask several students and have them answer.
- Divide the class into pairs and have them take turns asking and answering questions about different kinds of transportation.

C **GOAL 3:** Describe Transportation

Language Expansion: Ground transportation

From the Airport to Downtown

There are many ways to get downtown from the airport.

▲ **Bus**
Take the A100 bus to the Central Bus Station. $4.50

▲ **Taxi**
Take a taxi. Approximately $50

▲ **Subway**
Take the subway direct to downtown. $2.50

▲ **Train**
Take the train. Change at Midway Station. $20

▲ **Car**
Rent a car. From $120 a day

▲ **Airport Shuttle Bus**
Take the airport shuttle bus to your hotel. $21–$25

A Complete the chart with the names of different types of ground transportation.

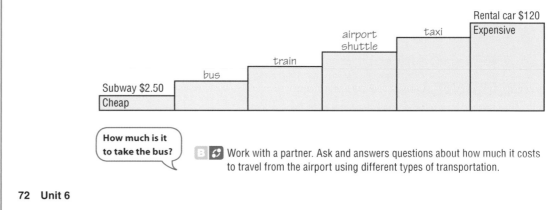

Rental car $120
Expensive

taxi

airport shuttle

train

bus

Subway $2.50
Cheap

How much is it to take the bus?

B Work with a partner. Ask and answers questions about how much it costs to travel from the airport using different types of transportation.

Word Bank: Using transportation

bus stop	stop
fare	subway station
line	ticket
schedule	transfer

Grammar: *Have to*

Have to is one way to express obligation in English. It is more common and less formal than *must* and is used in all tenses.

Don't/Doesn't have to expresses a lack of necessity.

We have to hand in our homework.

We don't have to hand in our notebooks. Our teacher doesn't check them.

Grammar: *Have to*

Statement	Question	Short answer
I/You/We/They **have to** take a taxi.	**Do** I/you/we/they **have to** change trains?	Yes, I/you/we/they **do**. No, I/you/we/they **don't**.
He/She **has to** change buses.	**Does** he/she **have to** take a taxi?	Yes, he/she **does**. No, he/she **doesn't**.

*Have to is used to show obligation.

A Complete the sentences with the correct form of *have to* or *do*.

1. Do we __have to__ take a bus? No, we __have to__ take a train.
2. __Do__ I have to change trains? Yes, you __do__.
3. __Does__ Susan have to take the subway? No, she __has to__ rent a car.
4. __Does__ he have to go to the meeting? No, he __doesn't__.
5. Do you __have to__ get up at 9:00 on Sundays? No, I __don't__.

B Write sentences using *have to*. Answers may vary.

1. Dan doesn't have any money. _He has to go to the bank_
2. It's 3:00 and your train leaves at 3:30. _I have to hurry_.
3. Mohamed goes to sleep at 10:00 and it's 9:30. _He has to get ready for bed_
4. I've got a toothache. _You have to see a dentist_.
5. Ann's cell phone is five years old. _She has to buy a new one_.

▲ To get to Boston Logan Airport, you can take the subway . . . under the water!

Conversation

A 🔊 32 Listen to the conversation. What time does the person have to get to the airport? _two thirty_

Tourist: Excuse me, how do I get to the airport?
Assistant: You can take <u>the subway</u>, but you have to change <u>trains</u>. It takes about an hour.
Tourist: Oh! But I have to get there by <u>two thirty</u>. And I have four bags!
Assistant: Two thirty! <u>In half an hour</u>? OK, you have to take <u>a taxi</u>! And quickly!

B 🔁 Practice the conversation with a partner. Switch roles and practice it again.

C 🔁 Change the underlined words and make a new conversation.

D 🔁 **GOAL CHECK** ✓ **Describe transportation**

Take turns giving directions from one place to another in your town. Say what transportation you have to take.

Getting There **73**

Grammar

- Tell the class, *We have some rules in our school. You have to go to class every day, You have to take a test every month*, and so forth. Elicit more examples.
- Go over the information in the box.

A • Have students work individually to complete the sentences.
- Have students compare answers with a partner.
- Check answers.

B • Have students work individually to write a sentence for each situation.
- Compare answers with the class. Answers will vary but should contain the correct form of *have to*.

Conversation

A • Have students close their books. Write the question on the board: *What time does the person have to get to the airport?*
- Play the recording. 🔊 32
- Check answers.

B • Play or read the conversation again for the class to repeat.
- Practice the conversation with the class in chorus.
- Have students practice the conversation with a partner and then switch roles and practice it again.

C • Have students work with the same partner to make a new conversation.
- Call on student pairs to present their conversation to the class.

D 🔁 **GOAL CHECK** ✓

- Divide the class into pairs and have them take turns giving directions from one place to another in town using different kinds of transportation.

Grammar Practice: *Have to*

What are the rules in your class? Have students work with a partner to write as many rules as they can with *have to* and *don't have to*. (For example, *We have to speak English with our partners*.) Call on student pairs to read their lists to the class and discuss any interesting "rules" you hear.

With a partner or in small groups, have students think of other places where there are rules and write a list using *have to*. For example, at school, at the library, at a hospital.

Lesson C **73**

Record a Journey

Reading

- Introduce the topic of the reading. Elicit examples of what people write in a diary. Have students look at the pictures and talk about the places in them. Are they hot or cold? Is traveling easy or difficult there?

A
- Have students read the diary. Point out the words in the Word Focus box.
- Go over the article with the class, answering any questions from the students about vocabulary.

B
- Have students answer the questions, referring back to the diary as needed. Point out that they need to think about the information in the diary. Some of the answers are not given directly.
- Check answers.

D GOAL 4: Record a Journey

Reading

A Read the diary and look at the pictures.

B Choose the correct answer.

1. The journey starts in __b__ .
   a. Elephant Island   c. South Georgia
   b. London

2. The *Endurance* breaks up on __b__ .
   a. October 26, 1914
   b. October 26, 1915
   c. October 26, 1916

3. __c__ men leave Elephant Island on a small boat.
   a. Four   c. Six
   b. Five

4. It takes __b__ to go from Elephant Island to South Georgia.
   a. one week   c. three weeks
   b. two weeks

5. Shackleton finds help in __a__ .
   a. Stromness   c. London
   b. Elephant Island

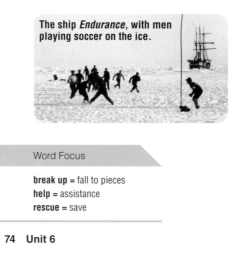

The ship *Endurance*, with men playing soccer on the ice.

Word Focus

break up = fall to pieces
help = assistance
rescue = save

For Your Information: Ernest Shackleton

Ernest Shackleton was born in 1874 and participated in several of the first expeditions to Antarctica. In 1914, he set out with a group of men to try to cross Antarctica. However, their ship the *Endurance* was caught in the ice and crushed. For four months, the crew camped on floating ice, until the men were forced to sail in open boats for five days to reach an uninhabited island far from any shipping routes. Shackleton took one lifeboat and sailed to the island of South Georgia, where there was a whaling settlement. The trip took more than two weeks, in appalling conditions, and they were unable to land near the settlement. Instead, Shackleton and two of the men hiked across the snowy, mountainous island to reach the settlement. Shackleton immediately sent out a ship to rescue the men from Elephant Island, but the first three attempts couldn't get through the ice. Finally, the fourth attempt was successful. Shackleton brought all of his men safely home, and he is regarded as one of the great heroes of exploration.

JOURNEY TO
ANTARCTICA

Reading Tip:
Using context
Teaching students to infer the meanings of unfamiliar words will help them become better readers. Tell students to guess the meaning of unfamiliar words using the words around them.

1914

August 8 Ernest Shackleton and his men leave London on their ship *Endurance*.

1915

January 18 The *Endurance* is trapped in the ice. The men play soccer on the ice.

October 26 It's very cold. The *Endurance* **breaks up.** The men have to leave the *Endurance*. They camp on the ice.

1916

April 9 The ice starts to break up. The men have to get into the small boats.

April 15 They land on Elephant Island.

April 24 Shackleton and five men leave Elephant Island in a small boat to find **help.** The other men stay on Elephant Island.

May 8 Shackleton lands in South Georgia.

May 19 Shackleton leaves three men with the boat. He crosses the mountains of South Georgia with two men to find help.

May 20 They arrive in Stromness, the main town in South Georgia. They find help.

August 30 Shackleton **rescues** the men on Elephant Island.

Getting There 75

After Reading
Have students work with a partner to make a list of ten things that they would take with them on a trip to Antarctica. Tell them to justify their choices. Compare lists with the class.

Record a Journey

Communication

A • Have students look at the pictures and describe what they see.

• Have students read the itinerary. Ask several comprehension questions: *Where do they eat in Paris? How do they travel to London?*, etc.

• Divide the class into pairs and have them plan their own trip or continue with the European Tour itinerary. Point out the questions in the speech bubble; model them with a student.

B • Have each pair tell another pair about their plan.

• Call on several pairs to tell the group their plan.

Writing

A • Have students write their itinerary individually for the trip they planned in **A**. Point out the information in the Writing Strategy box and tell students to use these words in their itinerary.

• Have students exchange papers with a partner. Ask students to mark corrections and suggestions for improvements on their partner's paper.

• If desired, have students rewrite their papers, to be collected for marking.

B 🔄 **GOAL CHECK** ✔

• Tell students to write a diary entry for the trip they wrote an itinerary for. Remind them of the journey diary they read on page 75.

• Call on students to read their diary entries to the class or have them read them to a small group.

D **GOAL 4:** Record a Journey

London, England

Writing Strategy

To put events in order, we use: **first, next, then,** and **finally.**

First we go to Sydney, ***then*** we go to Melbourne, and ***finally*** to Perth.

> **Where do we want to go?**

> **How long will we stay?**

> **What do we want to visit there?**

> **What will we do each day?**

Communication

A 🔄 Read the European Tour plan below. With a partner, plan an itinerary to another part of the world. Think about the questions to the left.

European Tour

Tour itinerary:

June 3: Arrive in Paris. First we visit the Louvre, next the Eiffel Tower, and finally we have dinner on the Champs Elysées.

June 4: Leave Paris. Take the train to London. First we visit the London Eye, and then the Tower of London, and in the evening we take a boat tour on the River Thames to see the city at night.

Paris, France

B ♻ Tell another pair about your plans.

Writing

A 🔄 Now write your itinerary in your notebook.

B **GOAL CHECK** ✔ **Record a journey**

Think about your itinerary. In your notebook, write a diary entry about the trip. Share your diary entry with the class.

Writing Tip

Encouraging students to use linking words such as those in the Writing Strategy box. These words will help them write more coherently. Help students see how the words (*first, then,* etc.) help the reader understand the ideas in a text.

lava lake

crater

eruption

lava

magma

Before You Watch

A Study the picture. Use the labels in the picture to complete the text.

A volcano is a mountain with a large hole at the top. This hole is called a ___crater___. A volcano produces very hot, melted rock. When it is underground, this hot, melted rock is called ___magma___. When it leaves, or comes out of the volcano, it is called ___lava___. When the lava stays in the crater, it forms a ___lava lake___. When lava leaves a volcano, we say the volcano erupts. We call it an ___eruption___.

▲ rocks and soil

While You Watch

A ▶ Watch the video. Match the sentence parts.

1. The geologists ___b___
2. The lava lake ___e___
3. Hot lava comes out of the earth ___f___
4. The team spends hours ___a___
5. It is not easy to stand near the crater ___d___
6. The professors are ___c___

a. collecting pieces of red-hot lava.
b. travel to the volcano on camels.
c. excited about studying the volcano.
d. because it is very hot.
e. is inside the crater.
f. and forms the lava lake.

After You Watch

A ⟳ Discuss these questions with a partner.

1. Do you want to explore a volcano? Why or why not?
2. How can people travel to difficult places?

Getting There   **77**

Video Journal:
Volcano Trek

Before You Watch

A • Have students look at the photos and the illustration and repeat with you the words related to a volcano.

• Have students work individually to complete the text.

• Have students compare answers with a partner.

• Check answers.

While You Watch

A • Tell students they are going to watch a video about a volcano. Tell students to watch and match the sentence parts.

• Play the video.

• Have students compare answers with a partner. Play the video again as necessary.

• Check answers.

After You Watch

A • Match students with a partner and have them discuss the questions.

• Compare answers with the class.

Teacher Tip: Roles in group work

It can be helpful to assign roles to students in each group. Some possibilities:

• Leader—asks questions and keeps the discussion on topic

• Secretary—takes notes on the group's ideas

• Reporter—tells the group's answers to the class

• Recorder—records the number of times each group member speaks, and tells each member how often they spoke when the activity ends

Be sure to rotate these roles often.

For Your Information: Volcanoes

Scientists study volcanoes to try to establish when they will erupt and thus prevent disaster. But most eruptions are unpredictable, and they can be devastating for the surrounding populations.

Volcanoes are commonly found at plate boundaries where the friction of the plates melts the rock. Many of the world's volcanoes are found in the Pacific. This area is called the Ring of Fire. It encompasses the west coasts of North and South America and the east coast of Asia.

The eruption of Vesuvius (in the Mediterranean) in 79 AD is one of the most famous. It buried several Roman cities, including Pompeii. Other famous eruptions are those of Krakatoa in Indonesia, Mount St. Helens in Washington State, and Mauna Loa in Hawaii.

Unseen Footage, Untamed Nature

Before You Watch

A • Have students look at the pictures of the different items. Ask, *What are these things? Who uses them?*

• Have students complete the sentences with the correct words.

• Check answers.

B • Have students read the words and the definitions. Have them try to complete the definitions with the words.

• Have them compare answers with a partner.

• Check answers.

C • Have students look at the photos and read the captions on page 79.

• Have students discuss the questions with a partner.

• Have several pairs share their ideas and write them on the board.

While You Watch

A • Have students look at the photos and read the sentences. Tell students that they are going to watch the video and match the sentences with the photos.

B • Have students compare answers to **A** with a partner.

• Check answers.

Challenge

• With their books closed, have students say what Karen's job is and what her activities are. Write their ideas on the board.

• In small groups, have students discuss the questions.

• Have groups share their answers with the class. Write their ideas on the board.

Karen Bass Filmmaker
UNSEEN FOOTAGE, UNTAMED NATURE

Before You Watch

A Complete the sentences with the correct words.

camera

brush

books

tools

helicopter

1. This _____camera_____ is the filmmaker's.
2. Those _____books_____ are the teacher's.
3. That _____helicopter_____ is the pilot's.
4. These _____tools_____ are the architect's.
5. This _____brush_____ is the artist's.

B Write the letter of the correct word to complete each sentence.

a. creatures	**d.** goose bumps
b. shoot	**e.** remote
c. den	

1. If a place is __e__ it is far away from everything.

> Karen Bass's idea worth spreading is that new photographic technology is changing how we tell stories about animal behavior. Watch Bass's full TED Talk on TED.com.

2. A __c__ is a place that animals use to sleep or hide.

3. You sometimes have __d__ on your arms when you are afraid or excited about something.

4. To __b__ something can mean to film it.

5. __a__ are the same as animals.

C Look at the pictures and quotes on the next page. What do you think the TED Talk is about? What type of job is the TED Talk about? Discuss with your classmates.

While You Watch

A Watch the TED Talk. Read the quotes and look at the pictures. What do you see? Write the number of the picture on the line.

__4__ **a.** Karen Bass uses a camera on a helicopter for her job.

__1__ **b.** Baby grizzly bears walk with their mother.

__2__ **c.** Karen Bass talks about her job.

__3__ **d.** Baby bears roll down the mountain.

B Compare your answers from exercise **A** with a partner.

Challenge! Why do you think Karen's job is interesting? Can you think of other jobs where people travel a lot? Discuss with your group. Then share your ideas with the class.

78

> "As a filmmaker, I've been from one end of the Earth to the other trying to get the perfect shot and to capture animal behavior never seen before."
>
> — Karen Bass

1. "Images of grizzly bears are pretty familiar. You see them all the time, you think. But there's a whole side to their lives that we hardly ever see."

2. "I love this shot. I always get goose bumps every time I see it."

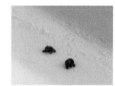

3. "Getting down can be a challenge for small cubs."

4. "We film the video from a helicopter using a special camera."

79

Working with authentic spoken language

When listening to authentic spoken English, such as in the TED Talks, it is important to help students be able to listen successfully. Pre-teaching key vocabulary, as in **Before You Watch, A** and **B** on the previous page, is a helpful pre-viewing step so that students will be able to focus on the main points of what they hear and be less distracted by unknown words. Therefore, it is essential to make sure that students have understood the new words presented, and that they know how they sound. You can do this by repeating the words with the students after they have completed the exercise.

After You Watch

A • Have students read the sentences. Tell them to match the questions and the answers as they watch the talk again.

• Have students compare answers with a partner.

• Check answers.

B • Have students read the sentences and answer *true* or *false*. Watch the video again as necessary.

• Have students compare answers with a partner.

• Check answers and correct any *false* sentences as a class.

C • Have students discuss the questions with a partner.

• Have several pairs share answers with the class.

D • Have students look at the map on page 81 (or draw the map on the board). Say, *I'm at the Diamond Hotel. How do I get to the university?* Ask several questions, and have students give you directions. Write the expressions for directions and the prepositions on the board.

• Have students read the sentences and match the people to the directions.

• Have students compare answers with a partner.

• Check answers.

TEDTALKS

Karen Bass Filmmaker
UNSEEN FOOTAGE, UNTAMED NATURE

A Watch the TED Talk. Match the questions with the answers.

Questions

1. Do the grizzly bears sleep in trees? _d_

2. Does Karen Bass go to Alaska to make her film? _c_

3. Do the grizzly bears climb mountains? _a_

4. Does Karen work at a travel agency? _b_

Answers

a. Yes, they do.

b. No, she doesn't.

c. Yes, she does.

d. No, they don't.

B Read the sentences. Circle **T** for true or **F** for false.

1. Grizzly bears have dens.   (T)   F

2. Karen doesn't have a special camera.   T   (F)

3. Grizzly bears don't have cubs.   T   (F)

4. A helicopter has wings.   T   (F)

5. Mountains sometimes have a lot of snow.   (T)   F

C ⚡ Work with a partner. What do you think? Discuss your answers to the questions.

1. Where do grizzly bears hibernate? Why?

2. Why do you think Karen films the bears?

D When Karen travels, she has to go to places she doesn't know. People in new places have to ask for directions. Locate the places on the map. Match the directions with the people.

1. The photographers have to go from the bus station to the museum. _c_

2. A hotel guest has to pick up her ticket from the travel agency. _d_

3. A college student has to meet his friends in the park. _e_

4. The banker has to buy his wife some jewelry. _b_

5. She has to meet her friend at the post office from the camera shop. _a_

a. Cross Grand Street. It's next to the Supermarket.

b. Cross Main Street. Go to the right. Turn left and walk down Grand Street. It's across from the Post Office.

c. Turn left on Long Avenue. Turn right on Main Street. It's across from the Italian Restaurant.

d. Turn right on Long Avenue. Turn right on Green Street. It's on the left.

e. Cross Grand Street. Turn right onto Lincoln Street. Turn left on Long Avenue. Turn right and walk one block down Green Street.

80

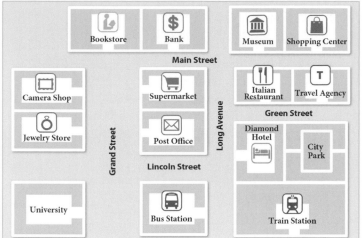

Main Street

Green Street

Lincoln Street

camera   books
photocopy machine
car   forest   airport
streets   school
office   university
mountains   plane

E Use the words to complete the chart. Write what each person **Uses** as part of their job and **Where** they work. Then, check if you **Like** or **Don't Like** the job. Some of the words can be used twice.

Job	Uses	Where	Like	Don't Like
Taxi Driver	car	streets		
Professor	books	university, school		
Wildlife Filmmaker	camera	mountains, forest		
Personal Assistant	photocopy machine	office		
Wildlife Photographer	camera	forest, mountains		
Pilot	plane	airport		

F Compare your chart with a partner's. Are your answers the same? Do you like the same jobs? Discuss.

Challenge! Find Alaska, British Columbia, and the Altiplano on a map or online. Are they close to each other? Make a list of the different kinds of transportation you think can be used to get to each place. Why do you think it is important to Karen to visit and show such different places in her work? Discuss with your group. Then share your ideas with the class.

E • Ask, *What does Karen use for her job? Where does she work?* Have students look at the information in the chart.

• Have students complete the chart with the items and places in the box and decide if they like the job or not.

F • Have students compare their completed chart with a partner.

• Have students identify which jobs they both like or dislike.

• Have several pairs share their answers with the class.

• Check answers.

Challenge!

• Provide students with access to a map of North and South America and have them locate Alaska, British Columbia, and the Altiplano.

• In small groups, have students make a list of the different kinds of transportation which could be used to get to each place. Have them discuss the question.

• Have groups share their answers with the class. Write their ideas on the board.

Expansion Activity

In groups, have students pick a place in their country, or another place that they have been to, and plan a photo shoot. Groups should say what equipment they will need, how many people will go on the shoot, what kind of transportation will be needed, and what they plan to shoot. Students should explain why they want to shoot this subject. Have students present their ideas to the class.

Free Time

About the Photo

This photo was taken by Paul Nicklen and appears in a *National Geographic* series called *Sacred Cenotes.* This image captures divers exploring a cenote, which is a deep sinkhole filled with water, near the ancient Maya ruins near Tulum, Mexico. Cenotes were important to the ancient Maya as sacred places that led to another world—the world of a god of rain called Chaak.

- Direct students' attention to the photo. Have them describe what they see.

- Introduce the concept of free time. Talk about free-time activities, and compile a list on the board. (Use the -*ing* form of the verb.) Ask students which activities they enjoy.

- Have students work with a partner to ask and answer the questions.

- Have several pairs share their answers with the class.

- Go over the Unit Goals with the class, explaining as necessary.

- For each goal, elicit any words students already know and write them on the board, for example, sports mentioned in the second step above, expressions used on the telephone, etc.

UNIT
7
Free Time

Divers explore a *cenote* in Mexico.
Cenotes are deep pits filled with water.

82

UNIT 7 GOALS	Grammar	Vocabulary	Listening
• Identify activities that are happening now • Make a phone call • Talk about abilities • Talk about sports	Present continuous tense *I'm not watching* TV. *I'm reading.* *Can* for ability *He **can** sing.* *He **can't*** play the guitar.	Pastimes Sports	Listening for specific information Telephone conversation

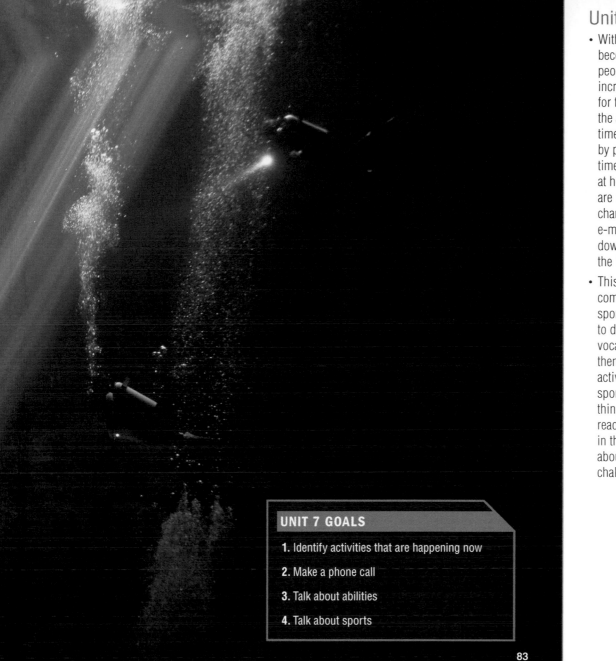

Unit Theme Overview

- With working hours gradually becoming shorter in most countries, people around the world have an increasing amount of time available for their leisure activities. Some of the activities they pursue in their free time are the same as those enjoyed by previous generations: spending time with family and friends, relaxing at home, or playing sports. Others are new and based on technological changes: sending and reading e-mail, playing computer games, or downloading music and movies from the Internet.

- This unit focuses on some of the most common leisure-time activities and on sports and things people have learned to do. Students begin by learning vocabulary for free-time pursuits and then learn to talk about their current activities. They acquire words for sports, and practice talking about things they can or can't do. Students read about the most popular sport in the world and finally, they learn about one man's unusual and exciting challenge.

UNIT 7 GOALS

1. Identify activities that are happening now

2. Make a phone call

3. Talk about abilities

4. Talk about sports

83

Speaking	Reading	Writing	Video Journal
Describing personal activities happening now **Pronunciation:** /ʃ/ and /tʃ/ sounds	**National Geographic:** "Soccer – The Beautiful Game"	Writing about abilities	**National Geographic:** "Danny's Challenge"

Identify Activities That Are Happening Now

Vocabulary

A • Have students look at the pictures. Elicit any words from the pictures that the students already know.

• Tell students to listen to the recording and write the activities under the correct pictures. Read the activities in the box to them.

• Play the recording one or more times. 🔊 2

• Check answers.

B • Have students copy the chart into their notebooks.

• Have students work individually to classify the activities in the chart.

• Have students compare their charts with a partner. Tell them to identify any activities that they both like or don't like.

• Call on students to tell you one thing they like or don't like.

Grammar

• Introduce the present continuous tense. Mime reading a newspaper and say, *I'm reading.* Write on the board, *I'm reading.* Repeat the process with several other verbs: *writing/eating/sitting.* Have students mime other actions and give/elicit the verbs.

• Introduce the negative: Mime and say, *I'm reading. I'm not writing.* Give/elicit more examples using mime.

• Introduce *Yes/No* questions and short answers. Point to a student and ask, *Is he eating/reading/writing?* Elicit *Yes, he is./No, he isn't.*

• Introduce *Wh-* questions. Ask a student to mime eating/reading and ask the class, *What is she eating?* Introduce *where* for location.

• Go over the information in the box.

A **GOAL 1:** Identify Activities That Are Happening Now

Vocabulary

A 🔊 2 Listen and write the words from the box under the correct picture.

> going to the movies   watching TV   playing the guitar   reading
> shopping   going for a walk   listening to music   cooking

1. _watching TV_

2. _playing the guitar_

3. _cooking_

4. _reading_

5. _listening to music_

6. _shopping_

7. _going to the movies_

8. _going for a walk_

B Write the activities from exercise **A** in a chart in your notebook. Your chart should look like this:

I like	I don't like

Grammar: Present continuous tense

Statement (negative)	*Yes/No* question	Short answer	*Wh-* question
I **am (not)** reading.	**Am** I reading?	Yes, **I am.** No, **I'm not.**	Where **am** I **going?**
You/We/They **are (not)** reading.	**Are** you/we/they **reading?**	Yes, you/we/they **are.** No, you/we/they **aren't.**	What **are** you/we/they **doing?**
He/She **is (not)** reading.	**Is** he/she **reading?**	Yes, he/she **is.** No, he/she **isn't.**	What **is** he/she **doing?**

*We use the present continuous tense to talk about things that are happening at the moment.

84   Unit 7

Word Bank: Activities

cleaning the house   shopping

exercising   studying

playing computer   visiting friends
games   writing e-mail

playing the piano

Grammar: Present continuous tense

The present continuous tense is used to talk about things that are happening at the moment of speaking:

I'm watching TV right now.

It contrasts with the simple present tense, which is used to talk about habits and facts:

I always watch the news at nine o'clock.

A Unscramble the words to write sentences and questions.

1. the guitar. is playing Charlie   _Charlie is playing the guitar._
2. Marian watching TV. is not   _Marian is not watching TV._
3. Asha listening to music? Is   _Is Asha listening to music?_
4. Ju What reading? is   _What is Ju reading?_

B 🔁 Work with a partner. Describe the picture at the top of the page. Take turns to ask and answer questions.

> **What is he/she doing?**

Conversation

A 🔊 3 Listen to the phone call. What is Dave doing?   _listening to music_

Dave: Hi, Mom.
Mom: <u>Dave</u>! Where are you? What are you doing?
Dave: Mom, don't worry! I'm at <u>Paul's</u>. We're <u>listening to music</u>.
Mom: Well, don't be home late.
Dave: Mom, I'm <u>17</u> years old. Relax!

B 🔁 Practice the conversation with a partner. Switch roles and practice it again.

C 🔁 Change the underlined words and make a new conversation.

D 🔁 **GOAL CHECK** ✔ **Identify activities that are happening now**

Work with a partner. Look at the pictures on page 84. Ask and answer questions. Then look around the room and describe what people are doing and not doing.

> ### Real Language
>
> We can use these expressions to tell someone not to worry.
> Formal ◄————► Informal
> *Don't worry! Relax! Take it easy!*

Grammar Practice: Present continuous tense

Mime an action and tell the class to guess what you're doing using the present continuous: *You're watching TV. You're watching a scary movie.* Tell the class when they have guessed correctly. Divide the class into pairs and have them plan a similar mime for the class to guess. Have each pair present their mime for the class to guess. At the end of the activity, talk about any funny/difficult/surprising mimes.

A • Have students work individually to write the sentences and questions.

• Have students compare answers with a partner.

• Check answers.

B • Divide the class into pairs. Model the question and have a student answer for one of the people in the picture. Ask one or two more questions about the picture. Provide vocabulary as necessary, for example: *crossing the street, going to work, going for a walk, shopping, taking a taxi.*

• Have students ask and answer questions about what the people in the picture are doing.

Conversation

A • Have students close their books. Write the question on the board: *What is Dave doing?*

• Play the recording. 🔊 3

• Check answers.

B • Play or read the conversation again for the class to repeat.

• Practice the conversation with the class in chorus.

• Direct students' attention to the Real Language box. Read the expressions.

• Have students practice the conversation with a partner and then switch roles and practice it again.

C • Have students work with the same partner to make a new conversation.

• Call on student pairs to present their conversation to the class.

D 🔁 **GOAL CHECK** ✔

• Have students work with a partner to talk about the pictures on page 84. Then have them talk about what people in the classroom are doing or not doing.

• Have several students share sentences about what people in the classroom are doing.

Make a Phone Call

Listening

A
- Have students look at the pictures and describe what they see in each one.
- Tell students they are going to listen to four phone conversations. Have them number the pictures according to the order in which they hear the conversations.
- Play the recording one or more times. 🔊 4
- Check answers.

B
- Tell students to listen to the conversations again and answer the questions. Go over the questions.
- Play the recording again one or more times. 🔊 4
- Have students compare answers with a partner.
- Check answers.

C
- Focus students' attention on the expressions in the Real Language box. Say each expression and have students repeat.
- Have students write the expression for each situation.
- Have students compare answers with a partner.
- Check answers.

B   GOAL 2: Make a Phone Call

Listening

A 🔊 4 Look at the pictures and listen to the telephone conversations. In what order do you hear the conversations? Write the numbers.

B 🔊 4 Answer the questions. Listen again to check your answers.

1. What is Mr. Evans doing? _He's talking on the phone._
2. Is David's wife taking a walk? _No, she isn't._
3. What is she doing? _She's meeting some clients._
4. Is Salma playing the guitar? _No, she isn't._
5. What is she doing? _She's watching TV._
6. What is Tracey doing? _She's driving. / She's talking on the phone._
7. Why doesn't Kenny want to talk? _He's driving._

C What telephone expressions can you use in the following situations?

1. You can't hear someone. _Sorry, can/could you speak up?_
2. You don't know the caller. _Who is calling/speaking, please?_
3. You are busy and can't talk. _Can/Could I call you back?_
4. The person you are calling is not available. _Can/Could I leave a message?_

Real Language

Useful telephone expressions.
Who is calling/speaking, please?
Can/Could I call you back?
Sorry, can/could you speak up?
Can/Could I leave a message?

86   Unit 7

For Your Information:
Cell phone etiquette

A phone call can interrupt important activities. When calling someone on a cell phone, it's considered polite to ask, *Is this a good time to talk?* In some countries, it is illegal to talk on a cell phone while driving.

Pronunciation: /ʃ/ and /tʃ/ sounds

A 🔊 **5** Listen and check the word you hear.

1. watch ✓   wash
2. cheap   sheep ✓
3. chair   share ✓
4. chip ✓   ship

5. cash ✓   catch
6. chop   shop ✓
7. choose   shoes ✓

B 🔄 Take turns reading the words. Your partner points to the words you say.

Communication

A Look at the chart. Fill in your information to make it true for you.

Day	Time	Location	Activity
Friday	8:00 a.m.	on the train	going to school
	1:00 p.m.		
	8:00 p.m.		
Saturday	8:00 a.m.		
	3:00 p.m.		
	8:00 p.m.		

B 🔄 Choose a day and time from the chart. Role-play a phone call with your partner. Follow the model below. Change partners and repeat.

Hi. Where are you? What are you doing?

I'm watching the soccer game! Can I call you back?

Wait, who is winning?

C 🔄 **GOAL CHECK** ✓ **Make a phone call**

Work with a partner. Take turns talking about what a friend or family member is doing right now.

Free Time   87

Pronunciation

- Point out the difference between the /ʃ/ and /tʃ/ sounds in English. Read the pairs of words to the class for students to repeat.

- Point out that in English the /ʃ/ sound is most often associated with the letters -sh, while the /tʃ/ sound is most often associated with the letters -ch.

A
- Tell students they will hear one word in each pair. They should check the word they hear in the recording. Play the recording one or more times. 🔊 **5**
- Have students compare answers with a partner.
- Check answers.

B
- Divide the class into pairs and have them take turns reading a word from each pair in **A.** Their partner should point to the word they hear.

Communication

A
- Have students complete the chart with their own information.

B
- With their books closed, elicit telephone expressions from students. Have different students tell you when you use each expression. Write the expressions on the board.
- Focus students' attention on the example. Model the phone call with a student.
- Have students choose a day and a time from their chart. Model the phone call again and have the student say what they are doing.
- Have students role-play phone calls with different partners.
- Have several pairs role-play a phone call for the class.

C 🔄 **GOAL CHECK** ✓

- Divide the class into pairs and have them take turns talking about what a friend or family member is doing right now.
- Call on students to say the most interesting thing their partner said.

Expansion Activity

Have student pairs repeat **Communication B,** role-playing a conversation with a famous person about what he or she is doing now. Provide vocabulary as necessary. Call on student pairs to present their role-plays to the class.

Talk About Abilities

Language Expansion

A • Go over the words in the box, pronouncing them for students to repeat.

 • Have students work individually to label the pictures.

 • Check answers. For each picture, ask, *What's she/he doing?*

B • Have students answer the questions about themselves and then talk to two other students and record their answers.

 • Compare answers with the class. Which sports are the most popular?

 • Point out the spelling changes in the verbs chart and go over the verbs with the class.

Word Bank: Sports

baseball	martial arts
basketball	rowing
boxing	surfing
car racing	waterskiing
diving	windsurfing
horse racing	wrestling
ice hockey	

Grammar: *Can* for ability

English has several ways to express ability, including *can, know how to, be able to.*

Can is the most general expression of ability, including skills and physical ability. (*I can play the piano. I can run one mile in six minutes. I can meet you at ten o'clock.*)

---

ice skate	ski	play soccer
play tennis		play volleyball
play golf	swim	ride a bike

Language Expansion: Sports

A Match the words in the box to the pictures.

1. _____swim_____ 2. _____play soccer_____ 3. _____ride a bike_____ 4. _____play volleyball_____

5. _____ski_____ 6. _____ice skate_____ 7. _____play golf_____ 8. _____play tennis_____

B Answer the questions. Then interview two classmates.

Do you . . .	Me	Classmate 1	Classmate 2
play soccer?			
ski?			
ice skate?			
play golf?			
play tennis?			
swim?			
play volleyball?			
ride a bike?			

Spelling changes for verbs in the present continuous tense			
one-syllable verbs	verbs ending in *e*	verbs ending with one vowel then a consonant	
		one syllable	two syllables
read – reading eat – eating	take – taking have – having	swim – swimming run – running	listen – listening finish – finishing

88   Unit 7

Present Continuous: Spelling rules

To make the present continuous, we use the verb *be* (*am/is/are*) with a verb + *-ing*:

 • Add *-ing* to the base form of the verb: read – reading, stand – standing, jump – jumping

 • If a verb ends in a silent *-e*, drop the *-e* and add *-ing*: leave – leaving, take – taking, receive – receiving

 • In a one-syllable word, if the last three letters are consonant-vowel-consonant (CVC), double the last consonant before adding *-ing*: sit – sitting, run – running, hop – hopping
 *Do not double the last consonant in a word that ends in *w, x,* or *y:* sew – sewing, fix – fixing, enjoy – enjoying

 • If a verb ends in *-ie*, change the *-ie* to *y* before adding *-ing*: die – dying

Grammar: *Can* for ability

Statement	Negative	*Yes/No* question	Short answer
I/You/She/We/They **can** swim.	He **cannot** swim. He **can't** play the guitar.	**Can** you ski?	Yes, I **can**. No, I **can't**.

A Write about yourself. Complete the sentences with *can* or *can't*.

1. I _____ swim.
2. I _____ play soccer.
3. I _____ play golf.
4. I _____ ski.
5. I _____ play tennis.

B Complete the conversations.

1. **A:** _____*Can you*_____ play volleyball?
   B: No, I can't, but I _____*can*_____ play soccer.

2. **A:** _____*Can*_____ Damien swim?
   B: Yes, _____*he can*_____.

Pronunciation

🔊 6 Listen and check *can* or *can't*.

	can	can't
1.	✓	
2.	✓	
3.		✓
4.	✓	
5.		✓

Conversation

A 🔊 7 Listen to the conversation. What can the new classmate do? *She can play the guitar, ski, and ice skate.*

Julie: Hi, Yumi. I hear we have a new classmate.
Yumi: Yes, she's nice. She can play the guitar.
Julie: Wow!
Yumi: Yes, and she can ski and ice skate, but she can't swim. She's just learning.
Julie: Hey, I'm learning as well. Maybe I can invite her to my classes.
Yumi: Good idea. I'm sure she will like that.

B 🔄 Practice the conversation with a partner. Switch roles and practice it again.

C 🔄 Change the underlined words and make a new conversation.

D ♻ GOAL CHECK ✓ **Talk about abilities**

Ask questions to find someone in your class who can do TWO of the following: play the guitar, swim, cook dinner, ice skate, or play golf. Then tell the class about the person you found.

Can you ski?

No, I can't, but I can ice skate.

Free Time **89**

Grammar Practice: *Can* for ability

Say: *He can fly. He can jump over buildings. Who is he?* (Superman.) If students can't guess, let them ask questions with *Can he . . .?* until they find the answer. Give students time to write a similar description for an animal or person. Divide the class into groups and have students read their descriptions for the group to guess. Have each group choose a description for the class to guess.

Can is pronounced /kæn/ alone or at the end of an utterance. For example, *Yes, I can.*

When can is negative, the /æ/ sound is shorter because although the /t/ in *can't* is reduced by the /n/ through coarticulation, the /t/ shortens the /n/, reducing its voice and shortening the vowel.

Can usually becomes /kən/ in the affirmative and the interrogative. For example, *Can I help you?* and *We can do that.*

Grammar

- Introduce *can*. Tell the class, *I can swim. Can you swim?* Elicit *Yes, I can./No, I can't.* Ask about other sports. Have students ask new questions to you and the class.
- Go over the information in the box.

A
- Have students work individually to complete the sentences.
- Compare answers with the class.

B
- Have students work individually to complete the conversations.
- Have students compare answers with a partner.
- Check answers.

Pronunciation

- Have students listen and check the column for what they hear (*can* or *can't*). 🔊 6
- Check answers.

Conversation

A
- Have students close their books. Write the question on the board: *What can the new classmate do?*
- Play the recording. 🔊 7
- Check answers.

B
- Play or read the conversation again for the class to repeat.
- Practice the conversation with the class in chorus.
- Have students practice the conversation with a partner and then switch roles and practice it again.

C
- Have students work with the same partner to make a new conversation.
- Call on student pairs to present their conversation to the class.

D ♻ GOAL CHECK ✓

- Have students ask questions to find someone who can do two things on the list.
- Call on students to tell the class about the person they found.

Talk About Sports

Reading

A • Have students look at the picture and describe what they see.

• Have students discuss the questions with a partner.

• Call on students to share their answers with the class.

B • Direct students' attention to the Word Focus box.

• Have students read the article and answer the questions.

• Have students compare answers with a partner.

• Check answers.

C • Have students say what they think the number one sport in the world is.

• With a partner, have students make a list of the top five sports in the world.

• Have several pairs share their lists.

• Compare answers. According to most sources, the most popular sports in the world are:

1. soccer

2. cricket

3. field hockey

4. tennis

5. volleyball or baseball

D • Discuss with the class why they think these are the most popular sports.

E • Have students write a list of their five favorite sports.

• Have students compare their list with a partner and explain why they like each sport.

• Have several students share their lists and give their reasons.

• Remind students to use *can* where appropriate.

D **GOAL 4:** Talk About Sports

Reading

A With a partner, answer these questions.

1. Is soccer popular in your country?

2. Do you play soccer?

3. Do you have a favorite team?

4. Who is your favorite soccer star?

B Read the article and answer the questions.

1. Who is Pelé?
   a famous soccer player

2. How many people in the world play soccer?
   264 million

3. Can women play soccer?
   Yes, they can.

4. What equipment do you need to play soccer?
   a ball

5. Why is soccer so popular?
   Answers will vary: Anyone can play it./You can play it anywhere./You only need a ball.

C Can you guess what the top five sports in the world are? Work with a partner. Your teacher has the answers.

D As a class discuss why you think these sports are popular.

E Write a list of your top five favorite sports. Compare with your partner. Explain why you like these sports.

> **Word Focus**
>
> **equipment** = things used for an activity
> **famous** = very well known

90   Unit 7

SOCCER—THE BEAUTIFUL GAME

In 1977, the **famous** soccer player Pelé named his book *My Life and the Beautiful Game.* The Beautiful Game is, of course, soccer.

Soccer is the number one sport in the world. According to FIFA, 264 million people play soccer. But that is just people who *play* soccer. About 3.2 billion people watched the 2010 World Cup on television. That is a lot of people. In fact, it is almost half the people in the world.

So, why is soccer the number one game in the world? Well, anyone can play soccer. Women, men, girls, and boys can play. Even Buddhist monks play!

Also, you can play soccer anywhere. You can play soccer on the beach, in your backyard, or in a stadium. And, unlike many other sports, you do not need special **equipment**—all you need is a ball. You don't even need special shoes. You can play in sandals, like the Buddhist monks.

For Your Information: The top five sports in the world—Why are they popular?

Cricket: Only ten countries in the world play cricket at an international level, but they include countries with large populations, like Bangladesh, India, and Pakistan. You can play on any flat piece of land with a homemade bat and a small ball.

Field Hockey: Field hockey is the national sport in India and Pakistan. It is also popular in Australia, Germany, Japan, The Netherlands, and South Korea. Equipment is not very expensive.

Tennis: Tennis is popular in big, rich countries, the USA being the most notable. Equipment and tennis courts are expensive.

Baseball: Baseball is played in Canada, China, Latin America, the Philippines, Russia, and the USA. Equipment is not expensive, but in countries that play cricket (a very similar game), it is not as popular.

Volleyball: Volleyball is played worldwide and is popular in schools, which leads to its high ranking.

Free Time 91

Reading Tip

Have students look at and discuss the photos on reading spreads and use background information to talk about what the reading is about. This is called *schema building*.

After Reading

Have students research a sport they have never played. Have them find out:

- where the game originated
- what countries it is played in
- what equipment is needed
- where it is played (court/field/etc.)
- what the rules are

Have students present the information they find in small groups.

Talk About Sports

Writing

A • Choose one of the sports students named in **E** on page 90 and have them tell you the rules. Write on the board *can/can't*. Ask questions to prompt students as necessary, for example, *Can you kick the ball in volleyball?*

• Have students write the rules for their favorite sport. Provide vocabulary as necessary.

Communication

A • Have students ask and answer questions about the rules of their favorite sport with a partner. Model the questions with a student.

B 🔄 **GOAL CHECK** ✔

• Divide the class into pairs and have them talk about sports they enjoy watching and playing. Have them explain the rules of the sports they like to play. Provide vocabulary as necessary.

• Have several students explain to the class the rules of a sport they play.

Word Bank: Sports

(badminton/squash/tennis) racket

(baseball/cricket) bat

(baseball/hockey/soccer) field

(basketball/tennis/volleyball) court

catch (the ball)

catcher's mitt

golf club

hit (the ball)

hockey stick

jump

kick (the ball)

run

team

team captain

team member

throw (the ball)

D **GOAL 4:** Talk About Sports

▲ A woman skis down a mountain at the end of the day.

Writing

A Pick your favorite sport. Think of the rules. Write three things you can do and three things you can't do when you play the sport. Answers will vary.

Sport: _baseball_

Can:

throw the ball

use your hands

use a bat

Can't:

kick the ball

tackle other players

throw the ball at players on the other team

You can kick the ball.

Can you touch it with your hands?

Communication

A 🔄 With a partner, take turns asking and answering questions about your favorite sports.

B 🔄 **GOAL CHECK** ✔ **Talk about sports**

Work with a partner. Talk about your favorite sports. Say what sports you like to watch. Say what sports you like to play. Describe the rules to each other.

92   Unit 7

For Your Information: Stunt bike riding

Stunt bike riders do acrobatics while riding their bikes. They do wheelies (lifting one wheel and balancing on the other one), spins, jumps, and even flips. But they don't just do these things riding along the ground. They jump up onto objects like walls and fences and jump from one object to another, or down or up steps, spinning and flipping at the same time. It is an exciting sport, but it can be dangerous. Riders have to wear helmets to protect their heads. Most riders wear elbow and knee pads, too.

Danny MacAskill is a famous stunt bike rider. He was born in 1985 on the Isle of Skye in Scotland and has been riding since he was about 12. Danny does street stunt bike riding, and he became popular when he released a video on the Internet in 2009 showing his skills with his bike, jumping, spinning, and flipping around the city of Edinburgh.

Before You Watch

A You are going to watch a video about a stunt bike rider. Circle five words you think you will hear in the video.

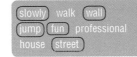

slowly walk wall
jump fun professional
house street

While You Watch

A ▶ People ride bikes for the following reasons:

(exercise) (fun) (the challenge) money

Watch the video and circle the reason, or reasons, why Danny rides his bike.

B Answer the questions.

1. Where does Danny come from? _Scotland_
2. Where does Danny ride his bike? _Edinburgh_
3. Do people think Danny is good? _yes_
4. What is Danny's challenge? _to ride over a bridge_

After You Watch

A Match the person and the challenge.

1. soccer player ___d___   **a.** get better grades
2. student ___a___   **b.** go faster
3. skier ___b___   **c.** hit the ball a long way
4. golfer ___c___   **d.** score more goals
5. basketball player ___e___   **e.** score more points

B 👥 Write down your own personal challenge. Form a group and ask others about their personal challenges.

Free Time **93**

Video Journal:
Danny's Challenge

Before You Watch

A • Have students look at the picture and describe what they see. Write on the board, *stunt bike rider,* and have students try to explain what it is.

• Tell students they are going to watch a video about a stunt bike rider. Have them circle the words in the box that they think they will hear.

While You Watch

A • Have students read the directions. Tell them to watch and circle the reasons why Danny rides his bike.

• Play the video.

• Have students compare answers with a partner.

• Check answers.

B • Have students read the directions. Tell them to watch again and answer the questions.

• Play the video again.

• Have students compare answers.

• Check answers.

After You Watch

A • Write on the board, *challenge.* Have students try to explain what it means. Give examples of challenges in your life and theirs.

• Have students work individually to match the challenges to the people.

• Have students compare answers with a partner.

• Check answers.

B • Have students read the directions and think about a personal challenge.

• Have students ask and answer questions about their personal challenges in small groups. Write on the board, *Why? How? When?* to prompt students.

• Have several students share their personal challenges with the class.

Teacher Tip: Checking answers

There are many ways to check students' answers to activities, all with advantages and disadvantages.

• Teacher reads the answers out loud, students check their work—the fastest way, but requires the least amount of student involvement.

• Teacher calls on students to give their answers—also fast, but may make students feel anxious.

• Students correct each other's work—gives students more responsibility, but they may not correct all the mistakes.

• Volunteers each write the answer to one question on the board—gives the class an opportunity to work with common errors, but uses a lot of time.

• Teacher corrects outside of class—an opportunity for detailed feedback, but requires a lot of work from the teacher!

Use a variety of different techniques for checking answers during your classes.

Clothes

About the Photo

Photographer J. Carrier spent many years working in Africa and the Middle East. This photo shows a Sudanese woman dressed in a traditional *tobe*, a large piece of material which women simply wrap around their body over a short-sleeved blouse. It appears to be both a simple and practical item of clothing, while at the same time being bright, colorful, and beautiful. Clothes are an important part of every culture, and there are differences and similarities in what people wear from culture to culture. Clothes may be chosen for tradition, utility, or fashion, but what we wear always says something about who we are and what is important to us.

- Introduce the theme of the unit. Direct students' attention to the photo. Have them describe what they see.

- Have students work with a partner to answer the questions.

- Compare answers with the class, compiling a list of colors on the board.

- Go over the Unit Goals with the class, explaining as necessary.

- For each goal, elicit any words students already know and write them on the board, for example, items of clothing, expressions used in stores, etc.

UNIT
8 **Clothes**

A Sudanese woman wears a traditional *tobe*, which she wraps around her body.

94

UNIT 8 GOALS	Grammar	Vocabulary	Listening
• Identify and shop for clothes • Buy clothes • Express likes and dislikes • Learn about clothes and colors	*Can/Could* (polite requests) **Can** I try on these shoes? Likes and dislikes I **love** your sweater! She **hates** pink.	Clothes Colors	Listening for specific details Listening to people shopping for clothes

Unit Theme Overview

- "Clothes make the man," according to an old English saying. What we wear expresses our personality, as well as our cultural values and our position in society. Because of this, clothing is a topic that fascinates people of all ages.

- In this unit, students begin by learning basic vocabulary and phrases to use in shopping for clothing. They learn to describe different kinds of clothing and to talk about their own preferences. Finally, they look at clothing in a wider context—both in its function to protect the wearer and in its cultural and historical context in the Video Journal.

UNIT 8 GOALS

1. Identify and shop for clothes

2. Buy clothes

3. Express likes and dislikes

4. Learn about clothes and colors

95

Speaking	Reading	Writing	Video Journal
Describing people's clothes **Pronunciation:** *Could you*	**National Geographic:** "Chameleon Clothes"	Writing about what people are wearing	**National Geographic:** "Traditional Silk-Making"

Identify and Shop for Clothes

Vocabulary

A • Have students look at the picture. Say the colors for students to repeat.

• Have students look at the clothes. Say the items of clothing and have students repeat.

• Model the example, then ask, *What are these?* Remind students of the difference between *this* and *these*. Divide the class into pairs and have them describe the clothing.

B • Have students read the sentences. Point out the pictures on page 97. Go over the meanings of the words and phrases in blue.

• Have students work individually to complete the sentences.

• Check answers.

C • Have students look at the pictures on page 97 again. Ask, *What's he wearing?*

• Divide the class into pairs and have them take turns describing what the people are wearing.

• Call on students to describe each person.

Vocabulary

This is a white shirt.

▲ shirt

A 🔁 Look at the picture. Then take turns describing the pictures below to a partner.

▲ dress   ▲ jacket   ▲ jeans   ▲ shoes

▲ sweater   ▲ tie   ▲ hat   ▲ skirt

▲ pants

B Look at the pictures on the next page. Complete the sentences. Notice the words in **blue**.

1. Ruben is **trying on** black _____shoes_____.
2. Lucy is **paying for** the _____coat_____ by credit card.
3. The sales assistant is **bringing** more _____sweaters_____.

C 🔁 Work with a partner. Take turns describing what the people are wearing in the pictures.

For Your Information:
Celebrating with dyes

The picture at the top of the page shows dyes used in the Holi festival. This Hindu festival signifies the arrival of spring and new beginnings. People light fires, cover each other with colored dyes, and go to parties.

Word Bank: More clothes

baseball cap	sneakers
boots	suits
gloves	sweatpants
mittens	sweatshirt
raincoat	uniform
sandals	vest
shorts	

Grammar: *Can/Could* (polite requests)

Using *Can/Could* with *please* softens a request and makes it more polite. English-speaking parents teach their young children that they must always say *please* when asking for something.

Grammar: *Can/Could* (polite requests)

Can/Could	
Can I try it on, please?	**Could** you bring another, please?

*Could is more formal than *can*.

A Write the polite requests.

1. You are looking at two dresses, a red one and a blue one. You want to try on the blue dress. <u>Can I try on the blue dress, please?</u>

2. You want to see some red shoes. <u>Could/Can I see some red shoes, please?</u>

3. You want to pay by credit card. <u>Can/Could I pay by credit card, please?</u>

4. You are looking at two sweaters, a red one and a green one. You want to try on the green sweater. <u>Can/Could I try on the green sweater, please?</u>

5. You want the sales assistant to bring a size 7. <u>Could/Can you bring a size 7, please?</u>

Conversation

A 🔊 8 Listen to the conversation. What color sweater does the customer want? <u>white</u>

Customer:	Do you have any <u>white sweaters</u>?
Sales Assistant:	Yes, we do.
Customer:	Could I see <u>them</u>, please?
Sales Assistant:	Yes, of course.
Customer:	Ah, <u>this one looks</u> nice. Can I try <u>it</u> on, please?
Sales Assistant:	Sure. The changing rooms are over here.
Customer:	OK. Back in a minute . . . . It fits great. I'll take it!

B 🔄 Practice the conversation with a partner. Switch roles and practice it again.

C 🔄 Change the underlined words and make a new conversation.

D 🔄 **GOAL CHECK** ✔ **Identify and shop for clothes**

Work with a partner. Take turns role-playing a sales assistant and a customer trying on clothes.

Word Focus

Wear is the verb you use with clothing.

Real Language

We can show we agree by saying:

Formal ←——————→ Informal
Of course   *Yes*   *Sure*

Grammar Practice: *Can/Could* (polite requests)

Explain to students that they can use *Can/Could* to make polite requests in the classroom, too, such as when they need a piece of paper or don't understand something. (*Could you give me a piece of paper/say that again, please?*) Have students work with a partner to role-play a classroom situation with a polite request. Call on student pairs to present their role-play to the class.

- Direct students' attention to the Word Focus box.

Grammar

- Go over the questions with *can* and *could* in the box. Point out that these sentences are used in stores to talk to sales assistants. Discuss other places where polite requests would be used (in a bank, post office, office, etc.). Point out the use of *please* to make requests more polite.

A • Have students work individually to write the requests.

- Have students compare answers with a partner.

- Check answers.

Conversation

A • Have students close their books. Write the question on the board: *What color sweater does the customer want?*

- Play the recording. 🔊 8

- Check answers.

- Direct students' attention to the Real Language box.

B • Play or read the conversation again for the class to repeat.

- Practice the conversation with the class in chorus.

- Have students practice the conversation with a partner and then switch roles and practice it again.

C • Have students work with the same partner to make a new conversation.

- Call on different pairs to present their conversation to the class.

D 🔄 **GOAL CHECK** ✔

- Have students work with the same partner to make new conversations about shopping for clothes.

- Call on student pairs to present their conversation to the class.

Buy Clothes

Listening

A • Have students look at the pictures and say what each person is shopping for. Tell them they are going to listen to four conversations.

• Play the recording one or more times and have students number the pictures in the order in which they hear the conversations. 🔊 9

• Check answers.

B • Listen again. Tell students to write the number of the conversation in which they hear each question.

• Play the recording 🔊 9

• Have students compare answers with a partner.

• Check answers. Play recording again as necessary.

C • Have students match questions and answers.

• Check answers.

Listening

A 🔊 9 Listen to the conversations. Number them in the order you hear them.

B 🔊 9 Listen again. In which conversation do you hear these expressions?

1. ☑ 2 The sale price is $29.99.
2. ☑ 1 Do you want to pay by cash or credit card?
3. ☑ 2 How much are they?
4. ☑ 3 What size are you?
5. ☑ 4 That's $36 in all.

C Match the questions and the answers.

1. Do you want to pay by cash or credit card? ___b___
2. What size are you? ___a___
3. Can I help you? ___e___
4. How much is it? ___c___
5. Do you have this in black? ___d___

a. I'm a 12.
b. I'll pay by credit card.
c. The sale price is $35.
d. No, I'm sorry. Only in brown.
e. Yes, I'm looking for a red tie.

98 Unit 8

Listening Tip

Remind students that when they listen they can use different strategies to help them understand. Before they listen, they should decide whether they need to focus on the main idea (as in **A**) or on specific details (as in **B**). If they know what kind of information they are listening for, they can focus on that and not worry about understanding every word. It is important to help students see that they can understand both main ideas and specific details even if there are words they don't know. It is also important to help students see how they can use these strategies when they are listening to English outside of class. For example, when listening to the news, sometimes we listen for main ideas to get a general idea of what's in the news; but on other occasions, we want specific details about a certain news story. In each case, what we pay attention to when we listen will be different.

Pronunciation: *Could you*

A 🔊 10 Listen and check (✓) the box of the form you hear.

	Full form	Reduced form
1. Could you call a taxi, please?	✓	
2. Could you call a taxi, please?		✓
3. Could you help me, please?		✓
4. Could you help me, please?	✓	
5. Could you repeat that, please?	✓	
6. Could you repeat that, please?		✓

Word Focus

The full form of *could you* is pronounced like "kud yu" (/kʊd ju/) and the reduced form is like "kudye" (/kʊdʒə/). The full form is used in formal speech and the reduced form is more informal.

B 🔄 With a partner, take turns reading the following sentences using the reduced form.

1. Could you bring me another pair of shoes, please?
2. Could you pass the water, please?
3. Could you say that again, please?
4. Could you tell me the time, please?
5. Could you bring my red scarf, please?
6. Could you repeat that, please?

Communication

A Complete the shopping list.

My shopping list			
clothes I would like to buy	shoes		
color	red		
size	8		
maximum price	$60		

B 🔄 **GOAL CHECK** ✓ **Buy clothes**

With a partner, role-play buying the clothes in exercise **A.** First, Student A is the customer and Student B is the sales assistant. Then switch roles.

Clothes **99**

Pronunciation

- Focus students' attention on the Word Focus box. Explain to students that in fast, casual speech, native English speakers often put words together and pronounce them in a reduced form. Emphasize that this is not incorrect English. Practicing reduced forms will help make students' English sound more natural.
- Introduce the full form and reduced form of *could you.*

A • Tell students to listen to the recording and mark the form they hear.
- Play the recording several times. 🔊 10
- Have students compare answers with a partner.
- Check answers.

B • Have students work with a partner to practice saying the sentences using the reduced form. Walk around checking for good pronunciation.
- Call on students to read a sentence to the class.

Communication

A • Have students complete the chart with items of clothing they would like to buy.

B 🔄 **GOAL CHECK** ✓

- Divide the class into pairs and have them role-play shopping for the clothes in their chart in **A.** Have students take turns being the customer and the sales assistant. Remind them to use the expressions in **Listening C.**
- Have several pairs role-play shopping for one of their items in front of the class.

Expansion Activity

For homework, have students find magazine or website photographs of clothes they like and bring them to class. Place or stick the photos around the classroom. Half the class will be sales assistants and the other half customers. Have students role-play being at a department store. The customers should move around the room and shop for different items.

Express Likes and Dislikes

Language Expansion

- Have students look at the picture. Say the names of the colors for students to repeat.

A • Have students work individually to fill in the names of the colors of the items of clothing in the pictures.

- Check answers.

B • Have students work individually or in pairs to list as many things as they can in the chart.

- Compare answers with the class, compiling lists on the board.

Grammar

- Explain that there are different ways of expressing degrees of *likes* and *dislikes*.

- Go over the sentences in the chart.

- Call on students to say their likes and dislikes using the expressions in the box.

1. ___beige___ coat

2. ___gray___ socks

3. ___dark purple___ blouse

pink/
4. ___dark pink___ scarf

5. ___orange___ T-shirt

Language Expansion: More clothes and colors

A Write the colors of the clothes shown in the pictures.

B Write all the clothes you can think of in the correct column.

Clothes men wear	Clothes women wear	Clothes men and women wear
		jeans

Grammar: Likes and dislikes

Likes and dislikes	
☺☺	I **love** jeans.
☺	I **like** pink T-shirts.
☹	I **don't like** hats.
☹☹	I **hate** white socks.
*We use these expressions to express likes and dislikes.	

100   Unit 8

Word Bank: More colors

gold	olive green
lavender	silver
lemon yellow	sky blue
navy blue	turquoise

Grammar: Likes and dislikes

These expressions can be used with all kinds of nouns and gerunds (for activities, *I love watching movies.*). Another very common expression for strong dislikes is *I can't stand (pizza)*.

A Complete the first column of the chart with other things like food, sports, and places. Then check (✓) the columns to show your likes and dislikes.

	😊😊 I love . . .	😊 I like . . .	😞 I don't like . . .	😫😫 I hate . . .
1. jeans				
2. the color red				
3. blue clothes				
4.				
5.				
6.				
7.				
8.				

B 🔄 Ask your partner's opinions about your chart. Write an ✗ in the chart for your partner's answers.

> Do you like strawberry ice cream?

> Yes, I love it!

C 🔄 Report to the class.

> I hate strawberry ice cream, but Rafael loves it.

Conversation

A 🔊 11 Chung and Brenda are buying a present for Brenda's brother. Listen to the conversation. What present do they buy? black T-shirt

Chung: What clothes does he like?
Brenda: He likes casual clothes. Jeans and T-shirts, you know.
Chung: What colors does he like?
Brenda: He loves dark colors. He hates colors like yellow or white.
Chung: OK, so buy him a black T-shirt.

▲ a present

B 🔄 Practice the conversation with a partner. Switch roles and practice it again.

C 🔄 Practice the conversation again, but buy a present for a person that you both know.

> What things do you love?

> I love basketball.

D 🔄 **GOAL CHECK** ✓ Express likes and dislikes

Tell a partner about things you love and things you hate.

Clothes **101**

Learn About Clothes and Colors

Reading

A • Match students with a partner and have them discuss their favorite color to wear. Are they wearing that color today?

B • Have students read the words and definitions and try to match them.
• Tell students to read the article and correct their answers, if necessary.
• Check answers.

C • Tell students to read the article again and answer *true* or *false*.
• Point out the words in the Word Focus box.
• Tell students to circle any other words they don't understand as they read.
• Check answers.
• Go over the article with the class and answer any questions from the students about vocabulary.

D • Have students discuss the questions with a partner.
• Compare answers as a class.

D | **GOAL 4:** Learn About Clothes and Colors

Reading

A ⚡ Tell a partner your favorite clothes color.

B Read the article. Match the word and the definition.

1. chameleon _b_
2. invisible _d_
3. to change _e_
4. soldier _a_
5. skin _c_

a. a person who fights in a war
b. an animal that changes color
c. the part of the body you can see
d. something you can't see
e. to make something different

C Circle **T** for *true* and **F** for *false*.

1. Chameleons change color when they are angry. (T) F
2. Dark blue is a powerful color. (T) F
3. Pink is the color of love. (T) F
4. You can buy clothes that change color. T (F)
5. Soldiers are invisible. T (F)

D ⚡ The reading says some colors make a person look a certain way. Do you agree? What do other colors say? Discuss with a partner.

Word Focus

calm = quiet
powerful = strong
romantic = loving

CHAMELEON CLOTHES

Chameleons can change the color of their skin. Sometimes they change color so that they are difficult to see and become almost invisible. Sometimes they change color to show that they are angry, or happy, or looking for a partner.

Of course, humans can't change the color of their skin, but we can change our clothes. Dark clothes make a person look more **powerful**. Pink is **romantic**; blue is **calm**. The color of your clothes says a lot about you.

Scientists are working on clothes that can change color when you press a button. They are not ready yet, but the idea is to make pants that can change from white to black or a shirt that can change from white to pink or red. Chameleon clothes!

For Your Information: Chameleons

There are about 160 different species of chameleons living in warm desert and tropical environments across Africa, Asia, and southern Europe. Some (but not all) chameleons can change their body color to fit in with their surroundings or to send a signal to other chameleons. The colors include blue, green, black, red, orange, brown, yellow, and turquoise. The color is produced by special cells in the lower layers of their skin. When a person is described as "a chameleon," it means that he or she is able to fit into different social situations easily by making changes in personality, behavior, and/or appearance.

Clothes that change color are also useful for soldiers. Like the chameleon, soldiers sometimes need to be invisible. Chameleon clothes make the soldiers difficult to see.

So, maybe someday you will be able to change your clothes from powerful to romantic to invisible—at the press of a button!

Reading Tip:
Unknown words

Tell students to circle or underline any words they don't know while reading. After they have finished, the meanings of the words may be clear based on context. After all students have finished, allow the class time to ask about the meaning of any words that are still unknown.

After Reading

Have students go online to a shopping website and find and print out a photo of clothes they like. If necessary, tell them which websites they should use. Divide the class into groups and have them take turns describing the pictures they found.

Learn About Clothes and Colors

Communication

A • Have students look at the pictures and say who they think the women are and what they are doing.

• Model the questions with a student.

• Divide the class into pairs and have them ask and answer questions about the women in the pictures.

• Call on students to describe one person's clothes to the class.

Writing

A • Have students work individually to describe the women in the pictures. Remind them that they should write about clothes, colors, and style.

• Have students exchange answers with a partner. Ask students to mark corrections and suggestions for improvements on their partner's paper.

• If desired, have students rewrite on a sheet of lined paper, to be collected for marking.

B 🔁 **GOAL CHECK** ✔

• Write on the board, *style*. Ask, *What's your style? What does it say about you?* Elicit ideas from the student, and write useful vocabulary on the board, for example: *casual, formal, serious, professional, fashionable,* etc.

• Have students work with the same partner to discuss the colors and clothes they like.

• Have several students report to the class on their partner's style or their own.

D **GOAL 4:** Learn About Clothes and Colors

> **What is she wearing?**

> **What color is it?**

> **Do you like it?**

> **Where do you think she is going?**

Communication

A 🔁 Take turns asking a partner about the clothes in the pictures. Use the questions to the left.

Writing

A Write a description of the pictures. Answers will vary.

She is wearing a yellow coat . . .

and black gloves. She has a black skirt on. She also has a black bag/ purse.

She is wearing a pink blouse and a light green skirt. She has red and yellow fabric in her hair.

_____

_____

_____

_____

B 🔁 **GOAL CHECK** ✔ **Learn about clothes and colors**

Ask your partner the following questions.

1. What is your favorite color?
2. What are your favorite clothes?

Then describe your style to your partner. What do you think your style says about you?

104   Unit 8

Teacher Tip: Giving students more responsibility

Giving students responsibility for everyday classroom tasks not only lightens the teacher's workload but also gives students more of a feeling of involvement. Here are some tasks that your students may be able to perform:

• calling the class to order at the beginning

• distributing papers

• erasing/washing the board at the end of class

• handing back homework

• setting up audio equipment

Before You Watch

A Match the opposites.

1. noisy ___b___   4. modern ___e___   a. different   d. quickly
2. same ___a___   5. beautiful ___c___   b. quiet   e. ancient
3. slowly ___d___   c. ugly

While You Watch

A ▶ Watch the video and circle **T** for *true* and **F** for *false*.

1. Florence is a modern city.   T (F)
2. The factory manager is a man.   T (F)
3. There are lots of women working in the factory.   (T) F

▲ loom

B ▶ Watch the video again. Circle the correct answer.

1. The Industrial Revolution, ((world wars,) | the cold war, | world laws,) and floods forced change.
2. The mechanical looms were made (in 1780. | (in the 19th century.) | 500 years ago.)
3. Other manufacturers threw away their old hand looms (after World War I. | 500 years ago. | (after World War II.))
4. The silk produced on antique hand looms has (4,000 threads. | (12,000 threads.) | 3,000 threads.)
5. Every damask and brocade is (man-made. | handmade. | (custom-made.))

After You Watch

A 🔁 Discuss these questions with a partner.

1. Why do you think Stefano Benelli is the only man in the video?
2. Are men better at some jobs than women? Are women better than men at some jobs? Why?

Clothes   **105**

Video Journal:
Traditional Silk-Making
Before You Watch

A • Have students look at the pictures and describe what they see.

• Have students match the opposites.

• Check answers.

• Have students predict which words in **A** they will hear in the video.

• Have students circle the words they think they will hear.

• After you play the video, have students check answers.

While You Watch

A • Have students read the statements. Tell them to watch and answer *true* or *false*.

• Play the video.

• Have students compare answers with a partner.

• Check answers.

B • Have students read the sentences. Tell them to watch the video and choose the correct answer to complete each sentence.

• Play the video again.

• Have students compare answers with a partner.

• Check answers.

After You Watch

A • Have students discuss the questions with a partner.

• Compare and discuss answers with the class.

For Your Information: Silk-Making in Florence

Silk-making became an important industry in Florence, Italy, in the early 14th century. Initially, the raw material—the silkworm eggs and cocoons, and the mulberry leaves that they ate—had to be imported from China. But as the industry grew, more raw materials were needed, so people started to cultivate mulberry bushes in the Tuscany region of Florence. This helped the industry become stronger,

and Florence became a center for silk producers from other regions of Italy who would go there to buy the raw materials.

Silk is still produced in Florence today, using the old-fashioned artisan techniques, and it is recognized around the world as being one of the finest silks. The beautiful silk scarves and wraps are popular with both locals and tourists.

Eat Well

About the Photo

Photographer Peter Menzel's project *What I Eat* shows people from all over the world posed with the food they eat in a typical day. The project includes 80 people from 30 countries. In this photo, we can see a baker baking flat bread in traditional clay ovens. As he works in the hot bakery, he eats many snacks, including food from his oven. These kinds of ovens are found in different countries around the world, such as Morocco in North Africa and in the Middle East. The flat bread may be used as a plate or as a spoon to eat a main mcal, or simply to accompany it.

Bread is a staple food for many cultures. Depending on the grains grown in a country, different types of "bread" are made, and often accompany meals. Bread is a staple in diets around the world. Examples include corn tortillas in Mexico, naan bread in India, and baguettes in France,

- Direct students' attention to the picture. Have students describe what thcy scc. Ask, *What is this man doing? What's his job? What country do you think he is in?*
- Have students answer the questions with a partner.
- Compare answers with the class, and write a list of favorite foods on the board.
- Go over the Unit Goals with the class, explaining as necessary.
- For each goal, elicit any words students already know and write them on the board, for example, food vocabulary, names of special occasions, etc.

Eat Well

A baker in Iran is shown with all the food he eats in a day, some of it cooked in his bakery.

106

UNIT 9 GOALS	Grammar	Vocabulary	Listening
• Order a meal • Plan a party • Describe your diet • Talk about a healthy diet	*Some* and *any* There's **some** ice cream in the freezer. How much/How many **How many** oranges do we need? **How much** chocolate do we have?	Food Meals Quantities Count and Non-count nouns	Listening for specific details Conversation to confirm a shopping list

UNIT 9 GOALS

1. Order a meal

2. Plan a party

3. Describe your diet

4. Talk about a healthy diet

107

Unit Theme Overview

- Food and food issues are in the news nearly every day. News reports talk about increases in food prices and changes in the way our food is grown. There is more and more debate about the healthiest way to eat and whether traditional or modern diets are better for us. Our choices in what to eat reflect many different factors: culture, economics, scientific information, and personal preference.

- In this unit, students approach the topic of food from a personal perspective (higher levels in *World English* look at the geographical and cultural aspects of food). Students learn the names of common foods and how to order in a restaurant. They practice the use of quantifiers such as *some* and *any* for food and learn to ask questions about amounts of count and non-count nouns. They consider whether their own diets are healthy or unhealthy. Finally, they read about TED speaker Ron Finley's idea for how to feed people in his neighborhood in Los Angeles.

Speaking	Reading	Writing	Video Journal
Planning a dinner Planning a garden **Pronunciation:** *And*	**TED Talks:** "Ron Finley: A Guerilla Gardener in South Central L.A."	Writing about a healthy diet	**National Geographic:** "Slow Food"

Order a Meal

Vocabulary

- Have students look at the pictures. Say the names of foods for the class to repeat.

A • Go over the terms on the menu. Have students work individually to list the items in the correct categories.

- Check answers.

- Have students say what they like to eat and drink at each meal.

B • Divide the class into pairs and have them discuss what they like to eat at each meal.

- Compare answers with the class.

A GOAL 1: Order a Meal

Vocabulary

▲ cereal and milk   ▲ eggs   ▲ steak   ▲ fish

▲ salad   ▲ pasta   ▲ chicken   ▲ fruit juice

▲ coffee   ▲ tea   ▲ chocolate cake   ▲ ice cream

A Write the foods pictured above in the correct place on the menu.

~~~ **Breakfast** ~~~
(7:00 a.m. to 12:00 p.m.)

cereal and milk, eggs

Lunch & Dinner
(12:00 p.m. to 8:00 p.m.) All served with salad

steak, fish, salad, pasta, chicken

Drinks

fruit juice, coffee, tea

Desserts

chocolate cake, ice cream

B Tell a partner the foods you like and don't like for breakfast, lunch, and dinner. Use a dictionary if needed.

108   Unit 9

Word Bank: More food

Breakfast: fruit, oatmeal/porridge, pancakes, toast, waffles, yogurt

Lunch/Dinner: beans, beef, ham, lamb, peas, potatoes, rice, soup

Drinks: iced tea, lemonade, mineral water, soda

Desserts: brownies, cookies, fruit salad, pastry, pie

Grammar: *Some* and *any*

Some is used in affirmative sentences; *any* is used in questions and negatives, and both are used in questions that make offers. This rule has been simplified here somewhat, but will always produce grammatical sentences.

(Native speakers generally use *some* in offers when they anticipate an affirmative answer: *Do you want some ice cream?* They use *any* when they anticipate a negative answer: *Do you want any more ice cream, or should I put it away?*)

Grammar: *Some* and *any*

Some and any		
Statement	**Negative**	**Question**
There's **some** ice cream in the freezer.	We don't have **any** chicken.	Do you have **any** chocolate cake?

*We use *some* for questions with *can* and *could*. Can I have **some** water, please?

A Complete the article with *some* or *any*.

In India, many people don't eat (1) ____any____ meat. They are

called vegetarians. That means they don't eat (2) ____any____

chicken or (3) ____any____ steak. So what do vegetarians eat?

They have (4) ____some____ delicious options. At an Indian

vegetarian restaurant, you can order (5) ____some____ delicious fruit

juices and enjoy (6) ____some____ wonderful salads. There are

also (7) ____some____ great desserts.

▲ About one-third of the people of India are vegetarians.

B Unscramble the words to write sentences and questions.

1. some coffee   There's   on the table.   _There's some coffee on the table._
2. some   I have   chocolate   Could   ice cream?   _Could I have some chocolate ice cream?_
3. have   We   don't   fruit juice.   any   _We don't have any fruit juice._
4. fish?   we have   any   Do   _Do we have any fish?_
5. eggs   next to   some   the milk.   There are   _There are some eggs next to the milk._

Conversation

A 🔊 12 Listen to the conversation. What does the customer order? *coffee and chocolate ice cream*

Waiter: Good evening.
Customer: Could I have some <u>coffee</u>, please?
Waiter: Sure.
Customer: Do you have any <u>strawberry ice cream</u>?
Waiter: No, I'm sorry. We don't have <u>strawberry</u>. We only have <u>chocolate</u>.
Customer: OK, I'll have some <u>chocolate ice cream</u>.

B 🔁 Practice the conversation with a partner. Switch roles and practice it again.

C 🔁 Change the underlined words and make a new conversation.

D 🔁 **GOAL CHECK** ✔ **Order a meal**

Change partners. Role-play ordering a meal.

- Go over the information about *some* and *any* in the chart.
- Point out that *any* is generally used in negative statements and questions. Point out that with polite requests, we use *some*.
- Elicit examples of food from students. List them on the board. Elicit sample sentences and questions from students.

A • Have students work individually to complete the article.
- Have students compare answers with a partner.
- Check answers.

B • Have students work individually to write the sentences.
- Have students compare answers with a partner.
- Check answers.

Conversation

A • Have students close their books. Write the question on the board: *What does the customer order?*
- Play the recording. 🔊 12
- Check answers.

B • Play or read the conversation again for the class to repeat.
- Practice the conversation with the class in chorus.
- Have students practice the conversation with a partner and then switch roles and practice it again.

C • Have students work with the same partner to make a new conversation.
- Call on student pairs to present their conversation to the class.

D 🔁 **GOAL CHECK** ✔

- Divide the class into pairs and have them role-play ordering some of their favorite foods in a restaurant.
- Call on student pairs to present their role-play to the class.

Grammar Practice: *Some* and *any*

Tell students to look at the restaurant menu in **Vocabulary A** and cross out any three items. These are things that the restaurant has "run out of." Then match students with a partner and have them role-play a scene in the restaurant. One student is the customer and the other is the server. The customer should order, and the server will tell the customer what they don't have. Then have students change roles and practice again.

Plan a Party

Listening

- Tell students they are going to hear two people planning a party. With the class, look at the picture and talk about the items in it.

A • Tell students to listen to the conversation and complete the shopping list.
- Play the recording one or more times. 🔊 13
- Check answers.

B • Divide the class into pairs and have them role-play a scene in a store where they ask for the items on the list.
- Model the question and answer with several students.

C • Say, *I'm inviting some friends for dinner. What can I make?* Write students' ideas on the board. Choose one or two dishes and drinks, and ask, *What do I need to buy?* Tell them how many people you are inviting. Have students help you write a shopping list on the board.
- Divide the class into pairs and have them plan a breakfast with friends. Have them decide how many people are coming, what they are going to prepare, and what they will need to buy. Then have them write a shopping list.
- Have several pairs share their shopping list with the class.

B | **GOAL 2:** Plan a Party

▲ loaf

▲ bottle

▲ bag

▲ carton

▲ box

110   Unit 9

Listening

Miguel and Diana are planning a party. Miguel is writing a shopping list.

A 🔊 13 Listen and complete Miguel's shopping list.

_____12_____	bottles of soda
1 bag of _____ice_____	
20 _____hamburgers_____	
10 _____hot dogs_____	

B 🔄 Role-play buying the food on Miguel's shopping list.

loaf		bread
bottle		soda, fruit juice
bag	of	ice
carton		milk, eggs, fruit juice
box		cereal

> Let's see. We need some soda.

> How many bottles do you want?

C You are inviting some friends over for breakfast. Write a shopping list.

SHOPPING LIST
2 cartons of milk
_____ _____
_____ _____
_____ _____

Word Bank: Party food

cake	peanuts
cheese and crackers	potato chips and dip
coffee, tea	pretzels
cookies	punch
corn chips	sandwiches
lemonade	

Pronunciation: *And*

A 🔊 14 Listen and check (✓) the correct column of the form you hear.

	Full form	Reduced form
1. pasta and salad	✓	
2. pasta and salad		✓
3. fruit juice and cereal		✓
4. fruit juice and cereal	✓	
5. chocolate cake and ice cream	✓	
6. chocolate cake and ice cream		✓

Word Focus

In conversation, the word *and* is often reduced to sound like *n*.

B 🔁 With a partner, take turns reading the following sentences using the reduced form.

1. I like hot dogs and hamburgers.
2. Jill and David are good friends.
3. How many brothers and sisters do you have?
4. We have strawberry ice cream and chocolate ice cream.

Communication

A 👥 In groups of three, plan a dinner party.

1. Decide how many people to invite. Write down their names.
2. Make a menu for the dinner.
3. Decide where the guests will sit. Make a seating plan in your notebook.

Does Sachin eat meat?

No, he's a vegetarian.

Emmanuel can sit next to Leo. They are good friends.

Let's put your brother between Gloria and Diana.

B 👥 **GOAL CHECK** ✔ **Plan a party**

Join another group. Explain your menu and seating plan.

Eat Well   **111**

Pronunciation

- Remind students that in fast, casual speech, native English speakers often pronounce words in a reduced form. Practicing reduced forms will help make students' English sound more natural.
- Point out the information in the Word Focus box and introduce the full form and reduced form of *and*.

A • Tell students to listen to the recording and check the form they hear.
- Play the recording several times. 🔊 14
- Have students compare answers with a partner.
- Check answers.

B • Have students work with the same partner to practice saying the sentences using the reduced form. Walk around helping with difficulties.
- Call on students to read a sentence to the class.

Communication

A • Divide the class into groups of three and have them follow the directions to plan an imaginary party. If desired, you can allow them to invite famous people to their party (living and/or dead!).

B 👥 **GOAL CHECK** ✔

- Combine the groups to form groups of six and have them take turns describing their party plans.
- Call on each group to tell the class about their menu, guest list, and seating plan.

Expansion Activity

If appropriate, have the students plan an actual party for class time, with snacks, music in English, and games in English (give help as needed in finding and setting up the games).

Describe Your Diet

Language Expansion

- Talk about the meaning of *diet*—all the food you eat. Ask students, *Is your diet healthy? Why or why not?*

- Have students look at the eatwell plate and talk about the foods on the plate. Elicit expressions to talk about likes and dislikes *(I love/like/ don't like/hate).* Ask, *Do you like (fish)? Is your favorite food here?*

A • Focus students' attention on the information in the box. Introduce the idea of count nouns (apples, oranges, hamburgers) and non-count nouns (coffee, tea, and water). Tell students that these are also sometimes called countable and uncountable nouns.

- Have students work individually to write the foods in the correct part of the chart.

- Have students compare answers with a partner.

- Copy the chart onto the board and check answers.

B • Have students add other foods to the chart.

- With the class, add to the chart on the board.

C **GOAL 3**: Describe Your Diet

Language Expansion: Count and non-count nouns

The Eatwell Plate

The eatwell plate helps you to eat a healthy diet. It shows the types of food to eat and also how much of each type of food to eat. Do you see any of your favorite foods?

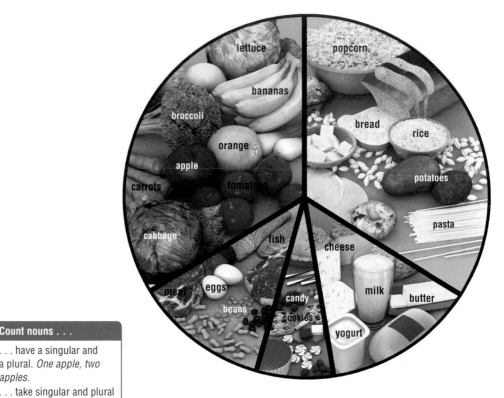

Count nouns . . .
. . . have a singular and a plural. *One apple, two apples.*
. . . take singular and plural verbs *The apple is red. The apples are red.*

Non-count nouns . . .
. . . only have a singular. *Water.*
. . . only take singular verbs. *The water is hot.*

A Write the foods from above in the correct column.

Count nouns (plural ending *-s*)		Non-count nouns		
oranges	potatoes	rice	meat	butter
apple	eggs	lettuce	fish	milk
bananas	cookies	broccoli	beans	candy
carrots		cabbage	cheese	
tomatoes		bread	yogurt	

B Add the names of other foods that you eat in your country to the chart in **A**.

Word Bank:
Fruit and vegetables

blueberries	melon	peppers
celery	onions	pineapples
cherries	papayas	spinach
cucumber	peaches	squash
grapes	peas	strawberries
mangoes	pears	zucchini

Grammar: Count and non-count nouns

Count nouns are things that are viewed as separate units: *one potato, two potatoes.*

Non-count nouns are things that are viewed as substances: *water, bread.*

For many non-count nouns, there are units that make them count nouns: *one <u>cup</u> of water, two <u>slices</u> of bread.*

Grammar: *How much / How many*

How much and How many	
Count nouns	**Non-count nouns**
How many oranges do you need?	**How much** milk do we have?

*How much and how many are used to ask about quantities.

A Complete the sentences. Use *how much* or *how many*.

1. _____How many_____ eggs do you eat every week?
2. _____How much_____ meat do you eat every week?
3. _____How much_____ fruit juice do you drink every day?
4. _____How many_____ cookies do you eat every day?
5. _____How much_____ bread do you eat every day?

B 🔄 With a partner, take turns asking and answering the questions in exercise **A**.

Conversation

A 🔊 **15** Listen to the conversation. Does the patient eat well? *no*

Doctor: Tell me about the food you eat. How much fruit do you eat?
Patient: I eat <u>an apple</u> every day. Sometimes I have <u>an orange</u>, as well.
Doctor: Very good! Do you eat meat?
Patient: <u>Yes, I love meat.</u>
Doctor: How much meat do you eat?
Patient: <u>I eat a big steak every day.</u>
Doctor: And vegetables. Do you eat any vegetables?
Patient: <u>No, I don't like vegetables.</u>

▲ How many count and non-count nouns can you see at this floating market in Indonesia?

B 🔄 Practice the conversation with a partner. Switch roles and practice it again.

C 🔄 Change the underlined words and make a new conversation. Make the diet more healthy.

D ♻ | **GOAL CHECK** ✔ **Describe your diet**

Make a list of the foods you eat on a normal day. Tell a partner or a group about your diet and decide with the group if it is healthy or not.

Eat Well **113**

Grammar

- Review the idea of count and non-count nouns. Go over the information in the chart. Have the class practice asking questions. Say, for example, *I eat hamburgers. (How many hamburgers do you eat?), I drink tea. (How much tea do you drink?)*

A • Have students work individually to complete the questions.
- Have students compare answers with a partner.
- Check answers.

B • Divide the class into pairs and have them practice asking and answering the questions. Remind them that they can also say (for example), *I don't eat meat.*

Conversation

A • Have students close their books. Write the question on the board: *Does the patient eat well?*
- Play the recording. 🔊 **15**
- Check answers.

B • Play or read the conversation again for the class to repeat.
- Practice the conversation with the class in chorus.
- Have students practice the conversation with a partner and then switch roles and practice it again.

C • Have students work with the same partner to make a new conversation.
- Call on student pairs to present their conversation to the class.

D ♻ | **GOAL CHECK** ✔

- Review the idea of diet. Have students write a list of what they eat on a normal day.
- Divide the class into groups of three or four. Within their groups, have students talk about their diet and discuss if it is healthy or not.
- Compare answers with the class. Discuss what kinds of food are in a healthy diet.

Grammar Practice: Count and non-count nouns

Divide the class into pairs. Have them close their books. Tell them to work together to list ten count nouns and ten non-count nouns as fast as they can. They should raise their hands when finished. Note the names of the first three pairs to finish. When all students have finished, call on the first three pairs to write their lists on the board. With the class, go over each list and correct any mistakes. The pair with the most correct answers is the winner.

Lesson C **113**

D TEDTALKS

Talk About a Healthy Diet

Reading

A • Have students look at the pictures and categorize the food into healthy and unhealthy. Provide vocabulary as necessary.

• Compare answers with the class.

B • Divide the class into groups of three or four and have students identify which foods in **A** they can buy in their neighborhood and where.

• Compare answers with the class.

C • Have students look at the pictures and the captions, then read the questions and guess the answers.

• Have students read the article and confirm their answers. Focus their attention on the Word Bank and go over any unfamiliar words.

• Have students compare answers with a partner.

• Check the answers.

D GOAL 4: Talk About a Healthy Diet

Reading

A Look at the pictures. Which foods are healthy? Which foods are unhealthy?

B Work with a group. Talk about the foods in exercise **A**. How many of these foods can you buy in your neighborhood? Where can you buy them?

C Read the article. Choose the words that correctly complete each sentence.

1. Ron Finley is an activist who likes to work in ((gardens) | restaurants).

2. He lives in a part of Los Angeles where there is a food (farmers market | (desert)).

3. In a ((food desert) | city), it is not easy to get fresh, healthy food.

4. In the (world | (United States)), more than 26 million people live in food deserts.

5. Ron Finley thinks that people should (eat more meat | (grow their own) (food)).

6. In South Central Los Angeles, there are many ((vacant lots) | empty streets) that can be made into gardens.

WORD BANK
access a way to get something
activist someone who works to solve a social problem
affordable does not cost too much money
garden area of land used for growing plants
gardener someone who takes care of a garden
vacant lot empty land in a city

114 Unit 9

Ideas worth spreading

Ron Finley Activist/Gardener

A GUERILLA GARDENER IN SOUTH CENTRAL L.A.

The following article is about Ron Finley. After Unit 9, you'll have the opportunity to watch some of Finley's TED Talk and learn more about his idea worth spreading.

Ron Finley is a **gardener** and **activist.** He lives in South Central, a low-income part of Los Angeles that Finley calls a "food desert." Food deserts are places with no access to fresh, healthy food.

How many people live in food deserts? In the United States, more than 26 million. In a food desert, people do not have **access** to food that is fresh, healthy, and **affordable.** There aren't many grocery stores or farmers markets. Instead, there are fast food restaurants and convenience stores. Many people in food deserts have bad health problems because of the unhealthy food.

Ron Finley wants to solve the problem of food deserts. He believes that people can grow their own food, even in the city. In Finley's neighborhood in Los Angeles, there are many **vacant lots** and other small areas of land that can be made into gardens. If there are **gardens** with vegetables and fruits, people will have access to healthy food and they can be more healthy.

For Your Information: Ron Finley

Ron Finley is an artist and designer from South Central, a part of Los Angeles. He became concerned about the health problems in his community, so he decided to take action. Finley co-founded L.A. Green Grounds, a charitable organization whose aim is to plant urban gardens all over L.A.—in empty lots, on sidewalks, and in any other suitable areas.

Finley's objective is to improve community life through these gardens by helping people learn about sustainability, gardening, and nutrition. He strongly believes that if people are involved in growing their own food, they will want to eat healthier, and at the same time become more involved in their communities. Diet and health problems, such as obesity and diabetes, are key issues in many areas due to the wide availability of processed food and relative unavailability of fresh, nutritious food. Finley is raising people's awareness of this issue and working creatively to make a change.

Urban gardening helps people in the city get healthy food.

"Food is the problem and food is the solution."

– Ron Finley

For Your Information: Farmer's markets

In the past five years, the number of farmer's markets in the United States has grown by 74%, from 4,685 to 8,144, and the number continues to grow. Almost 70% of these markets are in urban counties. The numbers show that as activists like Ron Finley fight to bring local, fresh food to communities, people are getting more and more access to these types of food.

After Reading

Ask students to find information about a fresh food that might be hard to get in a city. Where is the food from? What is in it? Why is it hard to find in urban areas?

Writing

A • Have students look at the picture and describe what they see.

• Tell students to read the directions and the words in the Word Bank.

• Have students complete the sentences.

• Have students compare answers with a partner.

• Check answers.

B • Discuss as a class if the sentences in **A** describe healthy or unhealthy eating habits.

C • Write on the board: *Mia wants to eat food that is healthier.* Ask, *Which word is the subject? Which is the verb?* Underline the verb and circle the subject. Focus students' attention on the Writing Strategy.

• Ask, *What can Mia do to have a healthier diet?* Write students' ideas on the board.

• Have students write their paragraph.

• Have students underline the verbs and subjects in their paragraph. Have them check that they have used *she* and the correct form of the verb.

Communication

A • Tell students they are going to plan a garden for the school.

• Divide the class into pairs and have students read the directions and plan their garden.

• Have pairs join together and explain their plans to each other.

B ⟳ **GOAL CHECK** ✔

• In the same pairs, have students plan a lunch to celebrate the new garden. Remind them to include food from the garden on the menu.

• Have several pairs tell the class about their lunch menu.

D | **GOAL 4:** Talk About a Healthy Diet

Finley says, "Growing your own food is like printing your own money."

WORD BANK
a. healthy
b. farmers market
c. dinner
d. ice cream
e. convenience store
f. favorite
g. potato

Writing

A Mia and her doctor are talking about what Mia eats. First, read all the sentences. Then complete the sentences with words from the word bank. Write the correct letter.

Mia says:

"I buy my (1) _f_ foods at a (2) _e_ near my house. For (3) _c_, I eat pizza. Also I eat some (4) _g_ chips. Later I eat a lot of (5) _d_ ."

Mia's doctor says:

"Mia needs to eat more fresh, (6) _a_ foods. She can buy them at a (7) _b_ ."

Writing Strategy

When you write, it is important to self-correct. As you correct your own writing, you can use visual cues to help you focus on certain words. Some visual cues you can use are underlining and circling.

B ♲ Do the sentences describe healthy or unhealthy eating habits? Discuss as a class.

C Mia wants to eat food that is healthier.

• Write a new paragraph about Mia, changing the unhealthy foods for healthy foods. Mia buys… For dinner, she…

• Underline the verbs and circle the subjects in your paragraph.

Communication

A ♲ Think of a place in or near your school where you could make a garden. With a partner, decide what you will plant there. Draw the shape of the area and mark it with the different plants. Decide how much or how many of each item you will grow.

- How many tomato plants do we need?

- Five tomato plants.

B ⟳ **GOAL CHECK** ✔ Talk about a healthy diet

With a partner, plan a lunch menu. Use foods from your school garden.

116 Unit 9

Before You Watch

A Write the food in the correct column. Add some more food items.

~~hamburger~~   ~~cheese~~   fish   mushrooms   pizza   hot dogs   french fries   fruit

Fast food	Slow food
hamburger	cheese
pizza	fish
hot dogs	mushrooms
french fries	fruit

While You Watch

A ▶ Answer the questions.

1. Is Greve a big city? _no_
2. What do the people of Chianti produce? _cheese and mushrooms_
3. Does the mayor want to change Greve? _no_
4. What is the goal of the Slow Food Movement? _keep good living, good food, family, and friends_
5. What do the farmers of Pistoia produce? _a special cheese_

After You Watch

A How can you slow down your life? Label the pictures with the phrases in the box.

spend time with friends and family   eat healthy food
get more exercise   take a nap in the afternoon

B 🔁 Discuss with a partner: In what other ways can you slow down your life?

eat healthy food

take a nap in the afternoon

get more exercise

spend time with friends and family

Eat Well   **117**

Video Journal:
Slow Food

Before You Watch

A • Have students look at the picture and describe what they see.

• With the class, go over the names of the foods in the pictures. Introduce the idea of *fast food*, and ask students for examples of it.

• Have students work individually to list the foods in the chart.

• Check answers.

• Divide the class into pairs and have them discuss foods they like and dislike (both foods from the chart and other foods).

While You Watch

A • Tell students to watch the video and answer the questions. Go over the questions with the class.

• Play the video one or more times.

• Have students compare answers with a partner.

• Check answers.

After You Watch

A • Talk about the idea of slow food and why people like to do things more slowly.

• Have students work individually to label the pictures.

• Check answers.

B • Divide the class into pairs and have them talk about more ideas for slowing down their lives.

• With the class, compile a list on the board. Ask students which ideas they would like to try.

For Your Information: Slow food

The Slow Food Movement was started in Italy in the 1980s to fight the rise of fast food and industrialized living. It was begun by Carlo Petrini. Now there are more than 100,000 members in 122 chapters in Italy, and 650 regional chapters of the organization around the world. The goals of the Slow Food Movement are to promote traditional foods, to start seed banks to save the seeds of traditional crops, and to organize celebrations of local cuisine in different regions of the world. It also tries to educate people about the problems and dangers of industrial agriculture.

Teacher Tip: Sharing students' work

• Make large posters to display in front of the class (brown wrapping paper for packages is cheap and works well for this).

• Tape students' papers around the classroom walls and allow time for students to walk around and read their classmates' work.

• Have students write or draw on a transparency and show these to the class on an overhead projector.

• Photocopy students' papers into a class magazine/newspaper and make a copy for each student.

A Guerilla Gardener in South Central L.A.

Before You Watch

A • Have students look at the words in the box and write them in the correct column in the chart.

• Check answers.

B • Have students read the words and the definitions in the box. Have them try to complete the sentences with the words.

• Have them compare answers with a partner.

• Check answers.

C • Ask, *What do you know about gardening?* Have students write down four things about gardening that they think will be in the talk.

• Have students compare their list with a partner.

• Have several pairs share their ideas and write them on the board.

• Have any students who have a home garden talk about their garden.

While You Watch

A • Have students read the items. Tell students they are going to watch the video and check the items they see in the talk.

• Have students compare answers with a partner.

• Check answers.

B • Have students look at the pictures on page 119.

• Divide the class into pairs and have students discuss what they think is happening in each picture.

• Call on pairs to share their answers with the class.

Ron Finley Activist/Gardener
A GUERILLA GARDENER IN SOUTH CENTRAL L.A.

Before You Watch

A Write the words from the box in the correct category.

> carrots   tomatoes   ice cream   pasta
> oranges   hamburgers   lettuce   candy
> pizza   beans

Garden Plants	Other Foods
carrots	ice cream
tomatoes	pasta
oranges	hamburgers
lettuce	candy
beans	pizza

B Look at the words in the box. Complete the sentences with the correct words.

> **food desert** a place with no fresh, healthy food
> **garden** land used for growing food
> **gardener** a person that works in a garden
> **grow** increase in size
> **plant** to put something in the ground to grow
> **vacant lot** an unused area of a city
> **volunteer** a person who works for free; to do work for free

1. He will _____grow_____ some food in his ___garden___.

2. The city has a ___food desert___ that has no markets or grocery stores.

3. She wants to ___plant___ some tomatoes on the land.

118

> Ron Finley's idea worth spreading is that we need to get smarter about the food we eat; and we should start by growing our own. Watch Finley's full TED Talk at TED.com.

4. The ___vacant lot___ was full of trash.

5. She is a ___volunteer___ at the garden two days a week.

6. The ___gardener___ picked many vegetables from his plants.

C You are going to watch a TED Talk about Ron Finley's gardens in the city of Los Angeles. What do you know about gardening? Write down four things you think you will see in the TED Talk. Compare your list with a partner's.

While You Watch

A Watch the TED Talk. Place a check mark next to the items that you see in the talk.

____ supermarkets
✓ wheelchairs
____ clothing stores
✓ Central Park
✓ seeds
✓ money
✓ Ron Finley's sons
____ orange trees
✓ volunteers
✓ children
____ soccer game
✓ farmers' market

B Look at the pictures on the next page. Explain to a partner what you think is happening in each picture.

> " Growing one plant will give you 1,000, 10,000 seeds. Growing your own food is like printing your own money."

— Ron Finley

Using Visual Cues

- Focus students' attention on the Strategy box.
- After watching the video, call on students to list any visual cues from the video that helped them understand the main idea.

"If kids grow kale, kids eat kale. If they grow tomatoes, they eat tomatoes."

"I have witnessed my garden become a tool for the education, a tool for the transformation of my neighborhood. To change the community, you have to change the composition of the soil. We are the soil."

USING VISUAL CUES

You do not need to understand every word you hear. Use visual cues such as photos in the TED Talk to help you understand the main idea.

"So with gardening, I see an opportunity where we can train these kids to take over their communities, to have a sustainable life."

119

Working with authentic spoken language

When listening to authentic spoken English as in the TED Talks, it is important that students remember that they don't need to understand every word. Remind them that in spoken English, words are often run together and reduced forms are used (as they saw in Unit 9 with *and*). Students should know that important (content) words are often stressed, so those are the words they should focus on to help them understand.

After You Watch

A • Have students read the sentences. Tell them to choose the correct word or words to complete each sentence as they watch the talk again.

• Have students compare answers with a partner.

• Check answers.

B • Have students read the sentences and choose *true* or *false*. Have them correct the false information. Watch the video again as necessary.

• Have students compare answers with a partner.

• Check answers.

TEDTALKS

Ron Finley Activist/Gardener
A GUERILLA GARDENER IN SOUTH CENTRAL L.A.

After You Watch

A Watch the TED Talk again. Choose the correct word to complete each quote.

1. More than 26.5 million Americans live in (Los Angeles | ⬡food deserts ⬡).

2. (Money | ⬡Food⬡) is the problem and (⬡food⬡ | water) is the solution.

3. L.A. leads the United States in (⬡vacant lots⬡ | supermarkets) that the city actually owns. That's enough space to plant 725 million (⬡tomato plants⬡ | apple trees).

4. One dollar's worth of (plants | ⬡green beans⬡) will give you 75 dollars' worth of produce.

5. (⬡Gardening⬡ | Shopping) is the most therapeutic and defiant act you can do, especially in the inner city. Plus you get (⬡strawberries⬡ | vegetables).

6. If kids (want | ⬡grow⬡) kale, kids eat kale. If they grow tomatoes, they (⬡eat⬡ | buy) tomatoes.

B Are these statements true or false? Circle **T** for true and **F** for false. Correct any false information in your notebook.

1. Ron Finley saw that many people in his neighborhood were unhealthy.   Ⓣ   F

2. Finley planted a food garden in the parkway in front of his house.   Ⓣ   F

3. At night, hungry people took food from Finley's garden, so he ~~stopped planting~~ gardens.   T   Ⓕ
planted more

4. Finley started L.A. Green Grounds, a group of volunteers who build ~~farmers markets~~ in the city.   T   Ⓕ
gardens

5. Green Grounds planted about ~~10~~ gardens.   T   Ⓕ
20

6. Finley believes that if kids learn to grow their own food, they will make the community better.   Ⓣ   F

C 🔁 Work with a partner to explain how Ron Finley's gardens help solve each problem. Answers will vary.

Problem	How gardening helps
1. Some people in South Central L.A. are unhealthy because of a poor diet.	More healthy food is available.
2. People do not have access to fresh, healthy food.	Gardens can be local, so everyone can get food.
3. The city has too many vacant lots.	The land is being used for something helpful.
4. Kids do not have a sustainable way of living or healthy habits.	Gardening gives kids healthy food and teaches them how to work hard for their community.

D 🔁 Write a list of the healthy foods you eat. Compare your list with a partner.

E 🔁 Work with a group to plan a small garden. Follow these steps:

* Say why your area should have a community garden.
* Use your lists from **D** to pick four foods that can be planted in the garden.
* Research the plants on the Internet or in the library to find out when they should be planted and what growing conditions (sunlight, weather, etc.) they need.
* Pick a place to build your garden. Plan your garden. Make a poster showing the garden's location and the foods that will be planted. Explain why you chose these plants.
* Present your garden poster to the class.

Challenge! Ron Finley is not the only person who believes that people need to grow their own food. Watch Roger Doiron's TED Talk on TED.com. How are their ideas similar? How are they different?

121

Expansion Activity

Have students research whether or not there are community gardens or farmers markets in their city or town. If there are, have students write a list of questions they would like to ask the people in charge. If there are not, have students write a list of reasons that the community would benefit from a community garden or farmer's market.

C • Have students read the list of problems and then decide with a partner how Finley's gardens help solve the problems.

* Have several pairs share their answers with the class. Answers will vary.

D • Elicit examples of healthy food. Have students write a list of the healthy food they eat.

* Divide the class into pairs, and have students interview each other to find out if they eat the same food. Model the questions, *Do you eat/drink…? How much/many… do you eat/drink?*

* Have several pairs share what they have in common with their partner.

E • Go over the steps with the class. Then with the same partner, have students work through the steps to plan a garden. **Note:** Depending on in-class access to the Internet, this activity may need out-of-class preparation time as well.

* Have students display their posters around the classroom and ask and answer questions about the gardens. Have one student from each pair stay by the poster to answer questions and the other student walk around looking at the other posters. Have them switch roles after a few minutes. If possible, invite other classes to come and see the posters and ask each group questions.

Challenge

* With their books closed, have students say what Ron Finley is doing, where, and why. Write their ideas on the board.

* Have students watch Roger Doiron's TED Talk in class, if possible, or outside class. Have them identify similarities and differences between his and Finley's ideas.

* Have students share their answers with the class. Write their ideas on the board.

Health

About the Photo

Chinese fan dancing has been a part of Chinese culture for at least 2,000 years, and it is still practiced today. The fan dances tell traditional stories and are a way of passing them on to younger generations. Fan dancing is also considered a form of exercise and a way to develop self-discipline.

This photo shows women dancing on the Bund, in Shanghai, with the Pudong district skyline in the background. The Bund is a famous waterfront area in central Shanghai. It has been considered the symbol of Shanghai for many years and is its most well-known tourist attraction. The Pudong district, across the Huangpu River from the Bund, is a modern urban district that opened in 1990 to be a center for international commerce and finance. It is an impressive mix of architectural styles that provides a stunning skyline for visitors viewing it from the Bund.

- Direct students' attention to the picture. Have students describe what they can see. Ask, *What are these people doing? Where? Why? What time of day is it?*
- Have students answer the questions with a partner.
- Compare answers with the class. Write what activities students do to stay healthy on the board.
- Go over the Unit Goals with the class, explaining as necessary.
- For each goal, elicit any words students already know and write them on the board, for example, parts of the body, illnesses.

Fan dancing is a beautiful form of exercise. These women perform a traditional fan dance in Shanghai.

122

UNIT 10 GOALS	Grammar	Vocabulary	Listening
• Identify parts of the body to say how you feel • Ask about and describe symptoms • Identify remedies and give advice • Describe how to prevent health problems	*Feel, look* John **looks** terrible. I **feel** sick. My back **hurts**. *Should* (for advice) You **should** see a doctor.	Parts of the body Common illnesses and ailments Remedies	Listening for general understanding and specific details Describing symptoms to a doctor

UNIT 10 GOALS

1. Identify parts of the body to say how you feel

2. Ask about and describe symptoms

3. Identify remedies and give advice

4. Describe how to prevent health problems

123

Unit Theme Overview

- The human body is the same all over the world, but people's experiences with health and illness vary widely, both among individuals and among cultures. For even a simple problem such as a cold, there are widely different reactions and remedies in different places. Some people will go to a doctor when they have a cold; others will use commercial medicines; others will employ old household remedies; some will just wait for the cold to pass.

- In this unit, students approach the topic of health by beginning with the universal. They learn to describe how they feel, and they learn the names of body parts to talk about problems. They talk about common conditions and learn to give advice about remedies. In the reading, they learn about preventing some of the most serious illnesses around the world and in the video, they learn that animals can get sick, too, just like people.

Speaking	Reading	Writing	Video Journal
Describing symptoms and illnesses Giving advice **Pronunciation:** Word stress	**National Geographic:** "Preventing Disease"	Writing rules for preventing health problems	**National Geographic:** "Farley, the Red Panda"

Identify Parts of the Body to Say How You Feel

Vocabulary

A • Have students look at the illustration of the body parts. Tell them to listen to the recording and repeat the words.

• Play the recording one or more times. 🔊 16

B • Direct students' attention to the pictures. Talk about the problems shown in each one, and pronounce the names of the health problems for students to repeat.

• Go over the words in the box for how people feel. Point out that they go from *terrible* (very, very bad) to *great* (very, very good).

• Have students complete the sentences, individually or with a partner.

• Check answers.

Grammar

• Go over the information in the chart. Point out the difference between feel (inside yourself) and look (outside to other people). Explain that sometimes people feel sick, but they don't look sick.

• Ask several students, *How are you feeling? How do you feel?*

Vocabulary

A 🔊 16 Listen and repeat the parts of the body.

B How are they feeling? Complete the sentences below with words from the box.

head
face
ear
chest
back
stomach
arm
hand
finger
knee
leg
foot/feet

▲ headache   ▲ fever

▲ cough   ▲ backache   ▲ stomachache

| terrible   sick   OK   well   great |

1. John is _____sick_____ . He has a fever, a cough, and a bad headache.
2. Mary isn't _____well_____ . She has a stomachache.
3. Michael is _____OK_____ . His fever is gone today.
4. Jane feels _____great_____ . She isn't sick, and today's her birthday.
5. Susan is feeling _____terrible_____ . She has a backache and can't move.

Grammar: *Feel, look*

Affirmative	Negative	*Yes/No* questions	Short answers	Information questions	Answers
I **feel** sick. He/She **looks** sick.	Hilary **doesn't feel** great. You **don't look** well.	**Do** you **feel** OK? **Does** he/she **look** tired?	Yes, **I do.** No, **she doesn't.**	How **do** you **feel?** How **are** you **feeling?**	I **feel** fine.

*The verbs *look* and *feel* are followed by an adjective.
**The questions *How do you feel?* and *How are you feeling?* are interchangeable.

Word Bank: Internal body parts

arteries	joints	muscles
bones	kidneys	nerves
brain	liver	stomach
heart	lungs	veins
intestines		

Grammar: *Feel, look*

Feel and *look* are stative verbs—verbs that describe states. They link the subject to additional information about the subject and are not usually used in continuous tenses.

A Match the questions and sentences with the responses.

1. How do you feel? __b__
2. Do you feel OK? __d__
3. Does Talib look well? __c__
4. How do they feel? __e__
5. Sarah doesn't look well. __a__

a. She isn't feeling well.
b. I feel fine.
c. No, he doesn't. He looks sick.
d. No, I feel terrible.
e. They feel OK.

B Complete the sentences.

1. **A:** Do you feel OK?
   B: Yes, I _____ *do* _____ .
2. **A:** How is Melanie?
   B: She doesn't _____ *feel* _____ well.
3. **A:** How *do you feel/are you feeling* ?
   B: I feel terrible.
4. **A:** What's the matter?
   B: I don't _____ *feel* _____ well.
5. **A:** Does Gerardo look OK?
   B: No, he _____ *he looks* _____ sick.

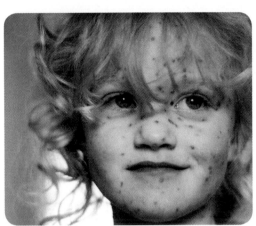

▲ Chicken pox affects many children. It causes blisters, fever, and headache.

Conversation

A  **17** Listen to the conversation. What's wrong with Kim? *her head hurts (and she feels sick)*

Boss: What's the matter, Kim? You don't look well.
Kim: I don't feel well. My head hurts.
Boss: Oh, no!
Kim: And I feel sick.
Boss: OK. You can go home.

B 🔄 Practice the conversation with a partner. Switch roles and practice it again.

C 🔄 You don't feel well at school. Ask the teacher (your partner) to let you go home. Then switch roles.

D 🔄 | GOAL CHECK ✓ **Identify parts of the body to say how you feel**

Take turns asking a partner how he or she feels today. Be creative with your aches and pains.

Real Language

We can ask about someone's health by using these questions:

Formal ◀━━━━━━━▶ Informal

| What's the matter? | What's wrong? | What's up? |

How are you? is a greeting. We do not normally use it to ask about someone's health.

A • Have students work individually to match the columns.
• Check answers.

B • Have students work individually to fill in the blanks.
• Check answers.

Conversation

• Direct students' attention to the Real Language box. Point out that we use these questions when we see a problem. Remind students about the difference between formal and informal. Ask, *Which question do you say to a friend? To a teacher?*

A • Have students close their books. Write the question on the board: *What's wrong with Kim?*
• Play the recording. ◀)) **17**
• Check answers.

B • Play or read the conversation again for the class to repeat.
• Practice the conversation with the class in chorus.
• Have students practice the conversation with a partner and then switch roles and practice it again.

C • Have students work with the same partner to make a new conversation.
• Call on student pairs to present their conversation to the class.

D 🔄 | GOAL CHECK ✓

• Divide the class into pairs and have them take turns talking about their health. Tell them to make up interesting health problems!
• Call on students to tell the class about their partner's problems.

Grammar Practice: *Feel, look*

Have students work with a partner to look through their books (both this unit and earlier units) to find pictures of people and talk about how they feel and how they look. Have them choose three photos and for each one write down the page number and two sentences. *(He feels cold. He looks happy.)* Call on each pair of students to tell the class about one picture.

Ask About and Describe Symptoms

Listening

A • Have students look at the picture and describe what they see. Introduce the topic. Ask students about when they go to the doctor. *What does the patient do? What does the doctor do?* Talk about the idea of symptoms—signs that you are sick.

• Direct students' attention to the Word Focus box, and point out how we use the verb *hurt*.

• Tell students they are going to hear two conversations in doctors' offices. Have them listen and write the patients' symptoms.

• Play the recording one or more times. ◀))) 18

• Have students compare answers with a partner.

• Check answers.

B • Have students look at the pictures. Ask, *What's the matter with him/her?*

• Have students read the list of symptoms and match them to the problems.

• Have students compare answers with a partner.

• Check answers.

B **GOAL 2:** Ask About and Describe Symptoms

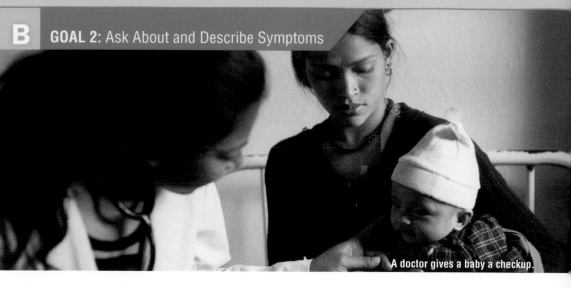

A doctor gives a baby a checkup.

Listening

A ◀))) 18 Listen to the conversations. List the patients' symptoms.

Patient 1	Patient 2
knee hurts, arm hurts, headache, foot hurts	cough, stomachache, fever

B Match the problems and the symptoms. Write the symptoms that go with each problem. You can use the symptoms more than once.

Symptoms

a. backache

b. fever

c. your arm hurts

d. headache

e. sore throat

f. cough

g. your knee hurts

h. toothache

Problems

1. cold: ____d, e, f____   2. flu: ____b, d, e, f____

3. bad tooth: ____d, h____   4. car accident: __a, c, d, g__

126   Unit 10

Pronunciation: Sentence stress

A 🔊 **19** Listen and notice the underlined stressed syllables.

Doctor: How can I <u>help</u> you?
Patient: I don't feel very <u>well</u>. I have a <u>head</u>ache.
Doctor: Anything <u>else</u>?
Patient: Yes, I have a <u>fev</u>er.
Doctor: OK. I think I need to ex<u>am</u>ine you.

B 🔊 **20** Listen to the conversation. Underline the stressed syllables.

Dentist: How are <u>you</u> today?
Patient: I have a terrible <u>tooth</u>ache.
Dentist: Where does it <u>hurt</u>?
Patient: Right <u>here</u>.
Dentist: I see the <u>prob</u>lem.

▲ Vaccines given to children can save many lives.

Communication

A 🔁 Role-play the following situations.

Situation 1	Situation 2
Student A You are a doctor. Ask your patient how he or she feels.	**Student B** You are a dentist. Ask your patient how he or she is.
Student B You are the patient. You have a cough, a headache, and a fever.	**Student A** You are the patient. You have a toothache.

Where does it hurt?

Does it hurt a lot?

Yes, when I eat or drink something hot!

B 🔁 Look at the pictures with a partner. Describe what is wrong with each child.

C 🔁 **GOAL CHECK** ✔ **Ask about and describe symptoms**

Look at the pictures above. Role-play a conversation between a doctor or dentist and these patients. Then switch roles.

Health **127**

Pronunciation

- Introduce the idea of stress—words and parts of words that sound "stronger" when we're speaking. Tell students that every language has its special pattern for stress. If desired, give examples from the students' language.

A
- Tell students that an English word has stress on one or more of its syllables. In English, the most important word in a sentence gets a strong stress on the syllable.
- Tell students to listen to the recording and read the sentences, paying attention to the underlined syllables.
- Play the recording one or more times. 🔊 **19**

B
- Tell students to listen to the recording and mark the stressed syllables.
- Play the recording one or more times. 🔊 **20**
- Check answers.
- Have students read the conversation with a partner, paying attention to the stressed syllables.

Communication

A
- Divide the class into pairs and have them work together to role-play the situations, switching roles for Situation 2.

B
- Divide the class into pairs. Have them look at the pictures and explain what is wrong with each child and what the symptoms are.
- Have pairs describe each child's problem and symptoms.

C 🔁 **GOAL CHECK** ✔
- Divide the class into pairs and have them role-play being the doctor and the patient using the pictures in **B**. Remind students to use the questions, *What's the matter? How do you feel? How are you feeling?*
- Have several pairs present their role-play to the class.

Expansion Activity

Have students discuss with a partner or a group which health problems are serious and which are not serious. Which ones should you go to the doctor for? Compare answers with the class.

Identify Remedies and Give Advice

Language Expansion

A • Introduce the idea of remedies—things you can do when you have a simple health problem.

• Read the remedies for students to repeat.

• Have students work individually to answer the questions. Tell them that more than one remedy may be correct for an ailment. Compare answers with the class.

Grammar

• Tell students, *I feel terrible. I have a cold. What should I do?* Model advice with *should: You should take some medicine.* Elicit ideas and write them on the board.

• Go over the information in the chart. Give/elicit more examples.

Language Expansion: Remedies

▲ go to bed   ▲ see a doctor   ▲ lie down

▲ see a dentist   ▲ take some cough medicine   ▲ take some pain reliever

A Answer the questions. Use the phrases above.

1. What do you do when you have a headache? _take some pain reliever_

2. What do you do when you have a very bad backache? _take some pain reliever, lie down, go to bed, see a doctor_

3. What do you do when you have a cough? _take some cough medicine, see a doctor_

4. What do you do when you have a toothache? _take some pain reliever, see a dentist_

5. What do you do when you have a fever? _take some pain reliever, lie down, go to bed, see a doctor_

Grammar: *Should* (for advice)

Statement	Negative	*Yes/No* question	Short answers	*Wh-* question
You **should** go to bed. He **should** take some cough medicine.	He **shouldn't** go to work today.	**Should** I see a doctor?	Yes, you **should.** No, you **shouldn't.**	What **should** I do?

*We use *should* to ask for and give advice.

Word Bank: Remedies

drink tea/hot water/orange juice
eat spicy food/chicken soup
go to bed early
put a cold cloth on your forehead
take a bath in warm/cool water
take vitamin C/garlic pills

Grammar: *Should* (for advice)

The modal *should* is used for various functions in English, including predictions, intentions, and advice. Native speakers often use the word *maybe* to soften the advice and make it more polite: *Maybe you should go home.*

Some people get *seasick* on boats. People who are seasick get stomachaches.

A Match the questions and the answers.

1. I feel sick. Should I see a doctor? __d__
2. I have a headache. What should I do? __a__
3. Nelson has a toothache. What should he do? __b__
4. Should Uzra see a doctor? __e__
5. Hilary has a cough. What should she do? __c__

a. You should take some pain reliever.
b. He should see a dentist.
c. She should take some cough medicine.
d. Yes, you should.
e. No, she shouldn't.

B Complete the conversations, and then practice them with a partner.

1. **A:** I have a backache. What should I do? **B:** *You should... take some pain reliever/lie down/see a doctor.*
2. **A:** I think I have the flu. What should I do? **B:** *You should see a doctor/go to bed.*
3. **A:** I have a stomachache. What should I do? **B:** *You should drink some tea/lie down.*
4. **A:** I have a cough. What should I do? **B:** *You should take some cough medicine.*

Conversation

A 🔊 21 Listen to the conversation. What does Casey think Brenda should do? *go home and go to bed*

Casey: Hi. What's up, Brenda?
Brenda: I don't feel well. I <u>think I have the flu</u>. What should I do?
Casey: I think you should <u>go home and go to bed</u>.
Brenda: Do you think I should see a doctor?
Casey: <u>No, I don't think so</u>.

B Practice the conversation with a partner. Switch roles and practice it again.

C Change the underlined words and make a new conversation.

> I have a toothache.

> You should go to the dentist.

D **GOAL CHECK** ✓ Identify remedies and give advice

Work with a partner. Take turns naming a medical problem and suggesting a remedy or giving advice.

Health **129**

Grammar: *Should* (for advice)

Talk about the idea of home remedies—easy things that people can do at home when they are sick to feel better. Point out that some remedies are very old. Choose a common health problem such as a cold or the hiccups (demonstrate this word), and ask students to tell you as many remedies as they can think of using *should: You should drink hot tea with lemon.*

Write them on the board. Ask, *Which ones are very old? Which ones really work?*

A
- Have students work individually to match the columns.
- Have students compare answers with a partner.
- Check answers.

B
- Have students work individually to complete the conversations.
- Have students compare answers with a partner.
- Check answers. Answers may vary.
- Have students practice the conversations with a partner.
- Call on student pairs to present a conversation to the class. Discuss any interesting remedies that students think of.

Conversation

A
- Have students close their books. Write the question on the board: *What does Casey think Brenda should do?*
- Play the recording. 🔊 21
- Check answers.

B
- Play or read the conversation again for the class to repeat.
- Practice the conversation with the class in chorus.
- Have students practice the conversation with a partner and then switch roles and practice it again.

C
- Have students work with the same partner to make a new conversation.
- Call on student pairs to present their conversation to the class.

D **GOAL CHECK** ✓

- Have students work with a different partner to talk about health problems and suggest advice.
- Call on student pairs to present a conversation to the class.

Describe How to Prevent Health Problems

Reading

- Introduce the topic of the reading. Talk about preventing something—stopping something bad from happening.

A • Have students work individually to check the things that people can prevent.
- Divide the class into pairs and have them compare answers and talk about ways to prevent flu and toothaches.

B • Tell students to read the article and answer *true* or *false*. Read through the statements with the class. Tell them to circle any words in the reading that they don't understand. Point out the words in the Word Focus box.
- Have students compare answers with a partner.
- Check answers.
- Go over the article with the class and answer any questions from the students about vocabulary.

C • Divide the class into pairs and have them talk about another disease that they think can be prevented. Have them explain how they think it can be prevented.
- Compare answers with the class.

D **GOAL 4:** Describe How to Prevent Health Problems

Reading

A 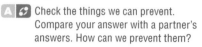 Check the things we can prevent. Compare your answer with a partner's answers. How can we prevent them?

- ☐ flu
- ☐ rain
- ☐ toothache
- ☐ headache

B Read the article. Circle **T** for *true* and **F** for *false*.

1. There is a vaccine for measles. (T) F
2. About 400,000 children die from malaria every day in Africa. T (F)
3. There is a vaccine for malaria. T (F)
4. Mosquito nets are expensive. T (F)
5. Influenza is a problem in hot countries. (T) F

C With a partner, talk about another disease you think we can prevent. How can we prevent it?

Word Focus

infectious disease = a disease you can get from another person

malaria = a sickness you can get from mosquitoes

prevent = avoid a problem before it happens

vaccine = medicine to prevent a disease

PREVENTING DISEASE

Many people, especially children, die from **infectious diseases** every year. We can **prevent** many infectious diseases. Let's look at some of the most dangerous ones.

Measles is mainly a children's disease. There is a very good, cheap **vaccine** for measles. All children should get the vaccine, but unfortunately not all do. About 900,000 children die every year from measles.

Imagine seven jumbo jets full of children. Now, imagine that all the jets crash and all the children are killed. That's how many children die from **malaria** in Africa *every day*. There is no vaccine for malaria, but it is not difficult to prevent. All you need is a $5 mosquito net.

Influenza (or flu) is caused by a virus. The virus changes, so scientists have to make a new vaccine every year. People at risk—for example, older people—should have a flu shot every year. In a bad year, influenza can kill millions of people.

Children and adults should sleep under a mosquito net.

For Your Information: Infectious diseases

Malaria: This disease is caused by microorganisms that are carried by mosquitoes. Every year, there are about 150–300 million cases of malaria in the world, which kill 500,000–800,000 people. Most of these deaths are in Africa.

Influenza/flu: This disease is caused by a number of different viruses and is spread through the air when people cough. New kinds of flu virus can develop and spread quickly around the world. In this unit, in the Student Workbook, a reading gives students more information about the flu.

All children should get a measles shot.

Reading Tip: Inference

When reading about a new topic, many learners will have to infer information. Inference is when a student uses facts (both previously known and presented in the reading), as well as their own logic and reasoning, to answer a question or understand a passage. Learning how to use inference will allow readers to understand reading passages more thoroughly and interact directly with the knowledge they are being presented with.

After Reading

With the class, talk about a serious health problem in the students' country, such as malaria, HIV/AIDS, or tuberculosis. What are the best ways to prevent this problem? Make a list on the board.

Describe How to Prevent Health Problems

Writing

A • Have students look at the picture and the caption. Ask, *How does exercise help prevent heart disease?*

• Have students look at the chart and read the sentence.

• Have students choose one of the health problems and write a paragraph using the advice in the chart and ideas of their own.

• Have students exchange paragraphs with a partner. Ask students to mark corrections and suggestions for improvements on their partner's paper.

• If desired, have students rewrite their papers, to be collected for marking.

Communication

A • Divide the class into pairs and have them choose one of the situations.

• Have them decide on three suggestions for that situation using *should/shouldn't*.

B 🔄 **GOAL CHECK** ✔

• Have each pair present their suggestions from **A** to the class.

D | **GOAL 4:** Describe How to Prevent Health Problems

Regular exercise helps prevent heart disease.

Writing

A Write a paragraph in your notebook about how to prevent one of the following health problems. Add your own ideas. Use a dictionary.

To prevent toothaches, you		wash fruit.
		eat candy.
		play sports.
To prevent heart disease, you	should shouldn't	eat uncooked food, like salads.
		go to the dentist every six months.
		exercise daily.
To prevent stomach problems when you are traveling, you		eat healthy food.
		brush your teeth after meals.
		eat lots of fast food.

To prevent toothache, you should brush your teeth after meals,
visit the dentist every six months, and you shouldn't eat candy.

Communication

A 🔄 Choose one of the following. With a partner, discuss and write down three things you should do to:

prevent car accidents.

prevent accidents in the home.

get good grades.

B 🔄 **GOAL CHECK** ✔ **Describe how to prevent health problems**

Present your ideas to the class.

Teacher Tip: "Fillers"

Here are some activities to "fill in" a few extra minutes at the end of a lesson:

• **The Blackboard Game** (if you have filled the board with vocabulary and other notes): Have a volunteer sit with his or her back to the board. Students take turns giving definitions of words on the board. When the volunteer says the correct word, you step up and erase it. The game ends when all the words are erased.

• **Error Quiz:** Write 10 incorrect sentences that you have seen in students' work. Have students work with a partner to correct as many as they can in 5 minutes. When the time is up, ask the class for corrections and rewrite the sentences.

• **Spelling Practice:** Dictate 10 to 15 words that students find difficult. Let them compare answers with a partner. Then give the correct answers.

Before You Watch

A Complete the Video Summary using the words in the box.

Video Summary

Farley is a red panda. He is cute, but he is a (1) _____fighter_____. He nearly
(2) _____dies_____ because his mother doesn't (3) _____look after_____ him. Then
he gets very sick. Zookeepers give him _____antibiotics_____ and he gets better.
Then they send him to another zoo to live with other red pandas.

> **antibiotics =** medicine that kills bacteria
>
> **die(s) =** not live
>
> **fighter =** someone who tries very hard
>
> **look after =** care for

While You Watch

A ▶ Circle **T** for *true* and **F** for *false*.

1. Farley grows ~~slowly~~ at first. *quickly*   T (F)
2. The zookeepers take Farley to the zoo's hospital. (T) F
3. Farley has ~~the flu~~. *an infection*   T (F)
4. Farley likes his new friend, Banshee. (T) F

B In your notebook, correct the *false* statements.

> food   water   love
> education   success
> family   friends
> medicine   water
> sleep   a job   shelter

After You Watch

A Humans also have needs. Write the words in the box in the correct place in the chart.

Answers will vary.

Self-esteem: *love, education, success, a job*
Social: *love, family, friends, a job*
Safety: *medicine, shelter*
Basic needs: *food, water, shelter*

B ⚡ Compare your answers with a partner and discuss any differences.

Health 133

Video Journal: *Farley, the Red Panda*

Before You Watch

A • Have students look at the picture and describe what they see.

• Have students read the words and definitions in the box and complete the video summary.

• Check answers.

While You Watch

A • Have students read the sentences. Tell them to watch the video and choose *true* or *false*.

• Play the video.

• Have students compare answers with a partner.

• Check answers.

B • Have students correct the false information in **A** in their notebooks.

• Play the video.

• Have students compare answers with a partner. Play the video again as necessary.

• Check answers.

After You Watch

A • Copy the chart onto the board. Check that students understand each category. Have students read the directions. Ask, *Where do we put food and water?* Go over the words in the box.

• Have students complete the chart.

B • Have students compare their chart with a partner and discuss any differences.

• Compare answers as a class and complete the chart on the board. Answers will vary.

For Your Information: Red pandas

Red pandas live in the mountains and forests of Nepal, Myanmar, and central China. They are distantly related to the panda, but they are much smaller; they grow to about the same size as a domestic cat. These pandas are a reddish-brown color and have big, bushy, ringed tails. They wrap their tail around their body to use it like a blanket to keep warm. Red pandas live in the mountains and spend most of their time high up in trees (they even sleep in trees), so they need to be able to keep warm. The red panda is now an endangered species because deforestation is destroying its natural habitat. More and more forests are being cut down because people want to use the wood or they want the land for agriculture. Unfortunately, this deforestation has put the red panda at risk.

Making Plans

About the Photo

This photo was taken by David Bowman, a National Geographic photographer based in Minneapolis, Minnesota. It captures the excitement of a fairground ride at the Minnesota State Fair. State fairs are an important part of the summer for many Americans; each state holds its own fair, which lasts for more than a week, and a visit to the fair is a must for many families. The Michigan State Fair is considered the oldest; it first took place in 1849. State fairs are a well-rooted tradition with a long history in the United States. The Minnesota State Fair is considered by many to be one of the best in the country. At the fairs, there are concerts, entertainment, fairground rides and games, animal shows, exhibitions, and many stalls selling food and drinks. As can be seen in this photo, state fairs are fun and exciting.

- Direct students' attention to the photo. Have students describe what they see.

- Have students answer the questions with a partner.

- Compare answers with the class. Write students' plans on the board. (Students will learn *be going to* and *would like to* in this unit. At this point, they can answer with phrases: *go shopping/ watch videos/get a job/study abroad.*)

- Go over the Unit Goals with the class, explaining as necessary.

- For each goal, elicit any words students already know and write them on the board. For example, special days and holidays and the activities/ traditions they have for these days.

A carnival ride lights up the night sky at a fair in Minnesota, USA.

134

UNIT 11 GOALS	Grammar	Vocabulary	Listening
• Plan special days • Describe holiday traditions • Make life plans • Express wishes and plans	*Be going to* What **are** you **going to** do? We **are going to** have a party. *Would like to* for wishes I **would like to** be a doctor.	Celebrating special days American holidays Professions	Listening for general understanding and specific details Conversations to discuss special dates or events

Look at the photo, answer the questions:

1 What are your plans for the weekend?

2 What are your plans for your life?

Unit Theme Overview

- Many students learn English with an eye to the future. They hope to use their new language to get a job, to interact with foreign colleagues, to study abroad, or to travel internationally. They may need English skills to qualify for higher levels of education, or they may just want to use their new language to gain access to a broader range of information or entertainment. English has also become a common language for communication between people from different non-English speaking countries. For any of these objectives, learning English is intimately linked with goals and plans—and this unit teaches students to explore and express theirs in English.

- They begin by learning to use *going to* and talking about short-term plans for special days, whether it's next weekend or an upcoming birthday or anniversary. They move on to learn the use of *would like to* to talk about future desires. They talk about their own life plans. They read about a TED speaker with an unusual opinion about making plans and then watch a video about the life plans of a group of young men in Thailand.

UNIT 11 GOALS

1. Plan special days

2. Describe holiday traditions

3. Make life plans

4. Express wishes and plans

135

Speaking	Reading	Writing	Video Journal
Talking about holiday celebrations **Pronunciation:** *Be going to* (reduced form)	**TED Talks:** "Derek Sivers: Keep Your Goals to Yourself"	Writing about wishes and plans	**National Geographic:** "Making a Thai Boxing Champion"

Plan Special Days

Vocabulary

A • Direct students' attention to the pictures and introduce the vocabulary. Ask, *Do you like to go to a game? Do you have a favorite team? Do you like to have a barbecue?* etc.

• Have students look at the year planner. Introduce/review the names of the months presented and the remaining months— September, October, November, and December—pronouncing them for students to repeat.

• Have students work individually to write their ideas about how to celebrate each occasion.

• Compare answers with the class. Answers may vary.

B • Divide the class into pairs and have them talk about how they usually celebrate their birthdays. Model the question and answer with one or two students.

• Call on students to tell the class about their partner's birthday activities.

go to a game

▲ have a party

▲ have a barbecue

▲ go to the movies

▲ have a family meal

▲ go out to eat

Vocabulary

Calendar		List	Day	Month		+
January			**May**			
7th, Dad's birthday			14th, My birthday			
February			**June**			
17th, John's birthday			3rd, Mom's birthday			
March			**July**			
			24th, Grandpa and Grandma's anniversary			
April			**August**			
1st, Mom and Dad's anniversary						

A Look at the planner and the pictures. Decide the best way to celebrate. Complete the sentences.

1. Dad likes sports, so on his birthday, we usually <u>go to a game</u>
   _____.

2. Mom and Dad like to eat outdoors, so for their anniversary, we usually <u>have a barbecue</u>.

3. John loves films, so on his birthday, we usually <u>go to the movies</u>
   _____.

4. Mom doesn't like cooking, so on her birthday, we usually <u>go out to eat</u>
   _____.

5. I like to see my friends, so on my birthday, we <u>have a party</u>
   _____.

6. Grandma loves cooking, so on her and Grandpa's anniversary, we go to their house and <u>have a family meal</u>.

B Tell a partner what you usually do on your birthday.

> What do you usually do on your birthday?

> On my birthday, I usually . . .

136 Unit 11

Word Bank: More plans

clean my house/apartment
get together with friends
go to bed early
go shopping
have a graduation party

have a housewarming party
have a picnic
have a wedding/baby shower
stay home

Grammar: *Be going to*

English uses a variety of different structures to talk about future time. One of them is *be going to*, which is used to talk about plans and intentions. It is also used informally for making predictions. One common error to watch out for is omitting the *be* verb—We always need *am/is/are* + *going to* + verb.

Grammar: *Be going to*

Be going to			
Statement	**Negative**	**Yes/No question**	**Wh- question**
I **am going to** have a party.	We **are not going to** have a big meal.	**Are** you **going to** go to the movies?	What **is** he **going to** do? When **are** we **going to** go?

*We use *be going to* for making plans.
*We also use these time expressions: *tomorrow, next Saturday/week/year.*

A 🔁 Complete the sentences. Use the words in parentheses and *be going to*. Then practice the conversations with a partner.

1. **A:** What ___are you going to___ (you) do for your birthday?

   B: I ___am going to___ have a BIG party! People are going to give me presents.

2. **A:** ___Are you going to___ (you) have a barbecue on the weekend?

   B: No, we ___are going to___ go to the movies.

3. **A:** Where ___are Courtney and___ (Courtney and Min) go on New Year's Eve? ___Min going to___

   B: They ___are going to___ go to Santo Domingo.

B 🔁 Discuss these questions with your partner.

1. What are you going to do after class?
2. What are you going to do this weekend?

Conversation

A 🔊 22 Listen to the conversation. When is Susan's birthday?

May 21

Sally: When is your birthday?
Susan: It's on <u>May 21st</u>.
Sally: Hey, that's next week. Are you going to <u>have a party</u>?
Susan: No, I'm going to <u>go out for dinner with my parents</u>.

B 🔁 Practice the conversation with a partner. Switch roles and practice it again.

▲ Santo Domingo is the capital of the Dominican Republic.

C 🔁 Change the underlined words and make a new conversation that is true for you.

D ♻ **GOAL CHECK** ✔ **Plan special days**

With a group, choose a special day, for example New Year's Eve or a graduation. Tell how you are going to celebrate it.

Making Plans **137**

Grammar Practice: *Be going to*

Have students take a piece of paper and make seven columns with the days of the week at the top. This is their "calendar" for next week. Then have them write an activity (real or imaginary) for five of the seven days (such as *see a movie, study English,* etc.). Have students work with a partner to plan an activity that they want to do together (such as *have a cup of coffee*). They should not look at their partner's calendar. Model sentences like, *I'm going to do the laundry on Monday night.* and *What are you going to do on Tuesday night?* When all student pairs have finished, call on students to talk about their plans.

Grammar

- Introduce the structure. Tell students, *I have a lot of plans this weekend. I'm going to read your homework papers. I'm going to see my friends.* Write the sentences on the board.
- Ask, *What are you going to do?* Elicit answers with *going to* and write them on the board.
- Go over the information in the chart, and give/elicit more examples.

A • Have students work individually to complete the sentences.
- Check answers.
- Divide the class into pairs and have them practice the conversations.

B • With the same partner, have students discuss the questions.
- Have several students tell the class their partner's plans.

Conversation

A • Have students close their books. Write the question on the board: *When is Susan's birthday?*
- Play the recording. 🔊 22
- Check answers.

B • Play or read the conversation again for the class to repeat.
- Practice the conversation with the class in chorus.
- Have students practice the conversation with a partner, then switch roles and practice it again.

C • Have students work with the same partner to make a new conversation.
- Call on student pairs to present their conversation to the class.

D ♻ **GOAL CHECK** ✔

- Divide the class into small groups and have them choose a special day and discuss how they are going to celebrate it.
- Have each group tell the class which day they chose and what each group member is going to do.

Lesson A **137**

Describe Holiday Traditions

Listening

A
- Tell students they are going to hear people talking about their plans for holidays.
- Have students look at the pictures and read the captions about American holidays.

B
- Tell students to listen to the conversations and write the name of each holiday. Tell them they will NOT hear the name of the holiday—they must think about the information in the conversation.
- Play the recording one or more times. 🔊 **23**
- Have students compare answers with a partner.
- Check answers.

C
- Tell students to listen again to answer the questions. Have them read the questions.
- Play the recording one or more times. 🔊 **23**
- Have students compare answers with a partner.
- Check answers.

B **GOAL 2:** Describe Holiday Traditions

▲ On New Year's Eve in New York City, people go to Times Square to celebrate.

▲ All over the United States, people celebrate Independence Day with fireworks.

Listening

A Look at the pictures. Read the captions about American holidays.

American Holidays

▲ On Thanksgiving Day, many people have a family meal.

B 🔊 **23** Listen and write which holidays the people are talking about.

1. Linda and Kenichi are talking about <u>New Year's Day</u>.
2. Tom and Maria are talking about <u>Independence Day</u>.

C 🔊 **23** Listen again and answer the questions.

1. Why isn't Linda going to go to Times Square? <u>There are too many people.</u>
2. What is she going to do? <u>stay home with her family</u>
3. Where is Kenichi going to go? <u>to a party</u>
4. What are Tom and Maria going to do? <u>go downtown and watch the fireworks</u>
5. What time is Tom leaving? <u>six o'clock</u>

138   Unit 11

For Your Information: American holidays

The activity talks about three of the most important holidays in the United States.

Thanksgiving is the fourth Thursday in November. People travel long distances to eat a traditional dinner with their family, often including turkey and pumpkin pie. They talk and think about all the good things in their life for which they are thankful.

Independence Day is July 4th. It is celebrated with parades (floats, marching bands, and patriotic displays), and many cities have fireworks in the parks at night.

On *New Year's Eve*, people usually have big parties with food and dancing. At midnight, people wish for good luck and welcome the new year.

Pronunciation: *Be going to* (reduced form)

A 🔊 **24** Listen and check the correct column of the form you hear.

	Full form	Reduced form
1. We're going to have a party.	✓	
2. We're going to have a party.		✓
3. I'm going to go to Paris.		✓
4. I'm going to go to Paris.	✓	
5. They're not going to come.	✓	
6. They're not going to come.		✓

B 🔄 Practice the dialogs with a partner. Use the reduced form of *be going to*.

A: What are you going to do on the weekend?
B: I'm going to go to the beach.

A: Are you going to go to Kim's party?
B: No, I'm going to stay home this weekend.

Communication

A 🔄 In your notebook, write a list of holidays in your country. With a partner, discuss what you are going to do on those days.

▲ Chinese New Year is celebrated all over the world. People give gifts, light lanterns, and watch parades.

B ♻ **GOAL CHECK** ✓ **Describe holiday traditions**

Join another pair of students and tell them about two holidays on your list.

Pronunciation

A • Explain to the class that in casual speech, *be going to* is pronounced with the reduced form *gonna*. This is very common, and practicing it will help make students' speech more natural. Emphasize that this form is used only in speaking, NOT in writing. (Learners sometimes write *gonna* in the mistaken belief that this makes their English more native-like.)

• Tell students to listen and check the form they hear.

• Play the recording one or more times. 🔊 **24**

• Have students compare answers with a partner.

• Check answers.

• Play the recording again, one or more times, for students to repeat. 🔊 **24**

B • Divide the class into pairs and have them practice the conversations, using the reduced form each time.

• Call on student pairs to present a conversation to the class.

Communication

A • Have students work with their partner to list holidays in their country. Help with vocabulary as needed. Then have them talk about their plans for each holiday using *going to*.

B ♻ **GOAL CHECK** ✓

• Combine student pairs into groups of four and have them take turns talking about their plans for two holidays. Assign students roles: leader, secretary, reporter, recorder (see p. 77).

Expansion Activity

As a follow-up to Goal 2, assign each group two different holidays and have them write descriptions similar to those of the American holidays on the previous page. Then have them share their descriptions with the class.

Make Life Plans

Language Expansion

- Introduce the idea of life plans. Ask, *Why do people usually choose a profession? Do people sometimes change their professions? Why?*

- Have students look at the pictures. Read the professions and have students repeat them.

- Clarify the difference between the person's job and the profession/field. Explain, *I'm a teacher. That's my job. I work in education. That's my profession.*

A • Have students work individually to match the columns.

- Check answers.

Grammar

- Introduce the idea of *would like to* for wishes in the future. Go over the information in the chart. Point out that *would like to* is used with a verb in the base form. Ask different students, *Would you like to study law? Would you like to be an actor?* etc.

C   **GOAL 3:** Make Life Plans

Language Expansion: Professions

▲ law

▲ information technology

▲ medicine

▲ music

▲ acting

▲ education

A Match the person to the profession.

1. nurse _b_
2. lawyer _e_
3. musician _a_
4. software engineer _f_
5. actor _d_
6. teacher _c_

a. music
b. medicine
c. education
d. acting
e. law
f. information technology

Grammar: *Would like to* for wishes

Statement	*Yes/No* question	Short answer	*Wh-* question
I **would like to** be a nurse.	**Would** you **like to** study engineering?	Yes, I **would**.	What **would** you **like to** be?
Danny **would like to** study law.	**Would** you **like to** be a nurse?	No, I **wouldn't**.	

140   Unit 11

Word Bank: Professions

agriculture   government
business   the military
education   science
engineering   technology

Grammar: *Would like to*

Would like to is considered slightly more polite and "softer" than *want to* in expressing a desire. It is used with the base form of the verb.

A Unscramble the words to write sentences and questions.

1. to be a would like I musician. _I would like to be a musician._
2. Eleanor like What would to be? _What would Eleanor like to be?_
3. to be Would you a doctor? like _Would you like to be a doctor?_
4. Deng medicine. would to study like _Deng would like to study medicine._
5. What like to be? would you _What would you like to be?_

B Write the wishes or plans. Add one of your own. Answers will vary.

Wish	**Plan**
1. _I would like to be an actor._	I am going to be an actor.
2. Danny would like to study medicine.	_He is going to be a doctor._
3. _I would like to study information technology._	I am going to be a software engineer.
4. We would like to leave at seven o'clock.	_We are going to (see the fireworks)._
5. _They would like to be musicians._	They are going to study music.
6. _Answers will vary._	_Answers will vary._

Conversation

A 🔊 25 Listen to the conversation. What would Wendy like to be? _a lawyer_

Father: So Wendy, you're <u>18</u> years old today. What are you going to do with your life?
Wendy: Well, I'd like to get married and have children.
Father: Whoa! Not so fast!
Wendy: Just kidding! I'd like to <u>study law and become a lawyer</u>.

> **Real Language**
>
> We can say *Just kidding* to show we are not serious.

B 🔄 Practice the conversation with a partner. Switch roles and practice it again.

C 🔄 Change the underlined words and make a new conversation.

D 🔄 **GOAL CHECK** ✔ **Make life plans**

Talk to a partner. What would you like to do with your life? What are you going to do to make your wishes come true?

▲ **Would you like to be a musician?**

Making Plans **141**

A • Have students work individually to write the sentences and questions.
• Check answers.

B • Have students work individually to write the wishes/plans.
• Have students compare answers with a partner.
• Check answers.

Conversation

A • Have students close their books. Write the question on the board: *What would Wendy like to be?*
• Play the recording. 🔊 25
• Check answers.
• Direct students' attention to the Real Language box.

B • Play or read the conversation again for the class to repeat.
• Practice the conversation with the class in chorus.
• Have students practice the conversation with a partner and then switch roles and practice it again.

C • Have students work with the same partner to make a new conversation.
• Call on student pairs to present their conversation to the class.

D 🔄 **GOAL CHECK** ✔

• Divide the class into pairs and have them talk about their life plans. Tell them that this can be a job or profession, or some other important plan. Tell them to say how they are going to make their wishes come true.
• Have students tell the class what their partner would like to do and what he or she is going to do to achieve it.

Grammar Practice: *Would like to* and *be going to*

Prepare a list of 8 to 10 sentences about yourself, using *am going to* and *would like to.* (For example: *I am going to take a vacation next week. I would like to go skiing.*) Some should be true, others not true. Dictate the sentences one at a time to the class. Tell them to think about the sentence and to write it down only if they think it's true. After you've dictated all the sentences, ask which sentences the students wrote down and give them the correct answers. You can repeat the activity by having students write their own list of true and false statements and dictate the statements to a partner. This activity can be done to practice many different structures.

Express Wishes and Plans

Reading

A • Have students look at the pictures and describe what they see.

• Divide the class into small groups of three or four and have them discuss their life plans. Remind them to say what they would like to do **and** how they are going to achieve it.

• Have several students share their plans with the class. If necessary, model the activity.

B • Have students look at the pictures and the captions, then read the sentences and guess the answers.

• Have students read the article and confirm their answers. Focus their attention on the Word Bank.

• Have students compare answers with a partner.

• Check the answers.

D   **GOAL 4:** Express Wishes and Plans

Reading

A What would you like to do with your life? How are you going to do it? Discuss as a group.
Answers will vary.

I would like to _____ .

So I am going to _____

_____

B Derek Sivers has some surprising ideas about how we can achieve our goals. Read the article about his ideas. Then choose the correct answers below.

1. Derek Sivers suggests we NOT tell anyone about our _____ .
   a. goals
   b. thoughts
   c. opinions

2. People usually don't _____ their plans if they say them out loud.
   a. forget
   b. complete
   c. share

3. Being quiet about a life plan means the same as _____ it.
   a. explaining
   b. talking about
   c. not talking about

4. How does Derek Sivers say people feel when they share their life plans?
   a. frightened
   b. cheerful
   c. sad

5. If you say a plan out loud, sometimes your brain _____ .
   a. assumes it is true
   b. slows down
   c. thinks it is already done

> **WORD BANK**
> **assume** to think something is true
> **motivated** have a reason to do something
> **psychologist** a doctor who studies the mind
> **secret** something hidden from others
> **trick** to confuse or fool

Derek Sivers Entrepreneur

KEEP YOUR GOALS TO YOURSELF

The following article is about Derek Sivers. After Unit 12, you'll have the opportunity to watch some of Derek Sivers's TED Talk and learn more about his idea worth spreading.

Many people **assume** that the first and most important step in making any kind of life plan is to tell someone about it. This makes the plan seem real—like it's definitely going to happen. But entrepreneur Derek Sivers thinks it's probably better to keep it **secret**. He says that studies have shown that announcing a goal doesn't actually bring you any closer to seeing it come true. In fact, the opposite usually happens. People rarely finish what they *say* they plan to do.

Psychologists say that talking about our plans **tricks** the mind into thinking they are already done. People get happy, as if they have already achieved the goal. This makes us less **motivated** to accomplish what we would like to do. This is called a "social reality." The plan is definitely real, but it often doesn't develop into anything more than an idea.

So the next time someone asks you about your life plans, you might want to keep quiet. By being quiet, you may actually put yourself closer to your goal.

For Your Information: Derek Sivers

Derek Sivers is a professional musician, a clown, and an entrepreneur. In 1998, he started a company called CD Baby, which sold music on the Internet for independent musicians. The website was very successful. However, he later sold this company to benefit a music education charity. Sivers is a frequent speaker at TED, and in addition to talking about not sharing our goals, he has given talks on starting a social movement and cross-cultural understanding. Sivers describes himself as a "student of life."

"Resist the temptation to announce your goal."

— Derek Sivers

143

Reading Tip

When using authentic materials, like TED Talks, ask students to think about how the material relates to their own lives. For this reading, ask students to think about a time when they had a plan or goal and what steps they took to achieve it.

After Reading

With the class, talk about the typical wishes and plans of people in their country. Are there certain things that people are expected to achieve in their life? (For example: going to college, getting married, buying a house, having children, traveling, etc.) Do these life plan expectations differ for men and women? Do they differ from country to country?

Writing

A • Have students read the directions and complete the sentences.

• Have students compare answers with a partner.

• Check the answers.

B • Have students write a list of plans they have for the future.

• Have students write a paragraph about their life plans. Have them say what they would like to do and how they are going to do it.

Communication

A • Divide the class into pairs and have them read the directions.

• Have students share their life plans from **Writing B** and identify any similarities or differences between their plans. Model the sample.

• Have several students share their partner's life plan with the class.

B **GOAL CHECK** ✔

• Divide the class into small groups and have them share and discuss their life plans. Have them give each other advice on what they should or shouldn't do.

• Have each group report back to the class on the group's discussion.

D **GOAL 4:** Express Wishes and Plans

> If you want to achieve a goal, you should spend your time working toward it, not telling people about it.

> I would like to be a teacher. I'm going to study every night.

Writing

A Help the people with their wishes. Complete the sentences with the correct plans.

save some money   invite her friends

have a family meal   find a good coach

1. Ben would like to take a long vacation. What is he going to to?
   He is going to *save some money*   .

2. Helen would like to have a party. What is she going to do?
   She is going to *invite her friends*   .

3. I would like to become a tennis player. What am I going to do?
   I am going to *find a good coach*   .

4. It is our father's birthday next week. What are we going to do?
   We are going to *have a family meal*   .

B What would you like to do with your life? How are you going to do it? Write a life plan.

Communication

A 🔁 Derek Sivers says you can still talk about a goal, but you should talk about it so it sounds hard to accomplish. Share your life plans with a partner. How are they the same or different? Discuss.

B 👥 **GOAL CHECK** ✔ **Express wishes and plans**

Share life plans. Is there anything in the life plans your classmates should NOT do? What should they do instead? Give your opinions and discuss as a group.

144   Unit 11

For Your Information: Thai boxing

Thai boxing is called Muay Thai in the Thai language and is a martial art and the national sport of Thailand. In contrast to western boxing, the hands, shins, elbows, and knees are all used against the opponent. It is performed in a ring and gloves are used. Training for a Thai boxer involves running, jumping rope, and intense daily practice of punches and kicks. Because of the difficulty of the sport, most Thai boxers retire from fighting after only a short career and work as trainers instead.

Video Journal: *Making a Thai Boxing Champion*

Before You Watch

A 🔁 Read the video summary. With a partner, try to guess the meanings of the words in **bold**.

While You Watch

A ▶️ Watch the video. Number the sentences in the order you see them.

 _4_ Manat doesn't win.

 _2_ Manat goes into the ring for a ceremony.

 _3_ The fight begins.

 _1_ Manat trains very hard.

 _5_ Manat will become a champion.

B ▶️ Watch the video again. Complete the sentences with words from the box.

1. Manat comes from a ___poor___ family.

2. Manat's coaches believe he will be a _champion_ .

3. When Manat wins, he wants to send the money to his ___family___ .

4. Manat doesn't ___win___ .

Video Summary

Thai **boxing,** or Muay Thai, is a traditional **martial art** from Thailand. Thai boxers use their hands, elbows, knees, and legs. Manat is a 12-year-old boy from a poor family who is living at a Thai boxing **training camp.** He trains seven hours a day, seven days a week. He wishes to become a boxing champion. He works very hard.

family   champion   poor   win

After You Watch

A 🔁 Answer these questions with a partner.

1. Do you think Manat will get his wish to become a Thai boxing champion?

2. What do you think about the camp? Name positive and negative things.

Making Plans 145

Video Journal: *Making a Thai Boxing Champion*

Before You Watch

A • Divide the class into pairs and have them read the video summary and discuss the meanings of the items in bold. Remind students that looking at the picture is a good strategy to help understand new vocabulary.

 • Go over the vocabulary with the class.

While You Watch

A • Tell students to watch the video and write numbers to put the events in order.

 • Play the video.

 • Have students compare answers with a partner.

 • Check answers.

B • Have students read the sentences and the words in the box. Have them complete any they think they already know.

 • Play the video and have students confirm or complete their answers.

 • Have students compare answers with a partner.

 • Check answers.

After You Watch

A • Divide the class into pairs and have them discuss the questions.

 • Compare answers with the class. Complete a chart on the board with positive and negative aspects of the training camps.

Teacher Tip: Fun with English outside of class

Encourage students to find language activities that they enjoy to get more practice outside of class. Some ideas:

 • sing along with English songs (lyrics can be found on the album liner or on websites)

 • speak in English with a friend or classmate outside of class time

 • read an English comic book or a magazine on a topic that is well-known in the native language (for example, soccer or fashion)

 • watch English-language movies

 • talk to yourself and describe things you see in English!

On the Move

About the Photo

This photo was taken by Joel Sartore, a photographer who specializes in photographing endangered species. His work raises awareness of the fact that losing species on our planet has consequences that affect all of us. In this photo, he shows a herd of elephants crossing the grassy savanna in the Queen Elizabeth National Park, Uganda. Thanks to the protection of the park, the elephant population in Uganda has now risen again to more than 2,500. In the park, the elephants are free to roam for miles and miles without the risk of poachers, and since they are migratory animals, it is important that they have these large protected spaces where they can roam safely.

- Introduce the theme of the unit. Talk about the meaning of *move*—to change your home to another place. Point out that sometimes one person or family moves; other times large groups of people move.

- Direct students' attention to the photo. Have students describe what they see. Ask, *What are these animals doing? Where are they going? Why?*

- Have students discuss the questions with a partner.

- Compare answers with the class. Write students' ideas on the board.

- Go over the Unit Goals with the class, explaining as necessary.

- For each goal, elicit any words students already know and write them on the board. For example, any verbs in the simple past, *I was born in . . ., I lived in . . .*, etc.

Elephants roam miles of grassy savanna inside Queen Elizabeth Park, Uganda.

146

UNIT 12 GOALS	Grammar	Vocabulary	Listening
• Use the simple past • Give biographical information • Describe a move • Discuss migrations	Simple past tense He **moved** to California. When **did** they **leave** Germany?	Moving Dates and years Preparations for a move	Listening for general understanding and specific details Biographies of famous American immigrants

Unit Theme Overview

- We live in an increasingly mobile world. Every day, countless people around the world move to a new city, or even a new country, to pursue better opportunities for work or education. And, tragically, large groups of people are forced to leave their homes because of war, hunger, or ethnic persecution.

- In this unit, students talk and think about why people move to a new home, both individually and in large groups, and learn to talk about past events. They begin by talking about individual changes in the past. They learn to talk about the dates when things happened. They consider how people prepared to move to a new home. Finally, they learn about larger patterns of human migration in the past and compare animals' migration across vast distances.

UNIT 12 GOALS

1. Use the simple past

2. Give biographical information

3. Describe a move

4. Discuss migrations

147

Speaking	Reading	Writing	Video Journal
Talking about people moving from place to place **Pronunciation:** -ed sounds	**National Geographic:** "Human Migration"	Writing a travel e-mail	**National Geographic:** "Monarch Migration"

Use the Simple Past

Vocabulary

- Introduce the vocabulary in the pictures. Explain that these words are verbs—words for actions— and that they are used together with the prepositions to show direction. Read the verb/preposition combinations for students to repeat.

A • Have students work individually to choose the correct verbs.

- Have students compare answers with a partner.

- Check answers.

Grammar

- Tell the class, *I usually leave school at four thirty. But yesterday, I left at six o'clock. What about you? When did you leave?* From different students elicit, *I left at (three thirty).* Write on the board, *I usually leave at four thirty. Yesterday, I left at six o'clock.* Tell students that this is the simple past tense. We use it to talk about things in the past, like yesterday, last year, and so forth.

- Go over the information in the chart. Point out that there are two kinds of verbs. Regular verbs use a rule to make the simple past tense: add -ed. Most verbs are regular. Some verbs are irregular; they don't use -ed to form the simple past tense. They are all different. Students have to memorize them. Go over the irregular verbs in the chart.

- Explain/review how the verb changes in the information question.

Vocabulary

▲ leave

▲ arrive in/at

▲ return to/from

▲ go to

▲ come from/to

▲ move from/to

▲ stay in/at

A Circle the correct verb in parentheses.

1. People (move | (leave)) their homes when they go to work.
2. They are going to (arrive | (come)) to our school tomorrow.
3. I am going to (come | (stay)) at Jim's house tonight.
4. At the moment, John is (staying | (returning)) to Toronto.
5. Children ((go) | stay) to school at eight o'clock.

Grammar: Simple past tense

Simple past tense		
Statement	**Negative**	***Wh-* questions**
He **moved** from New York to San Francisco.	I **didn't stay** in California.	When **did they leave** Germany? How long **did you stay** in France?

*We use the simple past tense to talk about completed actions.

*Some verbs are regular in the simple past. They have an *-ed* ending.		*Some verbs are irregular in the simple past. They have many different forms.	
return—returned stay—stayed arrive—arrived	move—moved live—lived	go—went come—came leave—left	do—did be—(I/he/she) was / (you/they) were

148   Unit 12

Word Bank: Useful irregular verbs

do–did	read–read
eat–ate	say–said
give–gave	see–saw
have–had	sit–sat
know–knew	take–took
make–made	think–thought
meet–met	write–wrote

Grammar: Simple past tense

The simple past is used to talk about actions that were completed in the past. Irregular verbs are those that don't follow the rule in forming the past tense and so must be learned individually (practicing with flash cards is a good way to do this). Tell students that if they are unsure about a verb, dictionaries usually have a list of irregular verbs in the back.

A Change the sentences to the simple past tense.

1. I live in Amsterdam. _I lived in Amsterdam._
2. They arrive today. _They arrived today._
3. When does Jenny arrive? _When did Jenny arrive?_
4. Do you live with your parents? _Did you live with your parents?_
5. I go to English class in the evening. _I went to English class in_ the evening.

B Fill in the blanks using the correct form of the verb.

1. When did you leave Canada? I _____left_____ in 2010.
2. How long _did you stay_ in Saudi Arabia? I stayed there for three years.
3. Did you live in Brazil for three months? No, we _____didn't_____.
   We _____lived_____ there for three years.
4. When did you arrive in the United States? I _____arrived_____ three
   years ago.

C Unscramble these questions and then ask them to your partner.

1. arrive at / When / did you / school? _When did you arrive at school?_
2. to school / Did you / by bus? / come _Did you come to school by bus?_
3. homework? / your / do / Did you _Did you do your homework?_
4. home? / did you / When / leave _When did you leave home?_

Conversation

A 🔊 26 Listen to the conversation. When did Abdul arrive in Canada?

Ed: Abdul, you're not Canadian, are you?   _five years ago_
Abdul: No, I'm from Syria, but later my parents moved to France.
Ed: How long did you stay in France?
Abdul: Twelve years. But then I left France when I was 18 to study in the United States.
Ed: And when did you come to Canada?
Abdul: I came here five years ago.

B 🔁 Practice the conversation with a partner. Switch roles and practice it again.

C 🔁 Change the underlined words and make a new conversation.

D 🔁 **GOAL CHECK** ✔ **Use the simple past**

Have you or your parents ever moved? With a partner, take turns asking each other about the moves.

▲ Stanley Park in Vancouver, Canada

On the Move **149**

A
- Have students change the sentences and questions to the simple past tense.
- Have students compare answers with a partner.
- Check answers.

B
- Have students work individually to complete the sentences with the correct form of the verb.
- Have students compare answers with a partner.
- Check answers.

C
- Have students unscramble the questions.
- Check answers.
- Have students take turns asking their partner the questions.
- Have several students tell the class one of their partner's answers.

Conversation

A
- Have students close their books. Write the question on the board: *When did Abdul arrive in Canada?*
- Play the recording. 🔊 26
- Check answers.

B
- Play or read the conversation again for the class to repeat.
- Practice the conversation with the class in chorus.
- Have students practice the conversation with a partner and then switch roles and practice it again.

C
- Have students work with the same partner to make a new conversation.
- Call on student pairs to present their conversation to the class.

D 🔁 **GOAL CHECK** ✔

- Divide the class into pairs and have students take turns asking and answering questions about the moves.
- Have several students tell the class something about their partner's (or partner's parents) move(s).

Grammar Practice:
Simple past tense

Have students work individually to write three sentences about themselves using the past tense verbs they have learned. Collect the papers, read each student's sentences to the class, and have them guess who wrote the sentences. Ask follow-up questions about any interesting statements.

Lesson A **149**

Give Biographical Information

Listening

- Go over the information in the Word Focus box. Tell students that in English, we say years as pairs of digits: *1850 is eighteen fifty.* The exception is 2000 to 2009, where we say (for example), *two thousand six.* Write more years on the board and have students practice saying them.

A
- Introduce the idea of an immigrant—a person who comes from another country to live in a new place.
- Tell students they are going to hear information about four immigrants in the United States. Have them match the name with the correct photo. Say the names so that students are familiar with how they sound before they listen.
  - Play the recording one or more times. 🔊 27
  - Check answers.

B
- Tell students to listen again for the dates and choose *true* or *false.* Have them read the sentences.
  - Play the recording one or more times. 🔊 27
  - Have students compare answers with a partner.
  - Check answers.

C
- Tell students to listen again and find the information. Have them read the questions.
  - Play the recording one or more times. 🔊 27
  - Have students compare answers with a partner.
  - Check answers.

B GOAL 2: Give Biographical Information

Listening

A 🔊 27 Do you know these people? Write the names under the photos. Listen and check.

| Albert Einstein   Jerry Yang   Salma Hayek   Albert Pujols |

We say years like this:
1990 = nineteen ninety
2000 = two thousand
2014 = two thousand fourteen
We say *When **were you/was she** born?* to find out someone's year of birth. The reply is *I/she **was** born in (1980).*

Famous Immigrants to the United States

1. <u>Albert Einstein</u>

2. <u>Salma Hayek</u>

3. <u>Jerry Yang</u>

4. <u>Albert Pujols</u>

B 🔊 27 Listen carefully for the dates. Circle **T** for *true* and **F** for *false*.

1. Albert Einstein moved to the United States in 1933.   (T)   F
2. Salma Hayek was born in 1976.   T   (F)
3. Jerry Yang moved to San Jose in 1976.   (T)   F
4. Albert Pujols moved to the United States in 1990.   T   (F)

C 🔊 27 Listen again and answer the questions.

1. Where did Albert Einstein go to school? <u>in Switzerland</u>
2. Who did Salma Hayek live with in the United States? <u>her aunt</u>
3. In what year did Jerry Yang start his company? <u>1994</u>
4. When did Albert Pujols become an American citizen? <u>2007</u>

150 Unit 12

For Your Information: Immigrants

Albert Einstein, a physicist, is best known for his theory of relativity. He received the Nobel Prize for physics in 1921.

Salma Hayek is an actress, director, and TV and film producer. She is also active in groups to stop violence against women.

Jerry Yang created a website in 1994 called "Jerry's Guide to the World Wide Web." This became yahoo.com.

Albert Pujols is a famous baseball player. He is a first baseman for the Los Angeles Angels of Anaheim.

Pronunciation: -ed endings

A 🔊 28 Listen and check (✓) the correct column.

B 🔄 Practice these sentences with a partner.

1. He moved to Peru in 1989.
2. They wanted to go to Egypt.
3. My mother cooked a delicious meal.
4. We walked to the beach.
5. I traveled from Buenos Aires by plane.
6. Kris wanted to buy a new coat.

	/d/ ending	/t/ ending	/ɪd/ ending
1. returned	✓		
2. moved	✓		
3. wanted			✓
4. traveled	✓		
5. cooked		✓	
6. stayed	✓		
7. lived	✓		
8. walked		✓	

Communication

A 🔄 Read the itineraries. Take turns asking where and when Jane Goodall and Zahi Hawass traveled.

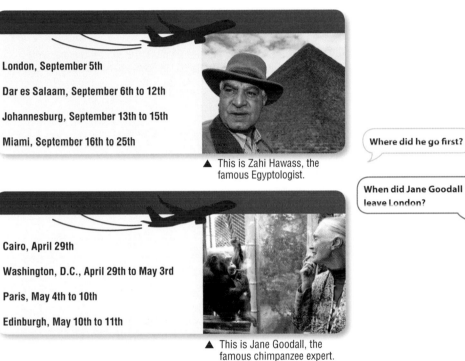

London, September 5th

Dar es Salaam, September 6th to 12th

Johannesburg, September 13th to 15th

Miami, September 16th to 25th

▲ This is Zahi Hawass, the famous Egyptologist.

Where did he go first?

When did Jane Goodall leave London?

Cairo, April 29th

Washington, D.C., April 29th to May 3rd

Paris, May 4th to 10th

Edinburgh, May 10th to 11th

▲ This is Jane Goodall, the famous chimpanzee expert.

B 🔄 | **GOAL CHECK** ✓ **Give biographical information**

Think of a friend or family member who has moved a lot in the past. Tell a partner where and when he or she moved.

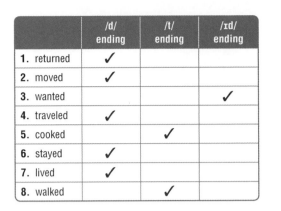

Pronunciation

A • Remind the class that regular verbs in the simple present tense add -ed at the end. Point out that the -ed has different pronunciations (/d/ after a voiced sound, /t/ after a voiceless sound, and /ɪd/ after t or d sounds).

• Many students will have an issue pronouncing the -ed of regular past tense verbs. It is common to hear them pronouncing an extra /ə/ when it is not necessary, such as in the word planned: /plænəd/ instead of /plænd°/. Teachers often add to the problem by exaggerating the final -ed pronunciation to "help" their students.

• Play the recording. 🔊 28

• Point out the differences in pronunciation.

• Play the recording again and have students check the sound they hear. 🔊 28

• Check answers.

• Tell students to listen again and repeat the words.

• Play the recording. 🔊 28

B • Divide the class into pairs and have them take turns reading the sentences. Walk around helping with difficulties.

• Call on students to read a sentence to the class.

Communication

A • Have students look at the two itineraries. Model the questions and answers with a student.

• Divide the class into pairs and have them take turns asking and answering questions about Hawass's and Goodall's travels.

• Call on different students to ask and answer the questions.

B 🔄 | **GOAL CHECK** ✓

• Have students tell their partners about a person they know who has moved a lot.

• Compare stories with the class.

Expansion Activity

With the class, talk about what kinds of people move frequently to other countries (businesspeople, diplomats, people in the military, etc.). Would students like to have this kind of a life? Why or why not?

Describe a Move

Language Expansion

- Go over the expressions for pre-moving activities. Point out the irregular past forms of the verbs in the Word Focus box.

A
- Look at the checklist with the class. Then have students work individually to write sentences.
- Have students compare answers with a partner.
- Check answers.

Grammar

- Review the simple past tense. Go over the information in the chart. Ask students a series of questions about their activities the day before: *Did you buy something new/go to a movie/get food at the supermarket?* and so on, to elicit, *Yes, I did./ No, I didn't.* Have students ask you questions.

C **GOAL 3:** Describe a Move

Language Expansion: Preparing to move

▲ close the bank account

▲ stop the mail

▲ have a going-away party

▲ get a passport

▲ pack

▲ sell the house

▲ buy the tickets

▲ sell the car

Word Focus

Note the following irregular past tenses:
sell—sold	buy—bought
get—got	have—had

Some verbs have a spelling change in the past tense.
stop—stopped

A Imagine that you and your family are moving to another country. Write sentences about what you did and didn't do from the checklist.

☑ sell the house ☐ get a passport ☐ have a going-away party

☑ buy the tickets ☑ sell the car ☑ stop the mail

☐ pack ☐ close the bank account

1. We sold the house.
2. We bought the tickets.
3. We didn't pack.
4. We didn't get passports. /I didn't get a passport .
5. We sold the car.
6. We didn't close the bank account.
7. We didn't have a going-away party.
8. We stopped the mail.

Grammar: Simple past tense—*Yes/No* questions

Simple past tense	
Yes/No **questions**	**Short answers**
Did they **return** to New York?	Yes, they **did.** No, they **didn't.**

Word Bank: Moving activities

buy a house

find a new school

get a new driver's license

get the water/electricity/gas turned on

notify the post office

rent an apartment

For Your Information: Studying in the United States

To study in the United States, international students need to get a student visa. They must submit a document stating the institution they want to apply to and the type of course they want to study, records of their previous educational qualifications, and scores on an international English test. They must also pass a medical examination.

A Unscramble the words to write questions.

1. going-away party? have a Did they Did they have a going-away party?
2. you the sell house? Did Did you sell the house?
3. Did the tickets? Ian buy Did Ian buy the tickets?
4. close the Did we windows? Did we close the windows?
5. pack they their Did things? Did they pack their things?

B Complete the sentences. Practice them with a partner.

1. **A:** _____Did you_____ buy the tickets? **B:** Yes, I _____did_____.
2. **A:** Did you __answers will vary__? **B:** No, I _____didn't_____.
3. **A:** Did they _____sell/buy_____ the house? **B:** No, ____they didn't____.

C With a partner, take turns asking questions about the checklist on page 152.

> Did you sell your car?

Conversation

A 🔊 29 Where are David and Liana moving? Listen to the conversation. *Canada*

David: Did you <u>get the tickets</u>?
Liana: Yes, I did. Here they are.
David: Great!
Liana: And did you <u>sell the car</u>?
David: Yes, I did. I got <u>$3,000</u> for it.
Liana: Wow! <u>Now I can buy some nice warm clothes</u> for <u>Canada</u>.

B Practice the conversation with a partner. Switch roles and practice it again.

C Change the underlined words and make a new conversation.

D 👥 | **GOAL CHECK** ✓ **Describe a move**

Yesterday Jack got a great job in a new city, but now he has to move . . . this weekend! In a group, take turns asking questions like: What did he already do? What didn't he do yet? Use your imagination.

▲ It looks like he's already packed!

On the Move **153**

A • Have students work individually to write the questions.
• Have students compare answers with a partner.
• Check answers.

B • Have students work individually to complete the sentences.
• Check answers.
• Divide the class into pairs to practice the conversations.

C • With the same pairs, have students ask and answer questions about the checklist on page 152.
• Call on student pairs to present questions and answers.

Conversation

A • Have students close their books. Write the question on the board: *Where are David and Liana moving?*
• Play the recording. 🔊 29
• Check answers.

B • Play or read the conversation again for the class to repeat.
• Practice the conversation with the class in chorus.
• Have students practice the conversation with a partner and then switch roles and practice it again.

C • Have students work with the same partner to make a new conversation.
• Call on student pairs to present their conversation to the class.

D 👥 | **GOAL CHECK** ✓

• Elicit activities we do before we move. Write a list on the board.
• Read the directions. Explain the meaning of *already* and *yet.* Ask, *Who's moving? Where's he moving to? When?* Model possible questions with a student.
• Divide the class into pairs and have them ask and answer questions about Jack's preparation.
• Call on different students to ask and answer questions.

Grammar Practice:
Simple past

Have students choose a trip they took in the past and think about their preparations. Then match students with a partner and have them ask and answer questions to write a list of things their partner did before the trip. Whose list is longer? Did he or she have a good trip?

Lesson C **153**

Discuss Migrations

Reading

A
- Have students look at the pictures and describe what they see.
- Introduce the topic of the reading. Talk about the idea of ancestors—your relatives a long time ago. With the class, talk about where people's ancestors came from.

B
- Have students read the article and find all the regular and irregular verbs. Tell them to mark any words they don't understand. Point out the words in the Word Focus box.
- Check answers.
- Go over the article with the class, answering any questions from the students about vocabulary.

C
- Have students read the article again to answer the questions.
- Have students compare answers with a partner.
- Check answers.

D   **GOAL 4:** Discuss Migrations

Reading

A At some time in the past, your ancestors moved to your country. Maybe it was 100 years ago; maybe it was 100,000 years ago. Where did they come from?

B Read. Underline the regular verbs and circle the irregular verbs in the simple past tense.

C Answer the questions.

1. Where did humans first appear?

   in Africa

2. Where did they migrate to first?

   to the Middle East

3. How did Europeans move across the United States?

   from the East to the West

4. Give an example of economic migration.
   People move to find work/a good life.

5. Give an example of forced migration.
   Answers will vary.
   People move because of wars.

These people are from the Congo, in Africa. They left their homes during the war, but now they are returning.

Word Focus

economic = about money

forced = when something is not your choice

migrate = to move from one place to another

war = a fight

154   Unit 12

For Your Information: Early human migration

Scientists believe that the first humans (Homo sapiens) began to move out of Africa about 70,000 years ago and spread all across Australia, Asia, and Europe in the following millennia. Humans reached the Americas between 20,000 and 15,000 years ago. The Pacific Islands were the last places to be populated, around 2,000 years ago. There have been many other migrations of civilizations, such as the movement of the Turks east across Asia between the sixth and eleventh centuries AD. The Vikings, Germans, and Roma ("gypsy") people all migrated across Europe during medieval times.

HUMAN **MIGRATION**

We think that modern humans appeared in Africa about 200,000 years ago. But they didn't stay in Africa. They **migrated** out of Africa to the Middle East and then to the rest of the world. Throughout history, people have migrated from one place to another. People, it seems, like to move.

Since the 17th century, many European people moved from Europe to the Americas. They left Spain and Portugal and moved to South America.

Many Northern Europeans migrated to North America. In the United States, most people arrived in New York. Some stayed on the East Coast, but many people migrated to the West Coast using wagon trains.

So, why do people move? First, there is **economic** migration. People move to find work and a good life. Second, there is **forced** migration. People move because of **wars;** it is not safe to stay in their homes.

Of course, many people don't migrate. They stay in the same place all their lives. But people like to visit different countries on their vacations. People, it seems, just like to move.

For Your Information

Students will often want to find out more information about a subject. The National Geographic Society website has more information on many of the subjects covered in *World English*. For more information about human migration, visit https://genographic.nationalgeographic.com/human-journey/

After Reading

With the class, talk about groups of people who have migrated to the students' country. Where did they come from? Why did they migrate? How is their life different now?

Discuss Migrations

Communication

A • Divide the class into pairs and have them read the travel options.

• Have each pair choose one option and write notes about why they chose that option.

B • Have pairs ask questions to find another pair who chose the same option. Have them form a group of four.

• Have students discuss in their groups why they chose that travel option and what they need to do to prepare for the trip. Have them write a list.

• Have each group share their reasons and their list with the class.

Writing

A • Tell students which travel option you chose and why. Tell them you are on your trip and you are writing an e-mail to a friend about it. Begin writing an e-mail on the board and have students help you develop it. Point out the verbs in the box for students to use.

• Have students write an e-mail about the trip they chose with their group. Remind them to use the verbs in the box. Provide other vocabulary as necessary.

• Have groups exchange e-mails and, if time allows, have them write a reply.

B 🔾 **GOAL CHECK** ✔

• Divide the class into small groups and have them discuss animal migrations. If necessary, introduce/review names of animals and countries.

• Have one student from each group report to the class on the animals they talked about and where they migrate to. Write a list on the board.

D **GOAL 4:** Discuss Migrations

Maya Bay, Thailand

▲ Rome, Italy

▲ Rio de Janeiro, Brazil

Did you choose Italy?

visited went
stayed left
arrived

Communication

A 🔁 With a partner, read the travel options. Choose one together.

Option A   Three weeks in Thailand and Cambodia
Archaeology and relaxation! 21-day guided tour includes Ayutthaya, Angkor, and many beautiful beaches and islands.
Option B   Summer in Italy
Learn Italian! Live with an Italian family in Rome for ten weeks. Learn about Italy's history, food, and language.
Option C   A year in Brazil
Foreign workers welcome to work at the Olympics and World Cup! Possible opportunity to settle permanently if interested.

B 🔾 In a group, talk about what you have to do to prepare for your trip.

Writing

A 🔾 As a group, write an e-mail to a friend about your trip. Use the verbs in the box.

B 🔾 **GOAL CHECK** ✔ **Discuss migrations**

Animals also migrate. Which animals migrate? Where do they migrate to and from? Why do they migrate?

156 Unit 12

For Your Information: Monarch butterflies

The monarch butterfly lives mainly in North America but is also found in Australia, New Zealand, and occasionally in Western Europe. Its wingspan is about 3½ to 4 inches (9 to 10 centimeters). It was named *monarch* because of its large size and also its large range. To defend against predators, it produces a poisonous chemical with a bad taste, and its brilliant color pattern warns other animals not to eat it.

Before You Watch

A Complete the sentences with words from the box. Use your dictionary.

> spectacle forest
> fragile environment
> disaster logging
> destroy preserve

1. Monarch butterflies are very _____fragile_____. Cold temperatures can kill them.
2. The monarch migration is very beautiful. It is a _____spectacle_____.
3. Monarch butterflies migrate to a _____forest_____ in Mexico.
4. _____Logging_____, or cutting down trees, is going to _____destroy_____ the forest.
5. Governments and organizations want to _____preserve_____ the forest.
6. Millions of monarchs will die without their natural _____environment_____. It will be a _____disaster_____.

While You Watch

A ▶ Watch the video. Circle **T** for *true* and **F** for *false*.

1. Monarch butterflies migrate from Canada to Mexico every year. **T** F
2. The butterflies are very strong. T **F**
3. Trees do not protect the butterflies. T **F**
3. Loggers cut down the trees and destroy the forest. **T** F
4. The Mexican government is not helping to protect the butterflies. T **F**

After You Watch

A ⚡ With a partner, think of an animal or plant that has a similar problem in your country or region. Answer these questions:

1. What is the animal or plant?
2. What problem does it have?
3. How can this animal or plant be saved?

Video Journal:
Monarch Migration
Before You Watch

A • Have students look at the picture and say what they see.

• Have students compare answers with a partner.

• Have students complete the sentences, referring to their dictionaries as needed.

• Check answers.

While You Watch

A • Have students read the statements. Tell them to choose *true* or *false* as they watch.

• Play the video.

• Have students compare answers with a partner. Play the video again as necessary.

• Check answers.

After You Watch

A • Elicit the names of animals or plants that have a similar problem in the students' country or region. Write them on the board.

• Divide the class into pairs and have them choose an animal or plant that is in danger and answer the questions.

• Have pairs share their ideas with the class.

Teacher Tip: Self-evaluation

At the end of the course, it's useful to have students spend some time reflecting on the progress they've made and their goals for future learning. One way to do this is by having them fill in a questionnaire in English or their native language, and then (if time permits) having a brief meeting with each student to discuss his or her answers.

Here are some possible questions you could use:

How much have you improved in these areas? Write "A lot," "Some," or "A little": Speaking/ Pronunciation/Listening/Writing/Reading/ Vocabulary/Grammar

Which activities in class helped you the most?

Which activities didn't help you?

What will you do differently in your next class?

Weird, or Just Different?

Before You Watch

A • Have students look at the pictures and decide what they think is happening in each one. Elicit one or two sentences using *looks* for the first picture. For example, *She looks sick. She looks tired.*

• Have students discuss what is happening in each picture with a partner.

• Have different pairs report back to the class. Ask, *Did you have the same idea about what was happening?*

B • Have students match the headings with the pictures in **A** and check if their ideas were right.

• Check answers.

C • Have students look at the words in the Word Bank and complete the sentences.

• Have students compare answers with a partner.

• Check answers.

D • Have students think about assumptions they have made. Tell them to think about when they were traveling, met someone new, or started a new job, for example. Provide an example yourself: *When I visited Spain, I assumed that the stores closed at 5:30 p.m., like they do in my country, but they don't close until 8:30 or 9:00 p.m.*

• Have students discuss their assumptions with a partner and explain if their assumptions were true or not.

• Have several students share their assumptions and whether they were true or not.

TEDTALKS

Derek Sivers Entrepreneur
WEIRD, OR
JUST DIFFERENT?

Before You Watch

A ⚡ What do you think is happening in each picture? Discuss with a partner. Use *looks* to describe your ideas. Do you share the same ideas? Write down what you think in your notebook.

1.

2.

3.

4.

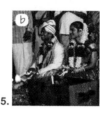
5.

Derek Sivers's idea worth spreading is that you shouldn't trust what you think you know; the opposite may also be true. Watch Sivers' full TED Talk on TED.com.

C Derek Sivers is interested in the assumptions we make in our lives. Here are some words you'll hear in his TED Talk. Complete the sentences with the correct words.

WORD BANK
assumption something believed to be true
block an area between two streets
brilliant very intelligent or skillful
imagine think about and make a picture of
obvious easy to understand

1. Marissa is a ____brilliant____ singer. She practices all the time.

2. Can you ____imagine____ how difficult it is to move to another country?

3. It's ____obvious____ that washing your hands helps prevent the spread of disease.

4. The wedding is not on this street, but one ____block____ from here at the Marina Hotel.

5. Your ____assumption____ is correct. Birds migrate to find food and stay warm.

D ⚡ You are going to watch a TED Talk about making assumptions. Think about an assumption you've made. Was it true? Discuss with a partner.

While You Watch

A Watch the video. Put the quotes in order. Write the number in the boxes provided.

B Look at the pictures from exercise **A** again. Check your ideas. Match the picture to the correct heading.

a. An infectious disease
b. A wedding
c. A singing lesson
d. Migrating to a new home
e. Lost in a strange city

Working with authentic spoken language

Activating prior knowledge of a subject is an important strategy to help students be effective listeners. Having students do pre-watching tasks, such as discussing concepts related to what they are going to listen to (as in the Before You Watch activities about assumptions), activates knowledge and ideas they already have about the topic. They can then use this knowledge to help them understand when they watch the video. These activities also help provide students with any necessary knowledge they may be lacking, so they can understand what they are going to see. Finally, the activities provide a bridge between what the students already know and the new information, which helps them process what they hear.

> "Sometimes we need to go to the opposite side of the world to realize assumptions we didn't even know we had, and realize that the opposite of them may also be true."
>
> — Derek Sivers

While You Watch

A • Have students look at the images and read the quotes on page 159. Tell students they are going to watch the TED Talk and number the quotes in the order they hear them.

• Have students compare answers with a partner.

• Check answers.

Challenge

• Have students think of an assumption people might have about their country that isn't true and discuss it with a partner.

• Have several pairs share the assumptions they discussed with the class. Write their ideas on the board. Have students think about why people from other countries have these assumptions, and discuss reasons with the whole class. Ask, *What assumptions do we have about other countries? Are they true?*

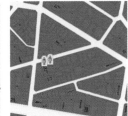

| 4 | "There's a saying that whatever true thing you can say about India, the opposite is also true." | 3 | "There are doctors in China who believe that it's their job to keep you healthy. So, any month you are healthy, you pay them." | 1 | "Excuse me, what is the name of this block?" | 2 | "All of these blocks have names, and the streets are just the unnamed spaces in between the blocks." |

Challenge! Can you think of an assumption that someone might have about your country that isn't true?

159

For Your Information: Intercultural Communicative Competence

As the world becomes more globalized, students will have the ability to communicate with people from many different cultures and backgrounds. As students use English with people from other cultures, they will need to be able to confront differences in background and ideas. It will be important for students to be able to find common ground with people from other cultures, recognize mistaken assumptions and stereotypes, examine their own culture, and practice empathy and respect for others.

After You Watch

A • Have students read the sentences. Tell them to choose *true* or *false* for each sentence.

• Have students compare answers with a partner. Play the video again as necessary.

• Check answers.

B • Have students read the sentences and complete them with the verb in the simple past.

• Have students compare answers with a partner.

• Check answers.

C • Have students read the assumptions and mark if they agree or disagree with each statement.

D • Divide the class into pairs and have them discuss whether they agree or disagree with each assumption.

• Have several pairs share their opinions with the class.

• As a class, discuss any differences in opinion.

TEDTALKS **Derek Sivers** Entrepreneur
WEIRD, OR
JUST DIFFERENT?

After You Watch

A Read the statements. Circle **T** for *true* and **F** for *false*.

1. In Japan, only the streets have names and numbers. T (F)
2. In the United States, the blocks have names and numbers. T (F)
3. In Japan, the houses are numbered by how old they are. (T) F
4. In China, doctors make money when people are healthy. (T) F
5. If you believe something, the opposite can also be true. (T) F

B Complete the sentences with the simple past tense form of the verb in parentheses.

1. The Japanese man _____asked_____ (ask), "What is the name of this block?"
2. We _____imagined_____ (imagine) standing on a street corner in America.
3. They _____paid_____ (pay) the doctors so they could stay healthy.
4. It was obvious that he _____was_____ (is) confused about the address.
5. I _____noticed_____ (notice) that the house numbers don't go in order.

C Read the assumptions. Do you agree or disagree?

1. If a street doesn't have a name, it's impossible to find the address. **Agree** **Disagree**
2. You should only see a doctor when you feel sick. **Agree** **Disagree**
3. There is only one correct way to show the size and location of a country on a map. **Agree** **Disagree**
4. You only cough when you have a cold. **Agree** **Disagree**
5. People only move to find a new job. **Agree** **Disagree**

D Talk about the assumptions with a partner. Discuss whether you agree or disagree with each other.

160

You might assume that a hotel can't be made of ice. You would be wrong!

E1 Look at the topics in the chart. What do you think about each one? Make a list of your assumptions. With a group, discuss your assumptions. Do the other people in your group share your ideas?

Medicine	A headache:
	A stomachache:
Jobs	A dentist:
	A lawyer:
Celebrations	A New Year's party:
	A Thanksgiving Day meal:
Migrations	Moving to a new apartment:
	Moving to a new country:

E2 Research one of your assumptions. Is it correct? Share what you find with the class.

Challenge! From watching the TED Talk, what would you assume about Derek Sivers? Read about Derek Sivers at TED.com. Were your assumptions correct? Discuss with a partner.

161

E1 • Have students read the topics in the chart and write their assumption(s) for each one.

• Divide the class into small groups and have them discuss and compare their assumptions. Have each group identify which assumptions they share.

• Have each group share their assumptions with the class.

E2 • With the same group, have students research one of their assumptions to find out if it is true or not.

• Have each group share what they found out.

Challenge

• With their books closed, have students say what Derek Sivers is interested in and what his ideas are. Write their ideas on the board.

• Have students write down what assumptions they think they can make about Sivers now that they have watched his talk.

• Have students share their assumptions with the class. Write them on the board.

• Have students read more about Derek Sivers at TED.com, and have them discuss with a partner whether their assumptions were true or not.

• With the whole class, look at the list of assumptions on the board and have students say whether they are true or not.

GLOSSARY

UNIT 1

black: the darkest color; the color at night if there is no light

blond: having light, yellowish hair

brother: a son with the same parents as another daughter or son

brown: the color of earth or wood

children: people who are not yet adults

curly: hair that forms into curves or spirals

daughter: a female child

family: people who are related to each other

father: a male parent

friends: a person who someone knows and likes

grandfather: the father of one's father or mother

grandmother: the mother of one's father or mother

gray: a color like black mixed with white

greeting: something friendly you say or do when you meet someone

hair: a thin fine growth on the skin and head of a person

handsome: good-looking or attractive

husband: a man who is married

introduce: tell someone your name so you can get to know them

married: having a husband or wife

mother: a female parent

old: having lived for many years

parent: a mother or father

pretty: lovely or attractive individual

red: the color of blood or fire

short: referring to below average height

single: one who is unmarried

sister: a daughter with the same parents as another daughter or son

son: a male child

straight: in the form of a line without bending

tall: referring to above average height

wavy: slightly curly, rippled or undulated

young: not old, of few years

UNIT 2

architect: a trained professional who designs buildings and is often in charge of their construction

artist: a person who creates art, such as a painter or musician

banker: an officer or manager of a bank

big: large

chef: the head cook in a restaurant

city: an area with many thousands of people living and working close together

cold (adj): having a low temperature

country: an area of land which is a nation

doctor: a physician or medical practitioner

dry: without water or moisture

engineer: a person highly trained in science and mathematics who plans the making of machines, roads, and bridges

hot: having a high degree of heat

maize: corn; a plant with long vegetables covered in yellow seeds

numbers 1-101: (see page 18)

small: not large

taxi driver: a person who is the driver of a car for hire

teacher: a person whose job is to instruct others

wet: to have a high degree of water

UNIT 3

apartment: set of rooms for living in within a building with other apartments

armchair: a chair with armrests

back yard: the land behind and belonging to a house

bathroom: room with a bath and toilet

bed: a piece of furniture for sleeping

bedroom: a room for sleeping

bookcase: a piece of furniture with shelves, sides, and usually a back

chair: a piece of furniture with a back, for a person to sit on

closet: a small room for storing clothes, towels, sheets, etc

coffee table: a long, low table often set in front of a sofa

dining room: a room for eating in, usually with chairs and a table

downstairs: in the direction of or located on floors below

front yard: an area in front of the house

garage: a building where a vehicle is kept

garden: an area of land used to grow flowers and vegetables

house: building in which people live

kitchen: a room where meals are prepared, usually having a stove, sink, and refrigerator

lamp: any variety of lighting devices using electricity, oil, or gas

living room: a room in a house where people sit, talk, read, or entertain

microwave: a small oven which uses short frequency electromagnetic waves

refrigerator: a storage box with cooling and usually freezing sections for keeping food fresh

sofa: a long, soft seat with a back, arms, and room for two or more people

stairs: a set of steps going up or down

stove: a piece of kitchen equipment with burners, usually containing an oven, used to cook food

swimming pool: an area that has been dug-out and filled with water for people to swim in

table: a piece of furniture with a flat top on legs

TV: a box-like device that receives and displays pictures and sound

upstairs: in the direction of the level or floor above

UNIT 4

backpack: a type of bag carried on the back with two shoulder straps

bag: a sack, a container made of paper, plastic, cloth, etc. used to carry things

book: pages of words kept together with a paper or hard cover

camcorder: a hand-held video camera and recorder

cell phone: a small telephone you can carry with you

dictionary: a book listing words and their meanings in alphabetical order

DVD player: a device that plays DVDs

earrings: pieces of jewelry that are attached to ears

glasses: two pieces of glass or plastic that one wears in front of the eyes to see better

gold: valuable yellow-colored metal

jewelry: ornaments that people wear

keys: pieces of metal used to lock or unlock a door, start or stop an engine, etc.

laptop: a small portable computer

MP3 player: portable device that plays music

necklace: chain or string of beads worn around the neck

notebook: a book with blank or lined pages to make notes in

pen: an instrument used to write or draw in ink

ring: a circular metal band worn on a finger

silver: a valuable pale gray metal

smart phone: an mobile phone that can access the Internet

speakers: piece of audio equipment that sound comes from

tablet: a small portable computer that is navigated through a touch screen

wallet: a small, folded case used to hold cash or credit cards

watch: a small clock worn on the wrist

check e-mails: to look at one's electronic mail

days of the week: (see page 58)

finish work: to reach the end of a work-day at one's job

get up: to wake-up and rise from sleeping

go to bed: the act of lying down in one's bed

go to meetings: the act of going to a gathering with work colleagues

go to the bank: the act of going to the place where one's money is kept

have dinner: to have something to eat in the evening

have lunch: to have something to eat in the middle of the day

make photocopies: to make copies of a document using a machine

meet clients: to get together with customers to whom a service is provided

start work: begin a work-day at a job

take a nap: to have a short sleep during the daytime

take a photo: to record an image using a camera

take a shower: to wash in the shower

talk on the phone: to communicate through a telephone

time: what people measure in years, days, hours, and minutes (see page 56)

travel: to go, journey

write reports: to write a document for work or school

across from: on the other side of the street

airport shuttle bus: a bus used to take people to and from, or within the airport

art gallery: a place to display works of art, such as paintings, sculptures, etc.

between: in the middle of two things

bus: a large vehicle used to carry people between places

bus station: a place or building where buses pick-up and drop-off passengers

car: an automobile

hotel: a building with bedrooms for rent

journey: act of traveling from one place to another

library: a building which holds books and other reference materials for borrowing

movie theater: a theater where movies are shown for entertainment

museum: a place that displays rare, valuable, and important art or historical objects

on the corner of: at the place where two streets meet

park: an area of land where people can exercise, play, or relax

post office: a building where mail is processed

restaurant: a business that serves food

subway: a public transportation system with trains that run underground

supermarket: a large store offering food and general household items

taxi: a car with a driver for hire

tourist office: a center that gives information to visitors or travelers

train: a line of vehicles, such as railroad cars pulled by a locomotive

train station: a place or building, where trains pick-up and drop-off their passengers

turn (left/right): change direction

cooking: preparing and serving food

free time: time not spent working or in school

going for a walk: the act of taking a walk outdoors

going to the movies: the act of watching a film in a movie theater

ice skate: to move over ice with ice skates

listening to music: to use our sense of hearing in order to enjoy music

play football: play a sport played by two 11-person teams, using an oval ball. In order to win one must pass or run the ball over the opponent's line

play golf: play an outdoors game in which people hit a small hard ball with a stick into a hole

play soccer: play a sport of two teams of 11 players, who kick a round ball into goals

play tennis: play a game on a court with two or four players who use rackets to hit the ball over a net

playing the guitar: using an instrument with six strings to make music

reading: to see and understand words in a book or magazine

shopping: the act of buying items at stores or online

ski: the sport of sliding down or across snowy surfaces on skis

sports: games that require physical skill

swim: to move through water by moving parts of the body

play volleyball: playing a sport played with players on each side of a net who score points by hitting the ball to the ground on the opponents' side

watching TV: the act of viewing the television

beige: a light-brown color

black: the darkest color; the color at night if there is no light

blouse: a woman's shirt

blue: the color of the sky and the sea

brown: the color of earth or wood

coat: warm clothing worn over other clothes

colors: (see pages 96 and 100)

dark: close to black

dress: a one-piece article of clothing worn by girls or women

gray: a color like black mixed with white

green: the color of grass or leaves

hat: a clothing item which covers the head

jacket: a short coat

jeans: informal pants made of denim

light: close to white

orange: a color between red and yellow

pants: a piece of clothing that covers the legs

pink: a color between red and white

purple: a color between red and blue

red: the color of blood or fire

scarf: a piece of cloth worn around the neck

shirt: a piece of clothing worn on the upper body

shoes: a covering for the foot

skirt: a piece of women's clothing that covers the waist, hips, and part of the legs

socks: a piece of cloth worn over the foot and under a shoe

sweater: a warm piece of clothing worn over the upper body

tie: a piece of cloth worn by men around the neck for formal occasions

t-shirt: a short-sleeved shirt worn over the upper body

white: the complete lack of color, or the lightest of all colors

yellow: the color of a lemon or the sun

apple: a round fruit with red, green, or yellow skin and firm, juicy flesh

banana: a long curved fruit with yellow skin

bean: an edible seed of many plants

bread: a food made of baked flour, water or milk, and yeast

butter: a yellowish fat made from milk or cream

candy: sweet food made with sugar

carrots: long, thin, orange vegetables

cereal: food made from grain

cheese: a solid food made from milk

chicken: a farm bird raised for its eggs and meat

chocolate cake: a sweet baked food made from flour, eggs, milk, sugar, and chocolate

coffee: a hot, brown, energy-giving drink made by water and coffee beans

cookies: a small, sweet cake

eggs: round or oval-shaped shell made by a female bird

fish: an animal with tails and fins that lives in water

fruit juice: a liquid drink made from fruit

ice cream: a frozen mixture of cream, milk, flavors, and sweeteners

meal: food you eat

meat: the flesh of animals

milk: a white liquid produced by some female animals such as cows

orange: a round, juicy, orange-colored fruit with thick skin

pasta: food made of flour, eggs, and water, formed in many shapes and boiled

potato: round or oval root vegetables with white insides

rice: white or brown grains from a cereal plant

salad: a mixture of vegetables, fruit, or other foods, served with a dressing

steak: a large piece of meat or fish, usually about an inch thick

tea: flowers and leaves that are dried, shredded, and brewed into a drink

tomato: a soft, red fruit

yogurt: a thick, creamy food make made from milk

UNIT 10

arm: one of two parts of the upper human body that extends from the shoulder to the hand

back: the side of the human body opposite the stomach and chest

backache: a dull, lasting pain in the back

body: all of a person or animal's physical parts

chest: the front of the human body above the stomach

cold (noun): an illness, usually with a blocked runny nose, sore throat, and a lot of sneezing

cough: to push air out of the throat suddenly with a harsh noise

cough medicine: liquid medicine taken for a cough

ear: one of the two organs used for hearing, located on either side of the head

earache: pain in the inside of your ear

face: the part of the head that has the eyes, mouth and nose

fever: higher that normal body temperature

finger: long, thin movable parts of the hand

foot: the body part attached to the lower leg and used for walking

hand: part of the body at the end of the arm

head: part of the body that has the face, ears, hair, skull, and brain

headache: a dull, lasting pain in the head

health: condition of a body

knee: where a leg bends

leg: one of the lower limbs of humans and many animals, used for walking and running

lie down: rest or sleep

pain reliever: a type of medicine taken to lessen aches in the body

patient: a person receiving medical care

sore throat: a pain in a person's throat

stomach: the front of the body below the chest

stomachache: pain in the belly

toothache: a pain in a person's tooth

UNIT 11

acting: performing in plays or movies

actor: a person who acts in plays or movies

anniversary: a date that is celebrated because of a special event

birthday: date somebody was born on

education: teaching people, usually at a school

go out for dinner: eat the main meal of the day outside of home

go to a game: watch a sports event in person

go to the movies: see a movie at a theater

have a barbecue: to cook food on a grill outside

have a family meal: eating with your family

have a party: have a get together or celebration with family or friends

holiday: a special day where people do not work or go to school

information technology: using computers to store and analyze information

law: rules made by a government body that must be followed by the people in a nation

lawyer: a professional who practices law

medicine: the science of curing sick people and preventing disease

months: (see page 136)

music: the art of putting sounds in a rhythmic sequence

musician: a person who writes, sings, or plays music

nurse: a person trained to take care of sick or injured people

plan: decide what you are going to do

software engineer: a professional who designs computer programs

special: more important than usual

teacher: a person who teachers or educates

wish: when someone wants to do or have something

UNIT 12

arrive in/at: to reach a place or destination

bank account: money in a bank

buy: to pay money for something

close: to shut down or bring to an end

come to: to arrive at a location

come from: location someone was in before

going-away party: a party arranged for a person who is leaving

go to: move or travel to

immigrant: a person who moves to another country to live

leave: to go away from

mail: letters, postcards, packages

move from: leaving a home to a new house or location

move to: a change of home to a new house or location

pack: to place, wrap, or seal objects in a container for transport of storage

passport: a small book issued by a government to a citizen of a nation

return to/from: to come back

sell: put something up for sale

stay in/at: to remain somewhere

ticket: a printed piece of paper bought for travel

GRAMMAR

adjectives, 8
    + *be,* 8–9
    demonstrative, 45
    possessive, 5
    some and *any,* 109
adverbs of frequency, 60
how much and *how many,* 113
indefinite articles, 16
nouns
    countable and uncountable, 112
    plural endings, 28
    possessives, 46
prepositions of place, 32–33, 69
there is/there are, 28–29
verbs,
    be + adjective, 8
    be + adjective + noun, 20–21
    be + *not,* 16
    be going to, 137
    can for ability, 89
    can/could (polite requests), 97
    contractions with *be,* 5, 16, 19
    feel, look, 124
    have, 49
    have to, 73
    imperatives, 69
    likes and dislikes, 100–101
    present continuous tense, 84–85
    present tense *be,* 5
    questions with *be* and short answers, 9
    should for advice, 128
    simple past tense, 148–149, 152
    simple present tense–questions and answers, 60–61
    simple present tense–statements and negatives, 56–57
    simple present tense–*What time* questions, 57
    simple present tense–*yes/no* questions, 152
    would like to for wishes, 140

LISTENING

biographical information, 150
conversations, 5, 9, 17, 21, 29, 33, 44, 46, 49, 57, 61, 69, 73, 85, 86, 89, 97, 101, 109, 113, 125, 126, 127, 129, 137, 149, 153
descriptions, 6, 30–31, 89, 98, 126, 138
discussions, 138
interviews, 18, 58, 61
introductions, 5, 6
party planning, 110
telephone conversations, 86
walking tours, 70

PRONUNCIATION

and, 111
be going to (reduced form), 139
can and *can't,* 88
contractions with *be,* 19
could you, 99
-ed endings, 151
falling intonations on statements and information questions, 59
final-*s,* 31
numbers, 19
/iː/ and /ɪ/ sounds, 46–47
/r/ sound, 7
sentence stress, 127
/ʃ/ and /tʃ/ sounds, 87
yes/no questions and short answers, 71

READING SKILLS 10, 18, 22, 34, 50, 62, 68, 74, 90, 102, 114, 130, 142, 154

READINGS

Chameleon Clothes, 102–103
Different Farmers, 22–23
Families around the World, 10–11
Human Migration, 154–155
Jewelry, 50–51
Journey to Antarctica, 74–75
Preventing Disease, 130–131
Soccer–The Beautiful Game, 90–91
TED Talks
    Brilliant Designs to Fit More People in Every City, 34–36
    A Guerilla Gardener in South Central L.A., 114–116
    Unseen Footage, Untamed Nature, 62–64
    Keep Your Goals to Yourself, 142–144

SPEAKING

asking for/giving directions, 71
asking/answering questions, 19, 21, 29, 45, 46, 47, 51, 58, 59, 61, 65, 69, 71, 73, 85, 104, 113, 115, 145, 151, 153, 157
comparing, 35
conversations, 5, 9, 17, 21, 29, 33, 45, 49, 57, 61, 69, 73, 85, 89, 97, 101, 109, 113, 125, 126, 127, 129, 131, 137, 141, 149, 151, 153
describing, 7, 11, 23, 25, 31, 99, 127
discussing, 23, 127, 139, 155
giving advice, 129, 131
greetings and introductions, 4
interviewing, 19, 61, 88, 113
making plans, 110, 111, 139, 141, 143
ordering food, 109
party planning, 110, 111

PHOTO

Cover Photo: Martin Roemers/Panos Pictures

2: (c) Martin Schoeller/AUGUST Image, LLC; **3:** (tl) (bl) (rc) Martin Schoeller/AUGUST Image, LLC; **4:** (tl) Jupiterimages/Photos.com/ Thinkstock, (tr) Ron Chapple Stock/Alamy, (bl) © Stuart Jenner/Shutterstock.com, (br) Bananastock/360/Getty Images; **6:** (bl) © iStockphoto.com/Aldo Murillo, (bc) Hill Street Studios/blend Images/Getty Images, (br) © iStockphoto.com/j-ezlo; **7:** (rc) jf/Cultura/Getty Images; **8:** (tl) © iStockphoto.com/Gisele, (tlc) © iStockphoto.com/Vetta Collection/naphtalina, (trc) Henglein and Steets/Cultura/Age Fotostock, (tr) Tim Robbins/Mint Images Limited/Alamy; **9:** (br) Radius Images/Corbis; **10–11:** (c) David Alan Harvey/National Geographic Creative; **10:** (inset) Peter Menzel Photography; **12:** (tl) (tc) (c) (tr) Martin Schoeller/AUGUST Image, LLC; **13:** (tc) Jed Weingarten/National Geographic Creative, (tr) Michael Nichols/National Geographic Creative, (rc) © iStockphoto.com/ EcoPic, (brc) © iStockphoto.com/skynesher, (br) © iStockphoto.com/Nealitpmcclimon; **14–15:** (c) China Daily Information Corp/Reuters; **16:** (tr) © iStockphoto.com/selimaksan, (trc) Craig Ferguson/Lonely Planet Images/Getty Images, (tlc) © Peter Close/Shutterstock.com, (tr) © Kzenon/Shutterstock.com, (blc) © iStockphoto.com/Casarsa, (blc) © iStockphoto. com/Gelpi, (brc) © iStockphoto.com/Pinopic, (br) Nicholas Cope/Stone/Getty Images; **17:** (tr) picturegarden/Photolibrary/Getty Images; **18:** (tl) © iStockphoto.com/bonnie Jacobs, (lc) © mangostock/Shutterstock.com, (bl) steve cicero/Flame/Corbis; **19:** (tr) Emil Von Maltitz/ Oxford Scientific/Getty Images; **20:** (lc) © iStockphoto.com/c-foto, (c) © iStockphoto. com/gioadventures, (bl) © iStockphoto.com/ michellegibson, (bc) © iStockphoto.com/ traveler1116; **21:** (tc) Audun Bakke Andersen/ Flickr/Getty Images; **22–23:** (c) James P. blair/ National Geographic Creative; **23:** (tr) David Alan Harvey/National Geographic Creative; **24:** (tc) Mauricio Handler/National Geographic Creative, (tl) Steve Winter/National Geographic Creative, (lc) Joel Sartore/National Geographic Creative; **25:** (tc) Darlyne A. Murawski/National Geographic Creative; **26–27:** (c) Courtesy Alexander Heilner; **29:** (tr) Urbanmyth/Alamy; **30:** (tl) Jaak Nilson/Spaces Images/Corbis, (tr) Simon Battensby/Image Source/Getty Images, (lc) © Rcpphoto/Shutterstock.ocm, (rc) © PeterG/Shutterstock.com; **31:** (bl) © Thierry Maffeis/Shutterstock.com, (br) Image Source/ Getty Images; **32:** (tr) © iStockphoto.com/ simonkr, (trc) © James Marvin Phelps/ Shutterstock.com, (tc) © iStockphoto.com/c-foto, (trc) © iStockphoto.com/adventtr, (tr) ©

iStockphoto.com/s-cphoto, (lc) © iStockphoto. com/tatniz, (lc) © iStockphoto.com/ blackwaterimages, (c) © iStockphoto.com/ Auris, (rc) © iStockphoto.com/claylib, (bl) © iStockphoto.com/deliormanli, (bc) © iStockphoto.com/eyecrave, (br) © iStockphoto. com/tiler84; **33:** (tl) © iStockphoto.com/CostinT, (tlc) © Juriah Mosin/Shutterstock.com, (tc) Stockbyte/Thinkstock, (trc) © iStockphoto.com/ Chuck Schmidt, (tr) © iStockphoto.com/Stacey Newman, (lc) © iStockphoto.com/Chuck Schmidt, (rc) © Rodenberg Photography/ Shutterstock.com; **35:** (C) Sheryl Lanzel/TED, (tr) Reed Kaestner/Corbis; **36:** (t) Xu Xiaolin/ Corbis; **37:** (tc) Claudio Camanini/Flickr Select/ Getty Images, (br) ©Dan Clausen/Shutterstock. com; **38:** (tl) © jason cox/Shutterstock.com, (tr) © Sean Nel/Shutterstock.com, (cl) ©Photographee.eu/Shutterstock.com, (cr) © blinka/Shutterstock.com, (b) © Elena Talberg/ Shutterstock.com; **39:** (t) Sheryl Lanzel/TED, (bl) WALTER ZERLA/Corbis, (bc) Sheryl Lanzel/ TED, (br) TED; **40:** (t) © IR Stone/Shutterstock. com; **42–43:** (c) Reed Young/Reedyoung.com; **44:** (tl) © iStockphoto.com/klikk, (tlc) © iStockphoto.com/JLGutierrez, (trc) AbleStock. com/Thinkstock, (tr) © iStockphoto.com/ WendellandCarolyn, (lc) © iStockphoto.com/ Floortje, (c) © Ian 2010/Shutterstock.com, (c) © iStockphoto.com/DarrenMower, (rc) © patpitchaya/Shutterstock.com, (bl) © iStockphoto.com/polusvet, (blc) © Nastya22/ Shutterstock.com, (brc) © jocic/Shutterstock. com, (br) © iStockphoto.com/Artzone; **45:** (tr) Jupiterimages/Pixland/Thinkstock, (tr) © iStockphoto.com/borisyankov, (rc) © iStockphoto.com/cotesebastien, (br) © iStockphoto.com/cynoclub, (br) © iStockphoto. com/Anna bryukhanova; **46:** (tl) Danita Delimont/Gallo Images/Getty Images; **47:** (tc) Ira block/National Geographic Creative, (rc) © iStockphoto.com/Jamesbowyer; **48:** (1) vetkit/ iStock/360/Getty Images, (2) © iStockphoto. com/Rouzes, (3) © iStockphoto.com/Nicolae Socaciu/marlanu, (4) © iStockphoto.com/4X-image, (5) Oleksiy Mark/iStock/360/Getty Images, (6) ekipaj/iStock/360/Getty Images, (7) © iStockphoto.com/Infografick, (8) Lusoimages/iStock/360/Getty Images; **49:** (br) Raul Touzon/National Geographic Creative; **50–51:** (rc) Sylvain Savolainen / Cosmos/Redux; **50 or 51:** Krista Rossow/National Geographic Creative; **52:** (tc) Pete Ryan/National Geographic Creative, (lc) Lisa B./Flame/Corbis; **53:** (tc) © iStockphoto.com/Nomadsoul1, (tr) O. Louis Mazzatenta/National Geographic Creative, (trc) B Christopher/Alamy, (rc) Buddy Mays/ Encyclopedia/Corbis, (brc) © Koroleva Katerina/ Shutterstock.com, (br) © iStockphoto.com/ samgrandy, (bl) © iStockphoto.com/wwing, (blc) © iStockphoto.com/DNY59, (bc) Jakub

Vacek/Dreamstime.com, (brc) © iStockphoto. com/pjohnson1; **54–55:** (c) RANDY OLSON/ National Geographic Creative; **56:** (tl) © iStockphoto.com/digitalskillet, (tlc) chris warren/CW Images/Alamy, (trc) © iStockphoto. com/RoyalFive, (tr) © iStockphoto.com/Mlenny, (bl) © iStockphoto.com/CharlesKnox, (blc) © iStockphoto.com/Diane Labombarbe, (brc) © iStockphoto.com/Leontura, (br) © iStockphoto.com/ monkeybusinessimages; **58:** (tc) Joel Sartore/ National Geographic Creative, (tlc) Joel Sartore/ National Geographic Creative, (lc) Joel Sartore/ National Geographic Creative; **59:** (tr) John W Banagan/Photographer's Choice/Getty Images; **60:** (tl) © iStockphoto.com/skynesher, (tlc) © Istockphoto/Michael DeLeon, (trc) © Andresr/ Shutterstock.com, (tr) © Dallas Events Inc/ Shutterstock.com, (bl) © Junial Enterprises/ Shutterstock.com, (blc) © iStockphoto.com/ Alina555, (brc) Fotosearch/Asiastock/Age Fotostock, (br) Jamie Grill/blend Images - JGI/ brand X Pictures/Getty Images; **61:** (tr) John W Banagan/Photographer's Choice/Getty Images; **63:** (C) James/Duncan/Davidson/TED, (tr) Mark Daffey/Lonely Planet Images/Getty Images; **64:** (t) brian Skyum/Alamy, (c) C. Douglas Peebles/ Douglas Peebles Photography/Alamy; **65:** (tc) Philip Pound/Alamy, (tr) © Johan Swanepoel/ Shutterstock.com, (trc) © iStockphoto.com/ GomezDavid, (rc) © iStockphoto.com/ GlobalStock, (brc) © iStockphoto.com/Roberto A Sanchez, (br) © iStockphoto.com/Chagin; **66–67:** (c) Sungjin Kim/National Geographic Creative; **69:** (rc) Pawel Libera/Robert Harding World Imagery/Alamy; **70:** (tc) Oliver Lopez Asis/Moment/Getty Images; **71:** (rc) Images&Stories/Alamy; **72:** (tl) © Tupungato/ Shutterstock.com, (lc) Jupiterimages/ liquidlibrary/Thinkstock, (bl) © iStockphoto. com/amriphoto, (c) Frank Short/E+/Getty Images, (tr) Fuse/Getty Images, (rc) © Robert Pernell/Shutterstock.com; **73:** (tr) Gavin Hellier/ Alamy; **74:** (b) Frank Hurley/Royal Geographic Society; **74–75:** (rc) Frans Lanting Studio/ Alamy; **76:** (tc) Chris Hepburn/Digital Vision/ Getty Images, (rc) Marina BW/Moment Open/ Getty Images; **77:** (tc) Paul Souders/Digital Vision/Getty Images, (rc) © iStockphoto.com/ barsik; **78:** (tl) © Andrey Zyk/Shutterstock.com, (cr) © sukiyaki/Shutterstock.com, (tr) © ILYA AKINSHIN/Shutterstock.com, (cr) © Lonely Walker/Shutterstock.com, (b) ©aragami12345s/ Shutterstock.com; **79:** (t) (c) (tr) TED, (t) James Duncan Davidson/TED; **82-83:** (c) PAUL NICKLEN/National Geographic Creative; **84:** (tl) © iStockphoto.com/Lisa-blue, (tlc) © arek_ malang/Shutterstock.com, (trc) © Toranico/ Shutterstock.com, (tr) © iStockphoto.com/ digitalskillet, (bl) © iStockphoto.com/TMSK, (blc) Xpacifica/National Geographic Creative, (brc) © iStockphoto.com/Deklofenak, (br)©

UNIT 1

🔊 6 **LESSON B, LISTENING**

Carlos: My name is Carlos and this is my family. These are my parents. This is my mother. Her name is Elena. This is my father. His name is Jose Manuel. This is my sister. Her name is Karina.

Now, these are my grandparents. This is my grandfather. His name is Pedro and this is my grandmother. She's Susana. Here's another photo. These are our dogs. Their names are Lucy and Lulu. I love my family.

UNIT 2

🔊 9 **LESSON A, VOCABULARY**

1. Oscar is a teacher.

2. Eun is an artist.

3. Jane is an engineer.

4. Dae-Jung is a chef.

5. Jim is a taxi driver.

6. Hannah is a doctor.

7. Harvey is a banker.

8. Fernanda is an architect.

🔊 11 **LESSON B, LISTENING**

Michelle: Hello, my name is Michelle. I'm 35 years old and I'm an artist. I love my job. It's very interesting.

Carlos: Hi! My name is Carlos. I'm 43 years old and I'm a taxi driver. My job is not very interesting.

Salim: Hello. My name is Salim and I'm an architect. I'm 34. I like my job. It's interesting.

UNIT 3

🔊 17 **LESSON B, LISTENING**

Heidi: Hello, my name is Heidi and I am from Norway. This is my house in winter. It is not a big house. There are just two bedrooms in my house. In Norway, it is cold in the winter but my house is warm inside.

Joe: My name is Joe and this is my house. It is a big house with a very big garden. On the first floor there is the kitchen, dining room, living room, and a bathroom. On the second floor, there are three bedrooms and two bathrooms. My favorite place though is the garden.

Ali: Hello, my name is Ali and I come from a small country called Oman. I have a big family and so I have a big house. There are seven bedrooms in the house. It is very hot and dry in Oman and our houses do not have big gardens.

Li: Hello! My name is Li, I am from Hong Kong and this is my apartment. I am single so I do not need a big apartment. This room is my bedroom and my living room. There is also a kitchen and a bathroom.

UNIT 4

 LESSON B, LISTENING

Conversation 1

Security: Excuse me, madam. Is this your bag?

Jill: Yes, it is.

Security: What do you have in it?

Jill: There are my books: a notebook, a dictionary, and my *World English* book.

Security: Is that all?

Jill: Oh, yes, and my wallet.

Security: OK, thank you.

Conversation 2

Security: Excuse me, sir. Is that your bag?

Lee: Yes, it is.

Security: What do you have in it, sir?

Lee: My cell phone and my wallet.

Security: Is that all?

Lee: Yes, that's all.

Security: OK, thank you.

UNIT 5

 LESSON B, LISTENING

Interviewer: This morning we have Joel Sartore, the photographer, with us. Good morning, Joel.

Joel: Good morning, Jane.

Interviewer:	First, can I say I love your photos.
Joel:	Thank you.
Interviewer:	So, what is your secret? How do you take such beautiful photos?
Joel:	It's easy. I get up early, like at six o'clock, and take some photos. Then I take a nap at twelve o'clock.
Interviewer:	You take a nap!
Joel:	Yes, I take a nap. And then in the evening, like about eight o'clock, I take some more photos. The secret is the light. The light is good early in the morning and late in the evening.
Interviewer:	I see. Thanks for the tip.

UNIT 6

◀)) 30 LESSON B, LISTENING

Tour guide:
Welcome to New York's Store Window Walking Tour. The tour starts at Bloomingdale's. From Bloomingdale's, walk two blocks along East 60th Street. Turn right on Madison Avenue and you will see Barneys. From Barneys, walk one block along East 61st Street and turn left on 5th Avenue. Walk for two blocks, and FAO Schwarz is on your left, on the corner of Fifth Avenue and East 58th Street. Then cross 5th Avenue and Bergdorf Goodman is on 5th Avenue between East 58th Street and East 57th Street. And finally, on the corner of East 57th Street and 5th Avenue is Tiffany & Co.

UNIT 7

◀)) 2 LESSON A, VOCABULARY

1. Katie is watching TV.
2. Lok is playing the guitar.
3. Ben is cooking.
4. Omar is reading
5. Mariko is listening to music.
6. Crystal is shopping.
7. Tom and Susan are going to the movies.
8. Tony is going for a walk.

Conversation 1

Helen: Hello, could I speak to Mr. Evans, please?

Receptionist: Yes. Who's calling, please.

Helen: It's Helen Daring.

Receptionist: Let me check if Mr Evans is available. I'm sorry, Mr Evans is not available at the moment. He is talking on the other line.

Helen: Can I leave a message?

Receptionist: Of course.

Helen: Please tell him the plans are ready.

Receptionist: Yes, of course. Thank you. Goodbye.

Conversation 2

Tracey: Hi Kenny, what are you doing?

Kenny: Hi Tracey, I'm driving. Can I call you back?

Tracey: I'm driving as well. It's OK. We can talk.

Kenny: No, it's dangerous.

Tracey: Don't worry. It's not dangerous. Kenny? Kenny?

Conversation 3

Husband: Hi!

Wife: Hi, David. Look, can I call you back?

Husband: Why? What are you doing?

Wife: I'm meeting some clients. It's important.

Husband: OK, but don't forget. *I'm* important, too!

Conversation 4

Ahmed: Hi, Salma. What's happening?

Salma: Sorry, can you speak up. I can't hear you.

Ahmed: Sorry. What are you doing?

Salma: Oh, I'm watching TV.

Ahmed: Well, turn it down!

LESSON B, PRONUNCIATION

1. watch
2. sheep
3. share
4. chip
5. cash
6. shop
7. shoes

UNIT 8

🔊 9 **LESSON B, LISTENING**

Conversation 1

Sales Assistant: Good afternoon. Can I help you?

Felix: Yes, I am looking for a blue tie. Do you have any?

Sales Assistant: Yes, we do. What about this one?

Felix: Do you have anything more formal?

Sales Assistant: Yes, of course. How about this one?

Felix: Yes. Very nice. I'll take it.

Sales Assistant: Do you want to pay by cash or credit card?

Felix: Credit card.

Conversation 2

Sales Assistant: Hi. Can I help you?

Julia: Sure. Could I see some shoes, please?

Sales Assistant: No problem. What color?

Julia: Do you have anything in green?

Sales Assistant: Yes. What about these?

Julia: OK! Cool! How much are they?

Sales Assistant: Normally they're $46 but the sale price is $29.99.

Julia: Great. I'll take them!

Conversation 3

Emre: Hi! Can I try on one of those jackets?

Sales Assistant: Sure. What size are you?

Emre: I think I'm a medium.

Sales Assistant: Here you are. How is it?

Emre: A little small.

Sales Assistant: I'm sorry, we don't have a large.

Emre: Oh no! OK, I'll leave it then.

Sales Assistant: Sorry!

Conversation 4

Emma: Hello. I'd like to look at the shirts, please.

Sales Assistant: Of course. Any particular color?

Emma: It's for school, so white or blue please. For a 10 year old.

Sales Assistant: Let me see. Yes, here we are.

Emma: OK. I'll take three please.

Sales Assistant: The shirts are $12 each. That's $36 in all.

Emma: Okay. Here's $40.

Sales Assistant: And $4 change. Thank you very much.

🔊 10 ## LESSON B, PRONUNCIATION

1. Could you call a taxi, please?

2. /kudjə/ call a taxi, please?

3. /kudjə/ help me, please?

4. Could you help me, please?

5. Could you repeat that, please?

6. /kudjɔ/ repeat that, please?

UNIT 9

🔊 13 **LESSON B, LISTENING**

Miguel:	OK, what do we need to buy for the party?
Diana:	Well, we need some drinks. Get 12 bottles of soda.
Miguel:	OK. And food?
Diana:	Wait a minute. We need some ice. One bag, I think.
Miguel:	OK, one bag of ice.
Diana:	Now food. Do we have any hamburgers?
Miguel:	No, we don't. So, we need, say, 20 hamburgers.
Diana:	OK. Let me see. Anything else?
Miguel:	Hot dogs?
Diana:	Good idea. OK, 10 hot dogs.

🔊 14 **LESSON B, PRONUNCIATION**

1. pasta and salad

2. pasta 'n' salad

3. fruit juice 'n' cereal

4. fruit juice and cereal

5. chocolate cake and ice cream

6. chocolate cake 'n' ice cream

UNIT 10

🔊 18 **LESSON B, LISTENING**

Conversation A

Doctor:	Oh dear! What is the problem?
Patient:	I had a bicycle accident. My knee hurts. And my arm hurts as well.
Doctor:	Mmm. Does your head hurt?
Patient:	Yes, I have a very bad headache.

Doctor:	Anything else?
Patient:	Yes, my foot hurts when I walk.
Doctor:	OK. I think you need an X ray.

Conversation B

Doctor:	Good morning, what can I do for you?
Patient:	Good morning doctor. I have a cough and I don't feel well.
Doctor:	You don't feel well? Can you explain?
Patient:	Well, I have a stomachache and I have a fever as well.
Doctor:	Mmm, oh dear! OK, I think I need to examine you.

UNIT 11

🔊 23 LESSON B, LISTENING

Conversation 1

Kenichi:	So Linda, what are you going to do for the holiday?
Linda:	Well, I'm not going to go to Times Square this year.
Kenichi:	Why?
Linda:	Because there are too many people.
Kenichi:	So what are you going to do?
Linda:	I'm going to stay home with my family. What are you going to do, Kenichi?
Kenichi:	I'm going to a party.
Linda:	Great. Hope you have a good time!
Kenichi:	And you!

Conversation 2

Tom:	What are you going to do for the holiday, Maria?
Maria:	I don't know. What are you going to do?
Tom:	Well, I'm going to go downtown and watch the fireworks. Do you want to come?
Maria:	Sure! What time?
Tom:	We're going to leave at about six o'clock. OK?
Maria:	Great!

LESSON B, PRONUNCIATION

1. We're going to have a party.

2. We're /ɡʌnə/ have a party.

3. I'm /ɡʌnə/ go to Paris.

4. I'm going to go to Paris.

5. They're not going to come.

6. They're not /ɡʌnə/ to come.

UNIT 12

LESSON B, LISTENING

1. Albert Einstein

Albert Einstein was born in Germany in 1879. His family moved to Milan, but Albert went to school in Switzerland in 1895. He graduated from college in Switzerland. He lived in Switzerland for 28 years and then moved to the United States in 1933.

2. Salma Hayek

Salma Hayek was born in Mexico in 1966. In 1978, at the age of 12, she moved to the United States to go to school, but soon returned to Mexico. Later, she again went to the United States to live with her aunt and did not return to Mexico until 1983. She moved to the United States again in 1991 and became an American citizen.

3. Jerry Yang

Jerry Yang was born on November 6, 1968, in Taipei, on the island of Taiwan. At the age of eight, in 1976, he moved to San Jose, California, with his mother and brother. When he arrived in America, he only knew one word of English—*shoe*. However, he learned quickly and, in 1994, with a partner started the company Yahoo! Inc.

4. Albert Pujols

Albert Pujols was born in the Dominican Republic in 1980. He started playing baseball in the Dominican Republic and then moved to the United States in 1996. He now plays for the Los Angeles Angels of Anaheim, in California. In 2007, Albert became an American citizen.

UNIT 1

VIDEO JOURNAL *ANIMAL FAMILIES*

NARRATOR: People live in families. Some families are big. Other families are small.

Some animals live alone.

But many animals live in family groups as well.

These are lions. They live in family groups. There are usually 5 to 7 females in the group.

In the group, there is usually only one male. He has long hair on his neck. He is very handsome. He is the father of all the young lions. These are his sons and daughters.

This is a family of meerkats. It is a big family. There are 20 to 30 meerkats in the family.

This is the alpha pair. They are the leaders. They are the mother and father of all the young meerkats. Aren't they pretty!

This is a family of gorillas. This is the leader of the family. He has silver hair on his back. He is the father of all the young gorillas in the group. There are seven females. They are the mothers of all the young gorillas.

Families are important for animals and for people.

UNIT 2

VIDEO JOURNAL *A JOB FOR CHILDREN*

NARRATOR: Einar and his sister Andrea are from Heimaey, in Iceland, a small country in Europe. They have a very interesting job. They have a box. In their box they have two young puffins, or pufflings. Einar and Andrea help these birds. They want to rescue them.

EINAR, Age 14, Heimaey Resident: They don't survive if they stay in the town. Cats and dogs eat them, or they just die. It's really good to rescue them.

NARRATOR: The children of Heimaey rescue young puffins, or 'pufflings'. Every summer, they help pufflings get to the sea. It is their job.

AGNES, Heimaey Parent: The children rescue the birds. If they don't do it, the puffins die. The children's job is exciting.

NARRATOR: They take the lost pufflings to the beach. Then they throw the pufflings into the sky. How do the pufflings get lost?

The pufflings leave their nests in the cliffs. They fly out to sea. They see the lights of Heimaey and they fly into the town! People find the puffins on the streets. The children of Heimaey help them.

Each night in summer, mothers and fathers go with their children to look for lost pufflings. They use flashlights. The pier is a good place to look for pufflings. They rescue the pufflings from the streets. It's hard work, Olaf Holm and his six-year-old son Andrew are looking for pufflings. They look carefully. They have a bird!

OLAF AND ANDREW, Puffling Patrollers: We found this puffling in the parking lot.

NARRATOR: The next day, the children take the birds to the beach. The children point the birds to the sea. They throw the young puffin to the sea. The little puffins swim or fly to safety. The children like their job. They are happy.

There are eight to ten million puffins in Iceland. Every year, the children work to look for puffins. Here, children of Heimaey rescue lost pufflings.

UNIT 3

VIDEO JOURNAL *A VERY SPECIAL VILLAGE*

NARRATOR: Camogli is a town on the Italian coast. The sun shines on the houses next to the sea. But, this town is different.

In the town of Camogli, things look real… but they're not.

This fishing village near Genoa is full of *trompe l'oeil*—a special art. In *trompe l'oeil* things are not real.

In this village, windows open—in solid walls. Beautiful stonework is paint! And the flowers are not real. They are painted on the buildings!

In the past, Camogli's fishermen painted their houses in bright colors and unusual designs. The fishermen wanted to see their homes from the water.

Then, in the 1700s, this art made small, simple buildings look special and expensive.

There are thousands of *trompe l'oeil* houses in this area. But only a few artists paint them.

Raffaella Stracca is an artist. Raffaella uses old and new methods in her work.

"You find a lot of these painted facades in the area of Liguria a lot.

NARRATOR: It is difficult to be a good *trompe l'oeil* painter. Rafaella has worked for 20 years to paint stone so it looks real.

Carlo Pere is an artist. He paints *trompe l'oeil* for people who live in small houses or city apartments. They want Pere's *trompe l'oeil* terraces and balconies.

Carlo feels that *trompe l'oeil* Is special.

"*Trompe l'oeil* means bringing the central city of Milan to the sea, or the sea to the mountains…or even the mountains to the sea."

NARRATOR: Carlos uses an art book from the 1300s to study *trompe l'oeil.* He uses traditional-style paints.

He wants to protect the *trompe l'oeil* traditions.

In this part of Italy, you can still see the local culture everywhere. It's in the street, in the bay and in the cafés of the town. But in Camogli what you see is not always real.

TED TALKS: KENT LARSON, *BRILLIANT DESIGNS TO FIT MORE PEOPLE IN EVERY CITY*

NARRATOR: What kind of house do you live in? In towns and in the countryside, houses are often big, with a bedroom for each person in the family, a living room, a kitchen, a dining room, and maybe a garden or back yard.

But there are not a lot of jobs in the countryside; most jobs are in the cities. More and more families move to the cities to live and work.

Many cities do not have a lot of space for housing. Families live in small apartments.

One architect, Kent Larson, has an idea for how to make a great home in a small space. His idea is that an apartment can use space in more efficient and changeable ways.

KENT LARSON: Housing is another place where we can really improve. Mayor Menino, in Boston, says lack of affordable housing for young people is one of the biggest problems the city faces. Developers say, "Okay we'll build little teeny apartments." People say, "Well we don't really want to live in a little teeny conventional apartment." So, we're saying let's build a standardized chassis much like our car. Let's bring advanced technology into the apartment, technology enabled infill. Give people the tools within this open loft chassis to go through a process of defining what their needs and values and activities are.

Now, the most interesting implementation of that for us is when you can begin to have robotic walls. So, your space can convert from an exercise to a work place, if you run a virtual company. You have guests over, you have two guest rooms that are developed. You have a conventional one bedroom arrangement, maybe that's most of the time. You have a dinner party: the table folds out to fit sixteen people in an otherwise conventional one bedroom. Or maybe you want a dance studio. I mean, architects have been thinking about these ideas for a long time. What we need to do now is develop things that can scale to those three hundred million Chinese people that would like to live in the city and very comfortably. We think we can make a very small apartment that functions as if it's twice as big by utilizing these strategies. I don't believe in smart homes; that's sort of a bogus concept. I think you have to build dumb homes and put smart stuff in it [them].

UNIT 4
VIDEO JOURNAL *UNCOVERING THE PAST*

NARRATOR: These people are archaeologists. They are looking for old things. Here, they find plates and bones.

Archaeology is the study of ancient things. They look at old buildings and houses. They look for things like jewelry, pots and plates.

Archaeologists also study paintings in caves. They also study fossils—the bones of old animals. And they study human remains, like these skulls.

To find things archaeologists get dirty. Teams work with shovels and spades. It is slow work. The work can be exciting.

This is a Mayan city. The beautiful carvings made by the Maya tell their history. The archaeologists who found these writings are discovering Maya civilization.

Archaeologists work in many places—in South America, in cities, in Asian jungles. Sometimes the work is dangerous. But it is always interesting.

UNIT 5
VIDEO JOURNAL *ZOO DENTISTS*

NARRATOR: When an animal has a toothache, it doesn't go to the dentist's office. Dr. Sarah de Sanz is a 'people dentist'. She treats human patients in her office in San Francisco. However, she sometimes treats patients who don't come to her office, or sit in her chair.

What kind of patients are these? Animals! Dr. de Sanz is a part-time zoo dentist. She and her father, Dr. Paul Brown, work in the San Francisco area. They do checkups, fillings, and other dental work on anyone—or anything—that needs them.

DR. BROWN: Yes, I'm happy. I think it's a wonderful job.

NARRATOR: Going to the dentist is frightening for a lot of people. But when a dentist treats a zoo animal, it's the patient that can be scary. Some of these patients can bite off a dentist's hand. Dr. de Sanz and Dr. Brown work in the most dangerous animal jaws. They're happy to do it. These animals need them.

NARRATOR: These dentists do checkups on zoo animals. Today, they start with Artie the sea lion, one of the dentists' best patients.

ZOO EMPLOYEE: He's an excellent dental patient; he's better than most people. Aren't you, Artie? Aren't you?

DR. DE SANZ: He is an old animal. He's 30 years old,... and he's happy about it... so we're going to just look at his teeth and see if he has any particular dental problems.

NARRATOR: They take an X-ray. They get a clear picture. Artie's checkup goes well. Artie's teeth are fine: not bad for a 30-year-old who's never brushed his teeth!

ZOO EMPLOYEE: Want to hear him say 'ah'?

DR. DE SANZ: Yeah! Could you say 'ah' please? You are an excellent patient!

NARRATOR: The next visit is Dr. Brown's favorite animal—the elephant. He likes elephants because they have interesting teeth.

DR. BROWN: This is an elephant molar.

NARRATOR: Elephants get six sets of teeth in a lifetime. When the last set is gone, they can no longer eat and will die.

ZOO EMPLOYEE: This is Sue. She's a ten-year-old little female African elephant.

NARRATOR: An elephant's tusks are really teeth. The dentists check the teeth in Sue's mouth, and her tusks.

DR. BROWN: Perfect! She's in great shape. Her teeth look wonderful!

NARRATOR: Sue is the perfect patient and gets an excellent report. But not all animals do so well...

The next patient is the San Francisco Zoo's rare black jaguar. Sandy has a terrible toothache and needs surgery.

DR. DUNKER: We can't walk up to her and say 'Can I look in your mouth?' You may lose a few fingers maybe your head! This animal has to be anesthetized in order for us to look at it.

NARRATOR: Making an animal sleep is difficult. Sandy is 21 years old, takes her to the operating room. Everybody is worried. They start the surgery. Suddenly there's a problem...

DR. DUNKER: Hey Ron, why don't you come over here?

NARRATOR: Sandy stops breathing! First the doctors give her oxygen. Sandy takes one breath per minute! The team acts quickly.

Sandy's teeth are very bad. She needs two root canals—and a filling! Dr. de Sanz and Dr. Brown must now work carefully and quickly to take out the nerve of each bad tooth and then put fillings in the holes that are left. After a lot of hard work—the surgery is over.

NARRATOR: The jaguar's visit with the dentists is finished. Sandy will feel well again. She won't have a toothache!

NARRATOR: As the zoo dentists finish another day. It's all in a day's work for these zoo dentists!

UNIT 6
VIDEO JOURNAL *VOLCANO TREK*

NARRATOR: In a region of Ethiopia, hot lava erupts from the Erta Ale volcano. The temperature of this lava is more than 2,000 degrees Fahrenheit.

Now, a team of explorers wants to see Erta Ale. They want to learn about the volcano. It's a difficult trek, and the team has to use camels.

They reach the crater. Franck Tessier and Irene Margaritis are geologists and professors at the University of Nice. They travel very far to see Erta Ale!

In the crater, they see the black lava lake.

"It is quite exciting. I want to see it now."

NARRATOR: Erta Ale is in the Afar area of Ethiopia. The Afar triangle is in an area where three continental plates meet. These plates move every year.

The Erta Ale volcano has the oldest lava lake in the world. The lake is one of the lowest points on Earth. At Erta Ale, geologists study how the world started millions of years ago.

Red hot lava comes out from the earth. This lava forms Erta Ale's lava lake. When the lava cools, it is hard and black. Hot magma breaks through when the volcano erupts.

The geologists stand at the top of the active volcano and wait next to the crater. It's difficult to be there; there is a strong smell of sulfur. It's very, very hot.

Then, the group goes down into the crater. Professor Tessier wants to collect pieces of the red-hot lava. It's 2:00 in the morning when they return. They're very tired and, as Professor Margaritis says; "very hot," "I think this is fresh lava,"

NARRATOR: The pieces don't come directly from the lava lake. However, the team decides they're fresh.

The team goes back to analyze the pieces of lava. They want to learn new information to teach to others. They want to know what the lava of Erta Ale can teach them about how the world started millions of years ago.

TED TALKS: KAREN BASS, *UNSEEN FOOTAGE, UNTAMED NATURE*

KAREN BASS: I'm a very lucky person. I've been privileged to see so much of our beautiful Earth and the people and creatures that live on it. And my passion was inspired at the age of seven, when my parents first took me to Morocco, at the edge of the Sahara Desert. Now imagine a little Brit somewhere that wasn't cold and damp like home. What an amazing experience. And it made me want to explore more.

So as a filmmaker, I've been from one end of the Earth to the other trying to get the perfect shot and to capture animal behavior never seen before. And what's more, I'm really lucky, because I get to share that with millions of people worldwide.

Images of grizzly bears are pretty familiar. You see them all the time, you think. But there's a whole side to their lives that we hardly ever see and had never been filmed. So what we did, we went to Alaska, which is where the grizzlies rely on really high, almost inaccessible, mountain slopes for their denning. And the only way to film that is a shoot from the air.

VIDEO NARRATOR: Throughout Alaska and British Columbia, thousands of bear families are emerging from their winter sleep. There is nothing to eat up here, but the conditions were ideal for hibernation. Lots of snow in which to dig a den. To find food, mothers must lead their cubs down to the coast, where the snow will already be melting. But getting down can be a challenge for small cubs. These mountains are dangerous places, but ultimately the fate of these bear families, and indeed that of all bears around the North Pacific, depends on the salmon.

KAREN BASS: I love that shot. I always get goose bumps every time I see it. That was filmed from a helicopter using a gyro-stabilized camera. And it's a wonderful bit of gear, because it's like having a flying tripod, crane and dolly all rolled into one. But technology alone isn't enough. To really get the money shots, it's down to being in the right place at the right time. And that sequence was especially difficult.

The first year we got nothing. We had to go back the following year, all the way back to the remote parts of Alaska. And we hung around with a helicopter for two whole weeks. And eventually we got lucky. The cloud lifted, the wind was still, and even the bear showed up. And we managed to get that magic moment.

UNIT 7

VIDEO JOURNAL *DANNY'S CHALLENGE*

NARRATOR: This is Danny MacAskill. He comes from Edinburgh in Scotland. Here he is riding his bicycle. But he is not riding his bicycle on the streets. He is riding on walls, stairs—anywhere! He can jump from one wall to another wall.

Danny was a mechanic but now he is a professional stunt rider. People come to watch Danny riding his bicycle.

SPECTATOR: He's awesome! He's really impressive!

NARRATOR: People like watching Danny. He is very good.

Can you jump from the wall to the mail box? No! But Danny can—even on his bicycle. Danny says that he sees the streets of Edinburgh differently now. He looks for more difficult places to ride his bicycle.

Danny wants to ride over this bridge. Not on the road, but on the bridge itself. It is a challenge. A difficult challenge. He tries many times and at last he climbs on to the bridge. Now he is riding up the bridge.

But Danny has a problem. Riding up the bridge is easy but it is difficult to ride down the other side. Slowly. Slowly. And at last he is safe on the other side of the bridge.

Danny conquered his challenge. But now he is looking for a more difficult challenge.

UNIT 8

VIDEO JOURNAL *TRADITIONAL SILK MAKING*

NARRATOR: In this ancient city, change comes slowly. Narrow stone streets are almost the same as they were when the Medici family ruled more than 500 years ago. The Industrial Revolution, world wars and a flood forced change but one factory , has not changed.

At the *Antico Setificio Fiorentino* or The Antique Silk Factory of Florence the sounds of mechanical looms remind us of the past. These noisy 19th century looms create some of the world's finest silk fabrics for drapery and upholstery. But here they are the new machines. On the other side of the factory are the real pieces of history. Stefano Benelli weaves silk fabric that machines cannot create.

And he does it slowly and carefully, one thread at a time. These looms were built in 1780 and they use the same principles of weaving used for centuries before that.

SABINE PRETSCH, Factory director: Everything is done like it was done in the ancient time. But we continue to do an evolution, continuously. We invent and we create continuously but using the old looms.

NARRATOR: All the other factories threw away their old hand looms after World War II. Only the Setificio now uses hand looms.

Usually silk has 3 to 4 thousand threads running in one direction, but the silk produced on the antique hand looms has 12,000 threads. It is much stronger and more beautiful.

Fabric from the Setificio cannot be found in stores and catalogues—it is custom made. Some people may think that making silk on a hand loom is difficult and boring but Benelli enjoys it.

STEFANO BENELLI, Silk craftsman: To the mind, is OK. Not stressful, yes.

NARRATOR: Perhaps no other city on earth has preserved the grandeur and the grace of the renaissance as well as Florence. It is appropriate then that here, at the *Antico Setificio Fiorentino* style and tradition are woven together.

UNIT 9

VIDEO JOURNAL *SLOW FOOD*

NARRATOR: This is Chianti, in Italy. Greve, is a small town in Chianti. The people produce cheese and mushrooms.

Life is slow in Chianti. Things do not change very quickly. The people like it that way.

"Our goal is to protect what makes Greve special. We want Chianti to remain a special place where things don't move too fast."

Greve's mayor helped start the Slow Food Movement. The goal of the Slow Food Movement is to keep the pleasures of good living, good food, family and friends.

Now the Slow Food Movement is international. It has more than 66,000 members worldwide.

"It's very nice to live here because we have a nice atmosphere, we have nice landscapes. And so, when you have nice things to see, a nice place to live in, it's very easy."

NARRATOR: Salvatore Tescano had an American style hamburger restaurant in Florence. Now he has a restaurant in Greve.

SALVATORE: You have to take your time. Slow down. What you eat is important.

NARRATOR: In the mountains of Pistoia, in northern Tuscany, the farmers make a special cheese. It is made from the milk of black sheep.

Many farmers stopped making the cheese. But the Slow Food Movement is helping. Now more farmers are making the cheese. It is very popular.

"Our cheese is famous now."

"From Singapore to Macao, in New York, in Rome, you always find the same pizza, the same hamburgers. Slow food doesn't want this. Slow Food wants the specialness of every product to be respected."

NARRATOR: Greve wants the best of both the modern world and the traditional life of Italy.

TED TALKS: RON FINLEY, *A GUERILLA GARDENER IN SOUTH CENTRAL L.A.*

NARRATOR: More than 26.5 million Americans live in "food deserts." Food deserts are places with no access to fresh, healthy food. Instead of grocery stores and markets, these places only have fast food restaurants. This is making a lot of people unhealthy around the world. More than half of the people living in food deserts in the United States are from low-income families. In activist Ron Finley's neighborhood of South Central Los Angeles the problem is very bad, but he has an idea to fix it.

RON FINLEY: I got tired of seeing this happening. And I was wondering, how would you feel if you had no access to healthy food, if every time you walk out your door you see the ill effects that the present food system has on your neighborhood? I see wheelchairs bought and sold like used cars. I see dialysis centers popping up like Starbucks. And I figured, this has to stop. So I figured that the problem is the solution. Food is the problem and food is the solution.

So what I did, I planted a food forest in front of my house. It was on a strip of land that we call a parkway. It's 150 feet by 10 feet. Thing is, it's owned by the city. But you have to maintain it.

So me and my group, L.A. Green Grounds, we got together and we started planting my food forest, fruit trees, you know, the whole nine, vegetables. What we do, we're a pay-it-forward kind of group, where it's composed of gardeners from all walks of life, from all over the city, and it's completely volunteer, and everything we do is free. And the garden, it was beautiful.

And then somebody complained. The city came down on me, and basically gave me a citation saying that I had to remove my garden, which this citation was turning into a warrant. And I'm like, "Come on, really? A warrant for planting food on a piece of land that you could care less about?" And I was like, "Cool. Bring it." Because this time it wasn't coming up. So L.A. Times got ahold of it. Steve Lopez did a story on it and talked to the councilman, and one of the Green Grounds members, they put up a petition on Change.org, and with 900 signatures, we were a success. We had a victory on our hands. My councilman even called in and said how they endorse and love what we're doing. I mean, come on, why wouldn't they? L.A. leads the United States in vacant lots that the city actually owns. They own 26 square miles of vacant lots. That's 20 Central Parks. That's enough space to plant 725 million tomato plants.

Growing one plant will give you 1,000, 10,000 seeds. When one dollar's worth of green beans will give you 75 dollars' worth of produce. It's my gospel, I tell people, "Grow your own food!" Growing your own food is like printing your own money.

See, I have a legacy in South Central. I grew up there. I raised my sons there. And I refuse to be a part of this manufactured reality that was manufactured for me by some other people, and I'm manufacturing my own reality.

So what happened? I have witnessed my garden become a tool for the education, a tool for the transformation of my neighborhood. To change the community, you have to change the composition of the soil. We are the soil. You'd be surprised how kids are affected by this. Gardening is the most therapeutic and defiant act you can do, especially in the inner city. Plus you get strawberries.

I remember this time, there was this mother and a daughter came, It was, like, 10:30 at night, and they were in my yard, and I came out and they looked so ashamed. So I'm like, man, it made me feel bad that they were there, and I told them, you know, you don't have to do this like this. This is on the street for a reason. It made me feel ashamed to see people that were this close to me that were hungry, and this only reinforced why I do this.

There's another time when I put a garden in this homeless shelter in downtown Los Angeles. These are the guys, they helped me unload the truck. It was cool, and they just shared the stories about how this affected them and how they used to plant with their mother and their grandmother, and it was just cool to see how this changed them, if it was only for that one moment.

So Green Grounds has gone on to plant maybe 20 gardens. We've had, like, 50 people come to our dig-ins and participate, and it's all volunteers. If kids grow kale, kids eat kale. If they grow tomatoes, they eat tomatoes.

I see young people and they want to work, but they're in this thing where they're caught up—I see kids of color and they're just on this track that's designed for them, that leads them to nowhere. So with gardening, I see an opportunity where we can train these kids to take over their communities, to have a sustainable life. And when we do this, who knows? We might produce the next George Washington Carver. But if we don't change the composition of the soil, we will never do this.

What I'm talking about is putting people to work, and getting kids off the street, and letting them know the joy, the pride and the honor in growing your own food, opening farmer's markets.

I want us all to become ecolutionary renegades, gangstas, gangsta gardeners. We got to flip the script on what a gangsta is. If you ain't a gardener, you ain't gangsta. Get gangsta with your shovel, okay? And let that be your weapon of choice.

UNIT 10

VIDEO JOURNAL *FARLEY, THE RED PANDA*

NARRATOR: This is Farley. He is a red panda. He's cute but he is also a fighter. When he was born, his mother didn't look after him. He was hungry and cold when zookeepers found him.

JANET HAWES: When we first got a look at Farley, we were mostly concerned about two things: his early poor nutrition—he had not been fed by the mother, and the fact that he was hypothermic, or had a low body temperature.

NARRATOR: Although nursery keepers here had never hand-raised a red panda before, it didn't take long to settle on a successful formula.

Zookeepers give Farley special milk. He likes the milk and starts to grow quickly

NURSE: Okay… That's enough… that's enough, slow down. It's been a little challenging. Ah, it's been a little nerve-wracking, It has been difficult but he's doing well. We're very pleased with his progress so far. Everything seems to be doing well and we're just keeping our fingers crossed.

NARRATOR: But Farley's problems weren't over just yet. At only three weeks, his once voracious appetite began to shrink and his breathing became heavy. Keepers rushed him to the zoo's hospital.

But then there is a problem. Farley stops drinking his milk. He is sick, so the zookeepers take Farley to the zoo's hospital.

JANET HAWES: He had has a very advanced and very severe infection going on inside of his body. and that he was indeed struggling for life

NARRATOR: For a while, it was touch and go. The massive infection required weeks of heavy antibiotics and regular tube feedings. Soon, Farley was well enough to move to his home at the nursery and ready to take the next step.

Farley is very sick. He has an infection and he needs antibiotics, lots of antibiotics. The keepers have to give Farley his milk with a tube. Farley is fighting for his life, But, good news! Farley is now feeling better.

ZOOKEEPER: The stage right now is just to try to get him to be a better climber. He's doing well, really well, exploring.

NARRATOR: What he needed next in life was at the Rosamond Gifford Zoo in Syracuse New York, another hand-raised red panda named Banshee.

But Farley has no friends. Pandas need other pandas to play with, so he goes to another zoo. Here he is, playing with his new friend, Banshee.

JANET HAWES: It's very important for red pandas as youngsters to have playmates, so that they don't bond so completely with human beings.

ZOOKEEPER 2: As you can see, they're really really active and they really like each other's company and they like to play and sleep together now.

NARRATOR: I think that the essential thing about Farley that sets him apart is his struggle was very difficult. He never lost his will to survive and the personality that emerged from those struggles is one that ass surprisingly affectionate and playful and he was just a great guy.

Farley has had a difficult life. He nearly died but he is a fighter and now he is a happy and well.

UNIT 11

VIDEO JOURNAL *MAKING A THAI BOXING CHAMPION*

NARRATOR: Thai boxing, or muay thai, is Thailand's oldest martial art. It looks like Western boxing, but it's very different. In Thai boxing you can use every part of your body: your hands, head, feet, knees—even elbows are okay.

The sport has a long history. Two thousand years ago, warriors trained in Thai boxing to protect their country from invaders. Now it's one of Thailand's most popular sports—everyone loves it. It's part of many festivals. You can see it on television around the country every day.

Many boxers in Thailand started boxing at the Lanna Muay Thai Training Camp in Chiang Mai. Right now, the camp is home for a 12-year-old boy named Manat. He and 15 other boys are here to become fighters.

The camp pays for their training. While they are here, they only box. The boys train for seven hours a day, seven days of the week.

They train hard. They wish to become the next great champion. For Manat and the others, success here can give them better lives and a higher status in Thai society. Canadian coach Andy Thomson started the camp.

ANDY THOMSON, Thai Boxing Coach: Thai boxing offers the boys a chance at status… improve status in their community, the opportunity to earn some money, and most of them will have a dream of being a champion one day in Lumphini Stadium in Bangkok. It's an opportunity to open up their world.

NARRATOR: For Manat and the other boys, this is their chance to see more than their home village. It's a chance to make their family and friends proud. Manat is getting ready for his second fight which is tomorrow. Thai boxers have to be strong, but they not only train their bodies. They prepare their minds and the way they think about the fight. Modern *muay thai* is about learning to think and fight like a warrior. And it's about achieving personal goals.

MANAT, Thai Boxer: If I move on to bigger fights, one day I'll be a champion—a champion of Chiang Mai. I'll feel very proud and good. And I'll send the money I win to my parents.

NARRATOR: Manat's big night finally arrives. The fight is in a small town outside of Chiang Mai.

Manat goes into the ring for the 'Rama Muay,' an ancient ceremony which focuses a fighter's strength and power. It helps him to get ready for the fight. After the ceremony, the fight begins.

THOMSON: The judges are looking for good, clean shot technique—both offensive and defensive. They are looking for the boxer who is in control of the fight.

NARRATOR: Manat fights hard, but for him, tonight is not the night. He doesn't win. Unfortunately, the boy Manat fought was taller, heavier, and more experienced than him. But even with these disadvantages, Manat did very well. He may have lost the fight, but his coaches now definitely believe that he can be a winner.

THOMSON: Manat's fight was very good. He fought really well. Good attitude... a good heart... very good heart. Even though he's not happy, he'll be all right tomorrow. He'll be back fighting again—no problem.

NARRATOR: Manat did not win tonight, but this was only one step in the long process of making a Thai boxing champion!

UNIT 12

VIDEO JOURNAL *MONARCH BUTTERFLIES*

NARRATOR: Every year's migration of North America's monarch butterflies is one of the great spectacles of nature.

Each year, up to 300 million monarchs travel more than 2,000 miles from northern America and Canada to a remote forest two hundred miles west of Mexico City.

But they are as fragile as they are beautiful.

Sudden changes in their environment can mean disaster.

A January 2002 rainstorm followed with freezing temperatures killed as many as 250 million butterflies, almost eighty percent of the population in the *El Rosario* butterfly sanctuary—just one of six sanctuaries in the area.

Their bodies covered the forest floor, giving off an unusual odor.

Mike Quinn is a Texas biologist with Monarch Watch—an organization based out of the University of Kansas.

He thinks logging, which happens more and more in these reserves, may have contributed to the death of the butterflies.

QUINN, Biologist: Logging is right up to the edge of the colony and logging opens up the forest and lets in the cold air and freezes penetrate into the forest whereas an intact forest acts as both an umbrella and as a blanket and that will severely protect the Monarchs.

NARRATOR: In the last 20 years, logging, mostly illegal, has destroyed nearly half the forests the monarchs need in this region.

The Mexican government, along with the World Wildlife Fund, has started efforts to preserve what is left. They offer to pay landowners to not cut trees.

But the money is very limited: 18 dollars for every cubic meter of loggable wood—not nearly as much money as they can make logging.

The 2002 storm wasn't the first to hit the monarch population, nor will it likely be the last.

For the moment, millions of the monarch butterflies still migrate each year.

TED TALKS: DEREK SIVERS, *WEIRD, OR JUST DIFFERENT?*

DEREK SIVERS: So, imagine you're standing on a street anywhere in America and a Japanese man comes up to you and says, "Excuse me, what is the name of this block?"

And you say, "I'm sorry, well, this is Oak Street, that's Elm Street. This is 26th, that's 27th."

He says, "OK, but what is the name of that block?"

You say, "Well, blocks don't have names. Streets have names; blocks are just the unnamed spaces in between streets."

He leaves, a little confused and disappointed.

So, now imagine you're standing on a street, anywhere in Japan, you turn to a person next to you and say,

"Excuse me, what is the name of this street?"

They say, "Oh, well that's Block 17 and this is Block 16."

And you say, "OK, but what is the name of this street?"

And they say, "Well, streets don't have names. Blocks have names. Just look at Google Maps here. There's Block 14, 15, 16, 17, 18, 19. All of these blocks have names, and the streets are just the unnamed spaces in between the blocks."

And you say then, "OK, then how do you know your home address?"

He said, "Well, easy, this is District Eight. There's Block 17, house number one."

You say, "OK, but walking around the neighborhood, I noticed that the house numbers don't go in order."

He says, "Of course they do. They go in the order in which they were built. The first house ever built on a block is house number one. The second house ever built is house number two. Third is house number three. It's easy. It's obvious."

So, I love that sometimes we need to go to the opposite side of the world to realize assumptions we didn't even know we had, and realize that the opposite of them may also be true.

So, for example, there are doctors in China who believe that it's their job to keep you healthy. So, any month you are healthy you pay them, and when you're sick you don't have to pay them because they failed at their job. They get rich when you're healthy, not sick.

And this map is also accurate.

There's a saying that whatever true thing you can say about India, the opposite is also true. So, let's never forget, whether at TED, or anywhere else, that whatever brilliant ideas you have or hear, that the opposite may also be true. Domo arigato gozaimashita.*

*Japanese for "Thank you very much."

UNIT 1 FRIENDS AND FAMILY

Lesson A

A. 1B. Fine. And you? 2A. Good morning. How are you? 2B. Fine thank you. And how are you? 3A. This is my friend Yong-Jun. 3B. Nice to meet you Yong-Jun. 3C. Nice to meet you too.

B. 2. He's Mr. Smith. 3. I'm Aisha. 4. You're Stefan. 5. They're Luis and Marta. 6. She's Noriko.

C. 2. My 3. Our 4. Their 5. Her 6. Your

Lesson B

A. 2. mother 3. brother 4. sister 5. grandfather 6. grandmother 7. husband 8. wife 9. parents 10. grandparents

B. 2. grandmother 3. mother 4. father 5. husband 6. sister 7. son

C. 1. their 2. are 3. Her 4. His 5. is

Lesson C

A. 1. young 2. tall 3. married 4. handsome 5. old 6. short 7. pretty 8. single

B. Answers will vary.

C. 1A. Is 1B. she isn't, short 2A. are 2B. is, is, isn't, he's

D. Answers will vary.

Lesson D

B. 1. Mari 2. Jeff 3. Yuji 4. Sara and Emma 5. Hiroshi Yamada 6. Yuji and Aya 7. David, Sara, Emma 8. Emma

C. 1. Yes 2. No 3. Yes 4. Yes 5. No 6. No 7. No 8. Yes

Review

A. Across 1. my 4. her 5. is 7. grandfather 11. his 12. young

Down 1. married 2. brothers 3. their 6. not 7. good 8. are 9. family 10. how's

B. 2. tall 3. long 4. sister 5. wavy 6. married 7. children 8. daughter

C. Answers will vary.

UNIT 2 JOBS AROUND THE WORLD

Lesson A

A. 2. She's a chef. 3. He's an engineer. 4. She's a banker. 5. She's an architect. 6. He's a teacher. 7. He's a doctor. 8. She's an artist.

B. 2. They aren't /They're not old. 3. She isn't /She's not an architect. 4. You're not/You aren't a teacher. 5. We're not /We aren't tall. 6. It isn't interesting.

C. 2. an 3. a 4. a 5. a 6. a 7. an 8. a 9. a 10. an

D. 2. They're good. 3. He's 23. 4. Yes, he is.

Lesson B

A. Written answers will vary. 2. How old are you? 3. What is your job? 4. Is your job interesting? 5. How old is your father now? 6. What is his job? 7. Is his job interesting?

B. 2. How old are you? 3. Are you married? 4. What do you do? 5. Is your job interesting?

C. 1. b 2. d 3. a 4. c

Lesson C

A. 2. The UK is a wet country. 3. Asia is a big continent. 4. Is Saudi Arabia a dry country? 5. Mexico isn't in South America.

B. Answers will vary. 2. Is the UK a wet country? 3. Is it in North America? 4. Is Russia a warm country? 5. Is Saudi Arabia a wet country?

C. 1. you 2. from 3. Russia 4. Europe 5. Is 6. very

D. Answers will vary.

Lesson D

A. 1. T 2. T 3. F 4. T 5. T 6. T 7. F 8. T 9. F 10. T

B. Answers will vary.

Review

A. Across 2. boring 3. country 4. Korea 6. Europe 8. continent 9. Argentina 11. China 12. small 13. driver

B. 2. in 3. a 4. dry 5. teacher 6. job

C. Answers will vary.

UNIT 3 HOUSES AND APARTMENTS

Lesson A

A. 1. stairs 2. bedroom 3. kitchen 4. closet 5. dining room 6. garage 7. living room 8. bathroom

B. 2. there is 3. Are there 4. there are 5. there is 6. Is there 7. there isn't 8. there is

C. Answers will vary.

Lesson B

A. 2. There are three closets in my house. 3. There are two bathrooms in her house. 4. There are two garages in their house.

B. /s/ closets /z/ bedrooms, bathrooms /iz/ garages

C. 1. Answers will vary. 2. Answers will vary.

Lesson C

A. 2. armchair 3. coffee table 4. TV 5. bed 6. bookcase 7. lamp 8. table 9. chair 10. stove 11. refrigerator 12. microwave

B. 2. next to 3. on 4. in 5. under 6. next to

C. in, next to, on, on

D. Answers will vary.

Lesson D

A. Yoshi's bedroom: 3, 4, 6; Jessie's bedroom: 2, 3, 4, 5, 6

B. Answers will vary.

C. Answers will vary.

Review

A. Across 3. in 5. next to 6. aren't 7. garage 8. are 9. kitchen 10. is 11. bedroom 12. there

Down 1. house 2. on 3. isn't 4. bookcase 6. apartment

B. 2. big 3. there is 4. There are 5. under 6. There isn't 7. in 8. dining room

UNIT 4 POSSESSIONS

Lesson A

A. 1. book 2. notebook 3. dictionary 4. ring 5. necklace 6. wallet 7. bag 8. keys 9. watch 10. glasses 11. handbag 12. pen

B. 2. Those 3. This 4. Those 5. These 6. This

C. 1. Are those your keys? 2. Is that your dictionary? 3. Are those your books? 4. Are those your glasses? 5. Is that your bag? 6. Is this your wallet? 7. Are those your notebooks? 8. Is this your watch?

Lesson B

A. 2. Francisco's 3. Paul's 4. Paul's 5. Francisco's 6. Jennie's

B. 2. That is Anita's car. 3. These are Martin's glasses. 4. This is Anita's handbag. 5. This is Martin's book. 6. This is Anita's wallet. 7. That is Martin's house.

C. 1. Answers will vary. 2. Answers will vary.

Lesson C

A. 1. MP3 player 2. smartphone 3. speakers 4. tablet 5. camcorder 6. laptop 7. cell phone 8. DVD player

B. Answers will vary.

C. 1. Do you 2. I do 3. you have 4. has 5. Do you have 6. I don't 7. have 8. has

Lesson D

B. 1. T 2. T 3. F 4. T 5. F 6. F

C. My special possession is a watch. It's very big and old. It's gold. It's special because it's my grandfather's watch and it's 100 years old.

D. Answers will vary.

Review

A. Across 1. do 6. aren't 7. wallet 9. possessions 10. No 11. cheap 13. Yes

Down 1. dictionary 2. player 3. laptop 4. have 5. Does 8. isn't 12. has

B. 2. but 3. and 4. or 5. have

C. Answers will vary.

UNIT 5 DAILY ACTIVITIES

Lesson A

A. 2. It's eleven. 3. It's seven thirty. 4. It's a quarter past nine. 5. It's two thirty. 6. Answers will vary.

B. Answers will vary.

C. 1. every 2. at 3. in 4. on 5. at

D. 2. takes 3. go to 4. has/eats 5. finishes 6. go 7. takes

Lesson B

A. 2. Monday 3. Tuesday 4. Wednesday 5. Thursday 6. Friday 7. Saturday

B. 3. What time does he start work? He starts work at eleven o'clock. 4. What time does he eat lunch? He eats lunch at four o'clock. 5. What time does he eat dinner? Answers will vary. 6. What time does he finish work? He finishes work at nine o'clock 7. What time does he go to bed? He goes to bed at one thirty.

Lesson C

A. 1. d 2. b 3. f 4. c 5. a 6. e

B. Dennis and Susan: 2. Do they talk to people? Yes, they do. 3. Do they go to meetings? No, they don't.; Melisa: 1. Does she travel? No, she doesn't. 2. Does she talk to people? Yes, she does. Does she go to meetings? Yes, she does.

C. Answers will vary.

Lesson D

A. 3, 2, 1

B. 1. F 2. T 3. T 4. T 5. T 6. F 7. T 8. F

C. early, every, to, and, sometimes

D. Answers will vary.

Review

A. Across 2. at 3. talk to 5. take 6. What 9. sometimes 12. go 13. on

Down 1. meet 2. activities 4. on 7. have 8. fill out 10. o'clock 11. every

B. 2. starts 3. always 4. at 5. bed 6. in 7. talks 8. writes

C. Answers will vary.

UNIT 6 GETTING THERE

Lesson A

A. 1. movie theater 2. restaurant 3. train station 4. library 5. bank 6. hotel 7. supermarket 8. park 9. museum 10. bus station 11. tourist office 12. post office

B. on, turn, walk, from, between

C. Answers will vary.

Lesson B

A. 1. Main Street 2. the Star of India Restaurant 3. do I 4. left 5. one block 6. Main Street and Lincoln Avenue 7. Thank

B. 1. Is there a bank 2. Long Avenue 3. King Street 4. go 5. two blocks 6. Mega Burgers/the art gallery

C. Answers will vary.

Lesson C

A. 1. bus 2. taxi 3. subway 4. train 5. rental car

B. 1. has to 2. has to 3. have to, don't have to 4. has to 5. doesn't have to 6. doesn't have to

C. Answers will vary.

Lesson D

A. 1. August 13 2. August 1 3. August 6 4. August 10 5. August 15 6. August 4

B. 1. T 2. T 3. F 4. F 5. T 6. T

C. Answers will vary.

Review

A. Across 3. blocks 5. have 6. cheap 11. restaurant 12. cross 13. on

Down 1. office 2. mall 4. shuttle 7. across 8. between 9. station

B. Answers will vary.

UNIT 7 FREE TIME

Lesson A

A. 2. He's reading. 3. She's cooking. 4. He's listening to music. 5. She's playing the guitar.

B. 1. d 2. a 3. e 4. b 5. c

Lesson B

A. 1. d 2. b 3. c 4. a

B. 1. Could I call you back? 2. Who is speaking, please?, Can I leave a message?

C. 1. I'm going 2. I'm watching, We're going 3. Are you cooking, I am

Lesson C

A. 1. swimming 2. skiing 3. ice skating 4. golf 5. soccer 6. biking 7. volleyball 8. tennis

B. Answers will vary.

C. can, can, can, Can you, can, can't, can't, Can you

Lesson D

A. 2. T 3. F, walk 4. T 5. F, eight 6. T 7. T 8. T

B. Answers will vary.

Review

A. Across 3. can't 5. listening 9. play 10. ice 11. watching 12. they can

Down 1. he is 2. they aren't 3. can 4. playing 6. I can't 7. going 8. where 11. what

B. 2. studying 3. listening 4. Can 5. Can't 6. can

C. Answers will vary.

UNIT 8 CLOTHES

Lesson A

A. 1. hat 2. coat 3. sweater 4. dress 5. shoes 6. jacket 7. shirt 8. pants

B. 1. red 2. white 3. black 4. brown 5. yellow 6. orange 7. green 8. blue

C. sweaters, Could, try, of course, Small

D. Answers will vary.

Lesson B

A. 2. The sale price is $29.99. 3. How much is it? 4. Do you have this in red? 5. That's $29.99 total.

B. 1. b 2. d 3. c 4. a

C. 2. I'm looking for 3. What size are you? 4. How much is it? 5. The sale price is 6. Do you want to pay by cash or credit card? 7. That's $49 total

Lesson C

A. 2. orange 3. red 4. dark blue 5. purple 6. beige 7. dark green 8. light blue

B. 1. T-shirt 2. socks 3. jeans 4. scarf 5. blouse

C. Answers will vary.

D. Answers will vary.

Lesson D

A. 1. f 2. e 3. b 4. a 5. c 6. d

B. 2. is wearing 3. T-shirt 4. shopping 5. looks 6. informal 7. beige 8. light 9. good

C. Answers will vary.

Review

A. Across 5. could you 9. course 10. try 11. assistant 12. light

Down 1. card 2. blouse 3. coat 4. dark 5. change 6. love 7. wearing 8. casual 13. hate

B. Answers will vary.

UNIT 9 EAT WELL

Lesson A

A. 1. cereal 2. eggs 3. fruit juice 4. steak 5. fish 6. pasta 7. chicken 8. salad 9. coffee 10. tea 11. chocolate cake 12. ice cream

B. 1. some 2. any 3. any 4. some 5. some 6. some 7. some 8. any

C. some, any, any, some

D. Answers will vary.

Lesson B

A. Answers will vary.

B. Answers will vary.

C. Answers will vary.

D. Answers will vary.

Lesson C

A. Non-count nouns: some coffee, some tea, some rice, some juice
Countable nouns: apples, steak

B. Answers will vary.

C. 2. How much meat do you eat? 3. How much coffee does he drink? 4. How much fruit does she eat? 5. How many eggs do you need? 6. How much tea do you drink?

Lesson D

B. cake, ice cream—United States; pie—Russia; cake, pasta—Philippines; soup—Korea

C. 1. F 2. F 3. T 4. F

D. I like my Birthday. My mother makes a great dinner with my favorite food. We eat steak and rice. She makes a chocolate cake. We sing Happy Birthday. We eat a lot of cake and ice cream.

E. Answers will vary.

Review

A. Across 3. juice 4. salad 5. meat 7. chocolate 11. some 12. fruit 13. many

Down 1. much 2. dessert 6. please 8. healthy 9. cream 10. menu 14. any

B. 2. vegetables 3. dessert 4. pie 5. ice cream

C. Answers will vary.

UNIT 10 HEALTH

Lesson A

A. 1. leg 2. head 3. ear 4. back 5. stomach 6. knee 7. face 8. hand 9. chest 10. finger 11. arm 12. foot

B. ☺: well, OK, great ☹: terrible, sick

C. 2. headache 3. fever 4. stomachache 5. backache

D. Answers will vary.

Lesson B

A. 1. toothache 2. cold 3. headache 4. backache 5. sore throat

B. 1. backache 2. cold 3. sore throat 4. toothache 5. headache

C. Doctor: <u>How</u> are you to<u>day</u>?
Patient: I have a <u>terrible</u> <u>sto</u>machache.
Doctor: <u>Where</u> does it <u>hurt</u>?
Patient: <u>Right</u> here.
Doctor: I <u>need</u> to ex<u>amine</u> you.

Lesson C

A. 1. go 2. see 3. take 4. lie 5. take 6. see

B. Answers will vary.

C. What should I do? You should go home. Should I go to English class? No you shouldn't. You should go to bed!

Lesson D

B. 1. F 2. F 3. T 4. T 5. F 6. T

C. Answers will vary.

D. should, shouldn't, shouldn't, should, should

E. Answers will vary.

Review

Across 1. flu 2. fingers 4. sore 6. examine 7. should 8. hurts 9. matter 10. shouldn't

Down 1. fever 2. feel 3. stomachache 5. great 6. ears 7. symptom

UNIT 11 MAKING PLANS

Lesson A

A. 1. e 2. b 3. a 4. c 5. f 6. d

B. 1. He's going to travel. He's going to the movies. 2. What is Mary going to do this weekend? She's going to have a family meal. She isn't going to travel. She isn't going to the movies. 3. What are Mr. and Mrs. Kim going to do this weekend? They are going to have a family meal. They are going to travel. They aren't going to the movies. 4. Answers will vary.

Lesson B

A. 2. sing Norwegian songs 3. He is going to walk around the city with Norwegian flags. 4. It's a Norwegian summer holiday, Jonsok. 5. He's going to make a big fire and sing all night. 6. He isn't going to go to bed. 7. There is a Norwegian winter holiday, Christmas. 8. He is going to make special cookies and cakes. 9. He is going to give presents to his family and friends.

B. Answers will vary.

Lesson C

A. 2. medicine 3. law 4. psychology 5. music 6. information technology

B. what would you like to do; Would you like to work; I wouldn't; Would you like to be; wouldn't; Where would you like to work?; would you like to work; would

C. Answers will vary.

Lesson D

A. doctor; piano teacher; actor; software engineer

B. I would like to travel in Europe. I want to visit France, England, Spain, and Germany. I need a lot of money. I'm going to get a weekend job and I'm going to work every Saturday and every Sunday. I'm going to save all my money. Then, I'm going to make plans for my trip. I would like to go to Europe next summer.

C. Answers will vary.

Review

A. Across 2. am going to 6. is going to 8. would like to 10. musician 12. medicine 13. holiday

Down 1. go 2. anniversary 3. wouldn't 4. meal 5. lawyer 7. out 9. have 11. the

B. 2. party 3. is going to 4. are going to 5. party

UNIT 12 ON THE MOVE

Lesson A

A. 1. leave 2. arrive 3. go, stay 4. return 5. come 6. move

B. 1. lived 2. went 3. arrived 4. came 5. moved 6. stayed 7. returned 8. left

C. 2. She went to Melbourne. She didn't go to Sydney. 3. She moved to Canberra. She didn't move to Perth. 4. She stayed in an apartment. She didn't stay in a hotel. 5. She returned to her home country. She didn't return to Australia.

D. 2. Why did they move to a new house? 3. When did he leave his hometown? 4. Where did she live in Europe? 5. Why did they go to a restaurant? 6. Where did we stay?

Lesson B

A. 2. two thousand and twelve 3. nineteen eighty-nine 4. two thousand and four 5. Answers will vary. 6. Answers will vary.

B. Reporter: When did you arrive; Javier: came, didn't know, went;
Reporter: Why did you leave; Javier: left, didn't have;
Reporter: Where did you live?; Javier: lived;
Reporter: When did you return; Javier: didn't return, returned, stayed

Lesson C

A. 1. have 2. sell 3. buy 4. pack 5. get 6. close 7. sell 8. stop

B. 2. Did he get money from the bank? Yes, he did. 3. Did he go to the supermarket? No, he didn't. 4. Did he call David? Yes, he did. 5. Did he check e-mail? No, he didn't.

C. Answers will vary.

Lesson D

A. 1. Yes, he did. 2. On April 1st. 3. To New York City. 4. 2 days 5. presents

B. New York, stores, Washington D.C., White, shopping, Miami, beach, presents

C. Answers will vary.

Review

A. Across 2. came 3. had 8. moved 10. nineteen ninety 11. bought 12. left 13. did you 14. stayed

Down 1. passport 4. account 5. farewell 6. arrived 7. went 9. didn't live

B. 2. sold 3. car 4. packed 5. got 6. tickets 7. going-away

Reasons for Writing

The Writing Program reinforce and complements the lessons in the Student Book. Writing gives students a chance to reflect on the English they've learned and to develop an indispensable academic skill.

The Writing Syllabus

The Writing Activities help students to develop all the building blocks of good writing: words, logical connectors, sentences, transitions, paragraphs, and short essays. As students progress through the levels of the **World English** series, the Writing Activities progress from the word and sentence level to the paragraph and composition level, allowing students to master the basics before they're asked to do more complex writing tasks.

The Writing Activities help students move from sentences to paragraphs as they show relationships between ideas and add detail and precision to their writing with descriptive adjectives.

Writing from Models vs. Process Writing

When students are provided with writing models—examples of completed writing tasks—they have a clear idea of what is expected from them as well as a model on which to base their own writing. Such models give students confidence and a sense of direction and can be found at all levels of the Writing Worksheets.

On the other hand, writers must also learn the writing process. They must generate ideas, plan their writing, perform the writing task, then polish their writing by revising and editing. The Writing Worksheets support process writing by providing activities to stimulate thinking, useful topics and vocabulary, graphic organizers for planning, and opportunities for students to share and refine their writing.

Ways to Use the Writing Program

In general, the Writing Activities are designed to be used after the class has covered all or most of a unit in the Student Book. The Writing Activities often contain grammar, vocabulary, and ideas from the units, which give students solid linguistic and conceptual ground to stand on.

On the other hand, it's not necessary to complete the Lesson D Writing task in the Student Book before using the Writing Activity for that unit. The worksheets complement the writing lessons in the Student Book, but can be used independently.

Here are some suggestions for using the writing activities.

- **In-Class Discussion**

  Discussion is an important way to stimulate thinking and to help students generate ideas they can use in their own writing. When an activity contains a preliminary matching or listing activity, for example, ask students to share and explain their answers. Ask specific questions about the writing models in order to check comprehension and to elicit opinions about the topics. And be sure to take advantage of opportunities for students to discuss their writing with you and their classmates.

- **Homework**

  Most of the Writing Activities are appropriate for self-study as long as follow-up discussion and feedback are provided later.

- **Vocabulary Practice**

  Many of the Writing Activities contain target vocabulary from the corresponding unit in the Student Book. Ask students to locate vocabulary from the unit in the writing models, or check comprehension by asking students to explain vocabulary words in the context of the worksheet.

- **Grammar Reinforcement**

  Many of the Writing Activities require the use of grammar points found in the Student Book units, and using the grammar in context supports real language acquisition.

- **Pronunciation Practice**

  Although oral skills are not the focus of the Writing Activities, you can do choral repetition of the word lists in the worksheets or use the writing models to practice pronunciation points from the Student Book. Students can also do read-alouds of their finished writing in pairs or small groups while the teacher monitors their pronunciation.

- **Personalization**

  When students complete unfinished sentences, paragraphs, and essays, or when they do less controlled original writing, they bring their personal thoughts and experiences into the classroom and take ownership of the writing task as well as the language they are learning.

- **Real Communication**

  Since the real-world purpose of writing is to communicate, be sure to respond not only to linguistic and technical aspects of student writing, but also to students' ideas. Make comments and ask questions that show genuine interest, either in class or when you collect and give written feedback on the worksheets.

	Writing Tasks	Language Focus
Unit 1 Describe Your Family	• Use *be* in a conversation. • Draw and describe family members.	*Hi, my name is Michael.* *This is Toby. He is my brother.*
Unit 2 Describe a Country	• Answer questions about yourself. • Write sentences about countries.	*No, I'm not a doctor.* *Brazil is a large country.*
Unit 3 Describe a Room	• Finish sentences about a house and an apartment. • Write sentences about a room.	*There are three bedrooms in my house.* *There is a lamp on the table.*
Unit 4 A Short Story	• Finish sentences about possessions. • Write questions with *have.* • Finish sentences in a story.	*There is a watch in the purse.* *Does Hanna have keys in her purse?*
Unit 5 Daily Schedule	• Write sentences about a person's schedule. • Write sentences about one's own daily routine.	*Jillian gets up at 7:30 every morning.* *I do homework at 6:30 every evening.*
Unit 6 Museum Tour	• Answer questions with *have to.* • Finish a paragraph about a tour.	*Do you have to arrive before 9:00 a.m.?* *No, you don't.* *Our tour started at 11:00.*
Unit 7 Showing Contrasts	• Write sentences about what's happening now. • Show contrasts with *but.*	*Right now, people are playing sports outside.* *Anita can't swim, but Peter can.*
Unit 8 Likes and Dislikes	• Write sentences about what people are wearing. • Write opinions about clothes and colors.	*My brother is wearing brown pants and a white shirt.* *I like pink and yellow.*
Unit 9 Restaurant Conversation	• Answer questions about favorite foods. • Use *and* to connect ideas in a conversation.	*I like mangos and strawberries.* *Could I have spaghetti and meatballs?*
Unit 10 Letters of Advice	• Give advice to people with health problems using *should* and *should not.*	*I have a terrible toothache.* *What should I do?* *You should see a dentist.*
Unit 11 Letter to a Millionaire	• Write answers to questions about your plans for the future. • Write a letter about your wishes for the future.	*I'm going to go shopping tomorrow.* *I would like to travel to China.*
Unit 12 Past Timeline	• Write sentences about past events.	*Kayo got her passport in 1998.*

UNIT 1 FRIENDS AND FAMILY

DESCRIBE YOUR FAMILY

A Read the conversation. Complete the conversation with *is*, *am*, or *are*.

Michael: Hi, my name _____ Michael.

Anna: Hi, Michael. Nice to meet you. I _____ Anna.

Michael: Nice to meet you, too. _____ you in my English class?

Anna: Yes, I am. We _____ in the same math class, too.

Michael: That's great!

✓ Practice the conversation with a partner.

B Write about your family members. Draw pictures then fill in the blanks. Use real names and words from the boxes.

Example:

This is _____ Toby _____. He is my _brother_.

He is _____ young _____ with _straight black_ hair.

family members	adjectives	hair types
grandmother grandfather sister brother mother father daughter son	tall short handsome pretty old young	curly wavy straight brown red black blond

This is _____. He/She is my _____.

He/She is _____ with _____ hair.

This is _____. He/She is my _____.

He/She is _____ with _____ hair.

This is _____. He/She is my _____.

He/She is _____ with _____ hair.

✓ Show your pictures to a classmate. Say the sentences about your family members.

UNIT 2 JOBS AROUND THE WORLD
DESCRIBE A COUNTRY

A Write answers to the questions that are true for you. Use *I'm* or *I'm not*.

Example: Are you a doctor? <u>Yes, I'm a doctor.</u> or <u>No, I'm not a doctor.</u>

Questions	Answers
1. Are you from Brazil?	
2. Are you a student?	
3. Are you an artist?	
4. Are you married?	
5. Are you from a small country?	
6. Are you an interesting person?	

B ✓ Ask and answer the questions with a partner.

B Finish each sentence with an adjective from the box. There may be more than one correct answer.

> hot   large   dry   small   wet   cold

1. Japan is a _____ country.

2. The United Kingdom is a _____ country.

3. Chile is a _____ country.

4. Korea is a _____ country.

5. The United States is a _____ country.

6. Russia is a _____ country.

C Read about Brazil.

> Brazil is a large country. It's in South America. Brasília is in Brazil. It's the capital city.

✓ Write a similar paragraph about Argentina.

UNIT 3 HOUSES AND APARTMENTS

DESCRIBE A ROOM

A Read about a house. Complete the paragraph with words from the box.

> is   sofas   next to   armchair   are

There _____ three bedrooms in my house. There _____ a big yard, too. There

are two _____ in the living room, and there is one _____. The kitchen is

_____ the living room.

B Read about an apartment. Complete the paragraph with words from the box.

> microwave   are   is   small   lamps

I live in a _____ apartment. There is a refrigerator and a _____ in the kitchen.

There _____ a table next to the bed. There are two _____ in the apartment.

C Draw one room in your house or apartment. Then write sentences about the room. Use *there is/there are* and some of the words in the boxes.

> in   on   under   next to

> table   bed   bookcase   stove   refrigerator   lamp   TV   sofa   chair

✓ Show your picture to a partner. Say your sentences.

UNIT 4 POSSESSIONS
A SHORT STORY

A Read about Esra's purse. Complete the paragraph with *there is* or *there are*.

Esra has many things in her purse. _____ keys to her apartment. _____ glasses because Esra doesn't see well. _____ a watch in the purse, too.

✓ Read about Bill's backpack. Complete the paragraph with *there is* or *there are*.

Bill has many things in his backpack. _____ pens and a notebook for class. _____ a book in the backpack, too. _____ a cell phone in the backpack because Bill likes to call his friends.

✓ Write questions with *have*.

1. Esra/keys? _Does Esra have keys in her purse?_ _____
2. Esra/cell phone? _____
3. Esra/glasses? _____
4. Bill/book? _____
5. Bill/wallet? _____
6. Bill/pens? _____

🔁 ✓ Ask and answer the questions with a partner.

B Read the story. Complete the paragraph with words from the box.

> have   keys   we   there   wallet   are   is

Bill doesn't remember things. Esra remembers everything. This morning, Bill asked Esra, "Where are my _____?" So Esra said, "_____ your keys on the coffee table?" But there were no keys on the coffee table. Then Bill asked Esra, "Do you _____ my wallet?" And Esra said, "No, I don't. _____ your wallet in the bedroom?" But _____ was no wallet in the bedroom. Finally, Bill asked Esra, "Do _____ have any eggs? I'm hungry!" Bill opened the refrigerator. In the refrigerator, there were some eggs, and some keys, and Bill's _____! So Esra asked Bill, "Why are your keys and your wallet in the refrigerator?" And Bill said, "I don't remember."

UNIT 5 DAILY ACTIVITIES

DAILY SCHEDULE

A Look at Jillian's schedule.

Monday	Tuesday	Wednesday	Thursday	Friday
7:30 get up	7:30 get up	7:30 get up	7:30 get up	7:30 get up
9:00 start work	9:00 start work	9:00 start work	9:00 start work	9:00 start work
12:30 have lunch	12:30 have lunch	12:30 have lunch	12:30 have lunch	12:30 have lunch
	3:00 finish work		3:00 finish work	
5:00 finish work		5:00 finish work		5:00 finish work
11:00 go to bed	11:00 go to bed	11:00 go to bed	11:00 go to bed	11:00 go to bed

✓ Use the words below to write sentences about Jillian's schedule.

1. get up/every morning ___*Jillian gets up at 7:30 every morning.*___

2. start work/every day _____

3. have lunch/every day _____

4. finish work/Tuesdays and Thursdays _____

5. finish work/Mondays, Wednesdays, and Fridays _____

6. go to bed/every night _____

✓ Compare your sentences with a partner.

B What do you do every day? Fill in the schedule with your information.

Monday	Tuesday	Wednesday	Thursday	Friday

✓ Write sentences about your schedule.

1. _____   4. _____

2. _____   5. _____

3. _____   6. _____

✓ Say your sentences to a partner.

UNIT 6 GETTING THERE
MUSEUM TOUR

A Read about a tour.

> ### Historic Village Tour
> - Tours every day from 10:00 a.m. until 4:00 p.m.
> - Tickets: $14 for adults and $9 for seniors over 65 years old
> - No children under 12 years old
> - Bus transportation to the village
> - Cameras allowed
> - No food inside the homes

✓ Write answers to the questions.

1. Do you have to arrive before 9:00 a.m.? _No, you don't._____

2. Do you have to arrive before 4:00 p.m.? _____

3. Do you have to pay $20 for the tour? _____

4. Do you have to be 12 years old or older? _____

5. Do you have to walk to the stars' homes? _____

6. Do you have to leave your camera on the bus? _____

⚙✓ Ask and answer the questions with a partner.

B Read the paragraph. Complete the paragraph with words from the box.

> for   to   afternoon   at   a   across

> ### My Tour of the Historic Village
> Last week, I went on a very interesting tour. Our tour started _____ 11:00 in the morning. I'm only 35 years old, so I had to pay $14 _____ my ticket. We took _____ bus to a historic village. The buildings were hundreds of years old! I really liked the lawyer's home. It was huge! And it was _____ the street from the blacksmith's. The tour ended at 1:30 in the _____. There was one bad thing about the tour. You have _____ leave your food on the bus when you go inside the buildings, so I was pretty hungry at the end.

UNIT 7 FREE TIME
SHOWING CONTRASTS

A What's happening right now? Make a check ✓ next to those things.

_____ It's raining.	_____ People are playing sports outside.
_____ I'm doing a worksheet.	_____ I'm sitting in a chair.
_____ The sun is shining.	_____ Someone is cooking.
_____ I'm listening to music.	_____ I'm talking on the telephone.
_____ My teacher is working.	_____ I'm studying English.

✓ Write sentences about what is happening or what is not happening.

1. *Right now, I'm doing a worksheet.* _____

2. *It's not raining at the moment.* _____

3. _____

4. _____

5. _____

6. _____

7. _____

8. _____

✓ You can connect two short sentences with *but*. Writers do this to show a contrast (very different meanings).

Example: Right now, people are playing sports outside, but I'm sitting in a chair.

B These people have different abilities. There is a check ✓ next to things each person can do.

Lin		Fernando	
✓ draw	✓ play the guitar	draw	play the guitar
✓ play golf	cook	play golf	✓ cook
ski	swim	✓ ski	✓ swim

✓ Write sentences with *but*.

Examples: Lin can play the guitar, but Fernando can't. Lin can't swim, but Fernando can.

1. _____   4. _____

2. _____   5. _____

3. _____   6. _____

UNIT 8 CLOTHES
LIKES AND DISLIKES

A What are you wearing? What are other people wearing? Write sentences with words from the boxes.

shirt	pants	skirt	shoes	sweater	jacket	coat	tie
hat	jeans	scarf	blouse	socks	T-shirt	dress	

red	(dark/light) blue	yellow	(dark/light) green	orange	white
brown	black	gray	purple	beige	pink

1. _My brother is wearing brown pants and a white shirt._ _____

2. _I am wearing_ _____

3. _____

4. _____

5. _____

6. _____

✓ Say your sentences to a partner.

B What do you like to wear? Write words for clothes in the columns.

clothes I love	clothes I like	clothes I dislike	clothes I hate

✓ Now complete the paragraph below. Use the plural form (*dresses, shoes,* etc.).

I have some strong opinions about clothes. For example, I like _____ and _____. And I really love _____. On the other hand, I dislike _____ and _____. And I really hate _____. They're the worst!

C Which colors do you like and dislike? Write sentences about your opinions.

_____

_____

_____

_____

UNIT 9 EAT WELL
RESTAURANT CONVERSATION

A What are your favorites? Complete with answers that are true for you.

Q.	A.
1. What are your favorite fruits?	**1.** I like _____ and _____.
2. What are your favorite vegetables?	**2.** I like _____ and _____.
3. What are your favorite drinks?	**3.** I like _____ and _____.
4. What are your favorite breakfast foods?	**4.** I like _____ and _____.
5. What are your favorite desserts?	**5.** I like _____ and _____.

✓ Ask and answer the questions with a partner.

B Writers use the word *and* to connect two or more ideas.

Two ideas: My favorite fruits are <u>mangos and strawberries</u>.

Three ideas: Could I have <u>soup, salad, and fish</u>?

Four ideas: We need to buy <u>pasta, soda, ice cream, and cake</u>.

✓ Look at the commas (,) in the sentences above.

C Complete the sentences in the conversation. Use your own ideas.

Larry: This looks like a nice restaurant.

Paula: It is nice. The food is good, too.

Larry: What should I have?

Paula: Well, the (*2 ideas*) _____ are both very good.

Waiter: Are you ready to order?

Paula: Yes, could I have (*3 ideas*) _____ ?

Waiter: No problem. And for you sir?

Larry: Could I have (*2 ideas*) _____ ?

Waiter: Very good. Anything else?

Larry: Well, I'll probably want dessert later. Do you have any desserts?

Waiter: Yes, we have (*4 ideas*) _____ .

Larry: Those sound good. I'll decide after I eat.

Waiter: Very good. Thank you.

Larry & : Thank you.
Paula

UNIT 10 HEALTH
LETTERS OF ADVICE

 Read about Chelsea's health problems.

> Dear Dr. Millham,
>
> My name is Chelsea. I have a terrible toothache. My mouth is very red inside, and I might have a fever, too. What should I do?

✓ Now read the doctor's letter to Chelsea.

> Dear Chelsea,
>
> You should take an aspirin. That will help the toothache and the fever. Then, you should see a dentist. You shouldn't wait. See a dentist today.

✓ Write a similar letter to each person below.

> Dear Dr. Millham,
>
> My name is Ryan. I think I have a cold. I'm coughing and coughing, and I also have a fever. What should I do?

> _____
>
> _____
>
> _____

> Dear Dr. Millham,
>
> My name is Lucinda. Everything hurts today! I have a bad headache. I have a backache, too. What should I do?

> _____
>
> _____
>
> _____

> Dear Dr. Millham,
>
> My name is Mi Young. I don't feel very well. Nothing hurts, but I'm very tired. What should I do?

> _____
>
> _____
>
> _____

UNIT 11 MAKING PLANS
LETTER TO A MILLIONAIRE

A Write answers to the questions. What are your plans?

Q.		A.	
1.	What are you going to do tomorrow?	**1.**	*I'm going to* _____.
2.	What are you going to do next week?	**2.**	_____.
3.	What are you going to do next month?	**3.**	_____.
4.	What are you going to do next year?	**4.**	_____.

✓ Ask and answer the questions with a partner.

B Read the letter. Why does the writer use *would like*?

Dear Mom and Dad,

Can you believe it? My birthday party is going to be next weekend! Thank you for having a party for me. If you don't mind, I would like to bring my friend Ayumi to the party. She's really nice, and I think you're going to like her. I would also like Mom to make her special lemon cake. (Would you do that, Mom?) It's my favorite!

See you soon,

Maria

C What are your wishes for your future? On the back of this paper, write several things you would like to do in your life:

Example: I would like to travel to Asia.

✓ Imagine this: There is a very rich person. This person wants to make someone's wishes come true! Write a letter to him or her about things you would like to do. (If you're lucky, the millionaire might decide to pay for everything!)

Dear Millionaire,

There are several things I would like to do in my life. First, I would like to _____

_____

_____

_____

_____ Thank you for reading my letter.

Sincerely,

_____

UNIT 12 ON THE MOVE
PAST TIMELINE

A Look at the dates and events on the timeline.

Kayo's Years in Australia

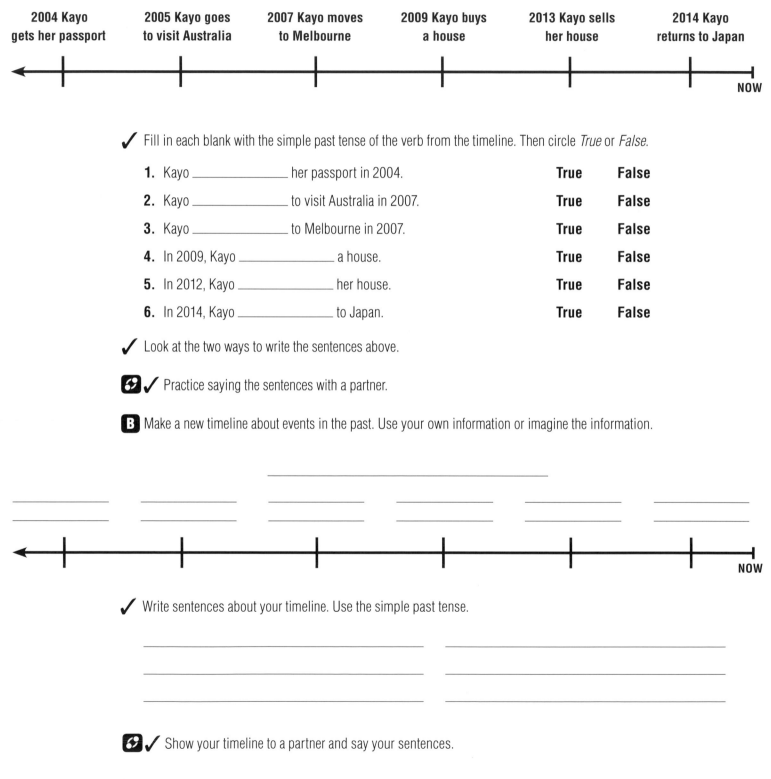

| 2004 Kayo gets her passport | 2005 Kayo goes to visit Australia | 2007 Kayo moves to Melbourne | 2009 Kayo buys a house | 2013 Kayo sells her house | 2014 Kayo returns to Japan |

NOW

✓ Fill in each blank with the simple past tense of the verb from the timeline. Then circle *True* or *False*.

1. Kayo _____ her passport in 2004.　　　**True**　　**False**

2. Kayo _____ to visit Australia in 2007.　**True**　　**False**

3. Kayo _____ to Melbourne in 2007.　　　**True**　　**False**

4. In 2009, Kayo _____ a house.　　　　　**True**　　**False**

5. In 2012, Kayo _____ her house.　　　　**True**　　**False**

6. In 2014, Kayo _____ to Japan.　　　　　**True**　　**False**

✓ Look at the two ways to write the sentences above.

⟳ ✓ Practice saying the sentences with a partner.

B Make a new timeline about events in the past. Use your own information or imagine the information.

_____

_____ _____ _____ _____ _____ _____

_____ _____ _____ _____ _____ _____

NOW

✓ Write sentences about your timeline. Use the simple past tense.

_____ _____

_____ _____

_____ _____

⟳ ✓ Show your timeline to a partner and say your sentences.

	Communication Goals	Language Focus
UNIT 1 Friends and Family	• Describe a person	*She/He's young, with straight _____ hair.* *His/Her name is _____.*
UNIT 2 Jobs Around the World	• Asking for and giving personal information • Talking about jobs • Talking about countries	*What's your name? How old are you?* *Where are you from?*
UNIT 3 Houses and Apartments	• Describing a house	*What's in the big bedroom?* *There are two beds.*
Unit 4 Possessions	• Talking about the personal possessions of others	*These earrings look cool.* *She already has earrings. What about this necklace?* *It's ugly! Look at this desk lamp . . .*
UNIT 5 Daily Activities	• Asking and answering questions about work activities	*What time do you start work?* *What time do you finish work?*
UNIT 6 Getting There	• Ask for and give directions	*You are in the _____. Cross _____ Avenue.* *Walk two blocks and _____. Turn left/right and _____.*
UNIT 7 Free Time	• Talk about abilities	*Can you speak _____?* *Can you play the piano?*
UNIT 8 Clothes	• Describing peoples' clothes	*He's wearing _____. What's his name?* *How do you spell it?*
UNIT 9 Eat Well	• Planning a dinner	*Could we have some soda, please?* *How many bottles do you want?*
UNIT 10 Health	• Describing symptoms and illnesses; giving advice	*What's the matter?* *You should . . .*
UNIT 11 Making Plans	• Express wishes and plans	*He would like to . . .* *She's going to . . .*
UNIT 12 On the Move	• Talking about people moving from place to place	*When did he leave _____?* *How long _____?* *Where did he live in _____?*

UNIT 1 FRIENDS AND FAMILY

Describe a person. Your partner says the name.

Student A: He's young, with straight black hair.
Student B: His name is Jason.

UNIT 2 JOBS AROUND THE WORLD

Student A

Ask and answer questions to fill in the information.

Name:		Rafael
Age:		48
Single/Married:		married
Country:		Argentina
City:		Buenos Aires
Job:		teacher
Interesting/boring		interesting

Student B

Ask and answer questions to fill in the information.

Name:	Maya	
Age:	30	
Single/Married:	married	
Country:	Russia	
City:	Moscow	
Job:	banker	
Interesting/boring	boring	

UNIT 3 HOUSES AND APARTMENTS

Student A

Talk to your partner. Ask and answer questions to complete the drawing.

What's in the big bedroom?

There are two beds.

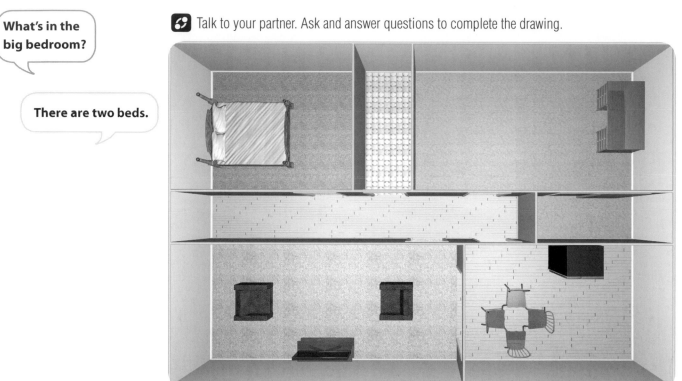

Student B

Talk to your partner. Ask and answer questions to complete the drawing.

What's in the big bedroom?

There are two beds.

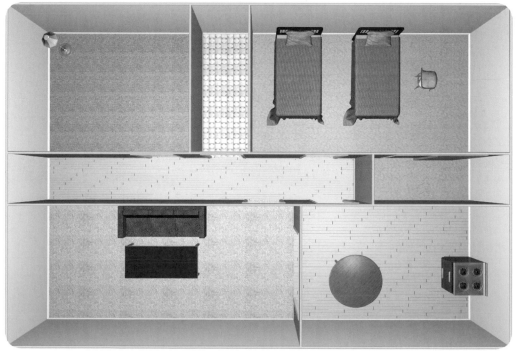

Photocopiable © 2015 National Geographic Learning

UNIT 4 POSSESSIONS

1. Your teacher will give you the names of two classmates. Look at the Web page and choose a present for each person.

1. Name:	Present:
2. Name:	Present:

2. Tell the class about the presents.

> These earrings look cool.

> She already has earrings. What about this necklace?

> It's ugly! Look at this desk lamp . . .

> Lily's present is a watch.

⊗⊖⊕

◄ ► C + http://www.GiftIdeas.com Q▾ ↺

Great gifts for every occassion!

Search [   ]

ALL NEW ! | Electronics | Home Goods | Books | Jewelry

ALL NEW !

Username:
[   ]

Password:
[   ]

Login

My shopping cart:

View cart 🛒

Tablet
Add to cart 🛒

silver necklace
Add to cart 🛒

DVD player
Add to cart 🛒

desk lamp
Add to cart 🛒

MP3 player
Add to cart 🛒

sunglasses
Add to cart 🛒

wallet
Add to cart 🛒

gold earrings
Add to cart 🛒

watch
Add to cart 🛒

SITE MAP | CONTACT US | OFFERS | TERMS AND CONDITIONS

UNIT 5 DAILY ACTIVITIES
Student A

Ask and answer questions to fill in the information. Are these good jobs?

Name:	Nathan	
Job:		baker
Get up:	4:00 p.m.	
Start work:	10:00 p.m.	
Have lunch:		8:15 a.m.
Finish work:	4:30 a.m.	
Go to bed:		6:30 p.m.

- -

Student B

Ask and answer questions to fill in the information. Are these good jobs?

Name:		Amanda
Job:	radio announcer	
Get up:		2:00 a.m.
Start work:		3:00 a.m.
Have lunch:	1:45 a.m.	
Finish work:		11:30 a.m.
Go to bed:	9:00 a.m.	

UNIT 6 GETTING THERE

Look at the map. Ask your partner for directions to these places.

Student A

1. the tourist office
2. the art museum
3. Beijing Restaurant

Student B

1. the train station
2. the post office
3. Burger World

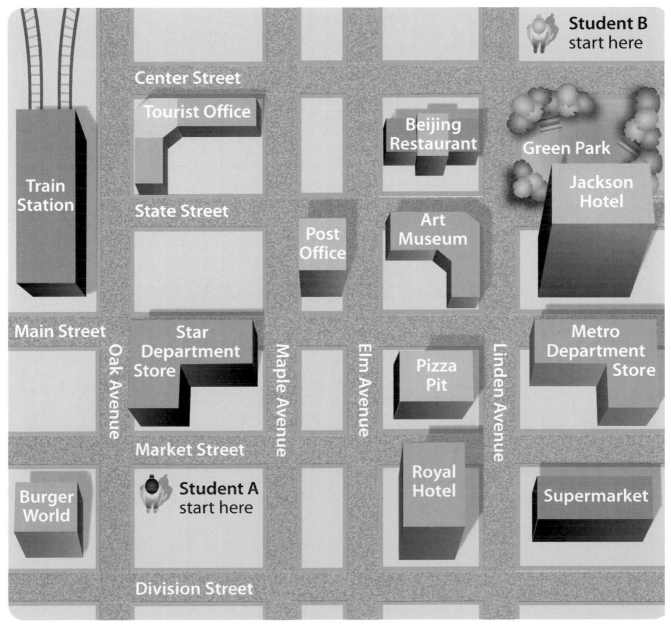

UNIT 7 FREE TIME

⚡ Ask and answer questions. Find a classmate who can do these things. Write the name.

Who can . . .	Name
1. speak two languages	
2. cook _____ (food)	
3. ice skate	
4. play the piano	
5. draw	
6. swim	
7. play _____ (sport)	
8. run fast	
9. play the guitar	
10. sing	

UNIT 8 CLOTHES

Student A

Listen to your partner's descriptions. Write the missing names.

He's wearing _____.

What's his name?

How do you spell it?

- -

Student B

Listen to your partner's descriptions. Write the missing names.

He's wearing _____.

What's his name?

How do you spell it?

UNIT 9 EAT WELL

👥 You and your group are planning a dinner for a special day.

1. Choose a special day: _____

2. Write the menu here.

   Foods: _____

   _____

   _____

   _____

   _____

   _____

3. Write the drinks here.

   Drinks: _____

   _____

   _____

4. What time does your dinner start? What time does it end?

   _____

5. What clothes do people wear for your dinner?

   _____

6. Now tell the class about your dinner.

UNIT 10 HEALTH

Make conversations. Give advice to these people

1. He feels tired all the time.
2. She feels nervous about the test.
3. He can't sleep.
4. She has a very bad cold.
5. He can't understand his English class.

What's the matter?

You should . . .

UNIT 11 MAKING PLANS

He would like to . . .

She's going to . . .

Look at the pictures. Talk about each person's goals and plans. Use your ideas.

UNIT 12 ON THE MOVE

Student A

1 Ask and answer questions to fill in the information.

2 With your partner, decide which person has a more interesting life.

Name:	Samuel	Ray
Born in:		1985
Home country:		The Philippines
Left his home country:		2005
Destination:		Australian College of Medicine and Science (Australia)
Migrated to:		Saudi Arabia (2007)
Moved to:		Riyadh, to work in a hospital as an x-ray technician

- -

Student B

1 Ask and answer questions to fill in the information.

2 With your partner, decide which person has a more interesting life.

Name:	Samuel	Ray
Born in:	1985	
Home country:	Nigeria (Africa)	
Left his home country:	2005	
Destination:	Oxford University (U.K.)	
Migrated to:	Canada (2011)	
Moved to:	Vancouver, to work in a bank	

Unit 1: Friends and Family

Lesson A

A Write the correct form of the verb *be*.

1. How __are__ you?

2. I _____ Yuina.

3. My name _____ Arjun.

4. We _____ classmates.

5. Lisa and Manuel _____ students.

B Circle the correct form of the verb *be*.

1. My name (am | (is)) Jack.

2. How (are | is) you?

3. I (am | is) a student.

4. She (are | is) Paola.

5. We (are | is) John and Feng.

C Write the sentences again. Use contractions with *be*.

1. My name is Jing. __My name's Jing__ .

2. Sarah is my classmate. _____

3. We are students. _____

4. They are David and Louis. _____

5. You are Carlos. _____

D Match the sentences with the same meaning.

1. You are Roberto. __d__   **a.** She's Anna.

2. They are teachers. _____   **b.** Their names are Isabel and Victor.

3. She is Anna. _____   **c.** My name is Cristina.

4. They are Isabel and Victor. _____   **d.** Your name is Roberto.

5. I am Cristina. _____   **e.** They're teachers.

E Write the correct possessive adjective.

1. He is a student. __His__ name is Justin.

2. I'm Ivan. _____ name is Ivan.

3. They are students. _____ teacher is Mrs. Hernandez.

4. _____ name is Kia. She is my friend.

5. You are Hiroto. _____ name is Hiroto.

Lesson C

A Unscramble the sentences and questions.

1. are The students young. _The students are young._

2. handsome is My brother. _____

3. are We married. _____

4. you single? Are _____

5. she attractive Is? _____

B Circle the correct form of the verb *be*.

1. You ((are) | is) pretty.

2. We (are | is) married.

3. I (am | is) tall.

4. She (are | is) old.

5. They (are | is) handsome.

C Use the words to write sentences. Use the verb *be* with adjectives and the word *with* to describe hair.

1. she / tall / straight red hair _She is tall with long red hair._

2. they / young / curly blond hair _____

3. he / short / curly gray hair _____

4. Anita / tall / wavy black hair _____

5. Teng / young / straight black hair _____

D Match the questions and the answers.

1. Is Miguel single? __d__

2. Are you tall? _____

3. Are they married? _____

4. Is Mariam young? _____

5. Is her sister married? _____

a. Yes, they are.

b. Yes, she is.

c. No, she is single.

d. Yes, Miguel is single.

e. No, I am short.

E Fill in the blanks with a question.

1. **Q:** _Is he old?_ _____

2. **Q:** _____

3. **Q:** _____

4. **Q:** _____

5. **Q:** _____

A: No, he isn't. He's young.

A: Yes, she is. Her husband's name is Jorge.

A: No, they aren't. They're single.

A: No, she isn't. She is old.

A: No, he is not. He's tall.

Unit 2: Jobs Around the World

Lesson A

A Fill in the blanks with *be* negative. Make negative sentences.

1. Elsa is a student. She _isn't_ a teacher.

2. Hao is a chef. He _____ a taxi driver.

3. You are a teacher. You _____ a banker.

4. They're students. They _____ artists.

5. I'm a doctor. I _____ an engineer.

B Make the sentences negative.

1. She's a student. _She isn't a student_.

2. I'm a doctor. _____.

3. They are artists. _____.

4. We're teachers. _____.

5. You're an architect. _____.

C Unscramble the sentences.

1. are / Julia and Carlos / doctors. / not _Julia and Carlos are not doctors._

2. not / teacher. / a / He's _____

3. students. / aren't / We _____

4. an / You / engineer. / not / are _____

5. chefs. / not / They're _____

D Circle *a* or *an*.

1. Larry isn't (a | (an)) engineer.

2. Yeeun is (a | an) student.

3. I'm not (a | an) taxi driver.

4. You're (a | an) doctor.

5. Ava isn't (a | an) artist.

E Complete the sentences with *be* negative contractions and an indefinite article, if needed.

1. Ali _____ doctor.

2. They _____ architects.

3. You _____ a student.

4. I _____ a teacher.

5. We _____ taxi drivers.

Lesson C

A Unscramble the sentences.

1. is / a / Canada / country. / big _Canada is a big country._

2. a / dry / Indonesia / hot / country. / is _____

3. Ecuador / small / Is / country? / a _____

4. country. / is / a / Iceland / cold _____

5. wet / Is / country? / Ireland / a _____

B Answer the questions.

1. Is Brazil a big country? _Yes, it is._

2. Is Egypt a wet country? _____

3. Is China a small country? _____

4. Is Malaysia a hot country? _____

5. Is Russia a cold country? _____

C Write the statements as questions.

1. The United States is a big country. _Is the United States a big country?_

2. Venezuela is a hot country. _____

3. Asia is a big continent. _____

4. England is a wet country. _____

5. The UAE is a hot, dry country. _____

D Match the questions and the answers.

1. Is Paraguay a big country? ___c___   **a.** No, it isn't. It's a dry country.

2. Is India in Asia? _____   **b.** No, it isn't. It's a wet country.

3. Is Morocco a wet country? _____   **c.** No, it isn't. It's a small country.

4. Is Belgium a dry country? _____   **d.** No it isn't. It's a cold country.

5. Is Canada a hot country? _____   **e.** Yes, it is.

E Unscramble the sentences.

1. wet a Costa Rica hot, country. is _Costa Rica is a hot, wet country._

2. is Russia country. a dry cold, _____

3. continent. a Australia big, is dry _____

4. a is hot small, country. Yemen _____

5. small, wet a Ireland country. is _____

Unit 3: Houses and Apartments

Lesson A

A Circle *There is* or *There are*.

1. (There is | (There are)) two bedrooms.

2. (There is | There are) a swimming pool.

3. (There is | There are) stairs.

4. (There is | There are) a bathroom upstairs.

5. (There is | There are) a car in the garage.

B Complete the sentences with *there is* or *there are*.

1. Upstairs _____*there are*_____ three bedrooms.

2. _____ a swimming pool in the backyard.

3. Downstairs _____ a bathroom.

4. _____ three closets.

5. _____ a kitchen downstairs.

C Unscramble the statements and questions.

1. two / there / apartment / the / bedrooms / Are / in _Are there two bedrooms in the apartment_ ?

2. garage / Is / a / there _____ ?

3. a / There / bathroom / is / a / small _____ .

4. are / There / downstairs / two / closets _____ .

5. garden / a / there / Is _____ ?

D Write the statements as questions.

1. There is a big kitchen. _Is there a big kitchen?_

2. There are cars in the garage. _____

3. There is a bathroom downstairs. _____

4. There are three bedrooms upstairs. _____

5. There is a swimming pool in the backyard. _____

E Write answers to the questions. Use (yes) or (no) below.

1. Is there a closet in the bathroom? (no) _No, there isn't_ .

2. Are there three bedrooms in your house? (yes) _____ .

3. Is there a garden in the backyard? (no) _____ .

4. Are there stairs? (no) _____ .

5. Is there a car in the garage? _____ .

Lesson C

A Look at the picture. Complete the sentences with *in*, *on*, *under*, or *next to*.

1. The book is __*on*__ the table.

2. The lamp is _____ the bookcase.

3. The laptop is _____ the table.

4. The laptop is _____ the book.

5. The chair is _____ the table.

6. The books are _____ the bookcase.

B Look at the pictures. Complete the sentences with *in*, *on*, *under*, or *next to*.

1. The lamp is __*next to*__ the chair.

2. The table is _____ the umbrella.

3. The pencils are _____ the cup.

4. The chairs are _____ the table.

5. The table and chairs are _____ the garden.

C Look at the picture. Circle **T** for *true* and **F** for *false*. Rewrite false sentences to make them true.

1. The glasses are on the book.   (**T**)   **F**

2. The lamp is under the book.   **T**   **F**

3. The book is under the glasses.   **T**   **F**

4. The lamp is next to the book.   **T**   **F**

5. The glasses are on the lamp.   **T**   **F**

Unit 4: Possessions

Lesson A

A Circle the correct demonstrative adjective to complete the sentence.

1. Is ((this) | those) your phone?
2. (That | These) are my books.
3. Are (these | this) your keys?
4. (That | Those) is my phone.
5. (That | These) is not your backpack.

B Unscramble the sentences and questions.

1. keys / not / These / your / are ___These are not your keys___ .
2. Is / notebook / this / your _____?
3. my / That's / phone _____ .
4. not / Those / my / are / glasses _____ .
5. your / dictionary / is / This _____ .

C Match the questions and answers. There is more than one right answer.

1. Are these your pens? __c, d__   **a.** Yes, it is.
2. Is this my backpack? _____   **b.** No, it isn't.
3. Are those your keys? _____   **c.** No, they aren't.
4. Is that your notebook? _____   **d.** Yes, they are.

D Complete the sentences with the correct demonstrative adjective. Use the clues.

1. Are (near) __these__ your books?   **3.** (far) _____ book is a dictionary.
   No, (far) __those__ are my books.   No, (near) _____ book is a dictionary.

2. (far) _____ are your keys.   **4.** Is (near) _____ this your notebook?
   No, (near) _____ are my keys.   No, (far) _____ that is my notebook.

E Cross out the word that does not complete the sentence.

1. (That | This | ~~Those~~) is my necklace.
2. Are (that | these | those) your books?
3. (That | These | This) is my laptop.
4. (That | These | Those) are your pens.
5. Is (that | this | those) is your backpack?

Lessons B and C

A Write the correct possessive form of the noun.

1. That is ____Jamal's____ (Jamal) mother.

2. The book is in _____ (Ploy) bag.

3. This is _____ (Ana and Jane) classroom.

4. The _____ (students) homework is on the desk.

5. The _____ (passengers) bags are in the bus.

B Circle the correct form of the verb *have*.

1. Ulli ((has) | have) a laptop in her bag.   **4.** She (has | have) a DVD player.

2. I (has | have) a tablet in my bag.   **5.** We (has | have) keys to the apartment.

3. You don't (has | have) an MP3 player.

C Write sentences with *have* or *has*.

1. My teacher _has_ a laptop.   **4.** He _____ a camcorder.

2. Ali and Tran _____ new touch phones.   **5.** I _____ a tablet in my backpack.

3. We _____ MP3 players.

D Write the sentences again. Make them negative.

1. Ri has a new watch _Ri doesn't have a new watch_____.

2. Kia and Juana have bracelets _____.

3. You have a cell phone _____.

4. I have a book _____.

5. She has rings _____.

E Write questions with *have*.

1. Javi/notebook? _Does Javi have a notebook_____?

2. you/keys? _____?

3. teacher/dictionary? _____?

4. they/big house? _____?

5. he/cell phone? _____?

F Write short answers to the questions.

1. Does he have glasses? (no) _No, he doesn't have glasses_____

2. Do they have laptops? (yes) _____.

3. Do you have a big apartment? (no) _____.

4. Do we have keys to the house? (no) _____.

5. Does she have a watch? (yes) _____.

Unit 5: Daily Activities

Lesson A

A Complete the sentences. Use the verbs in parentheses.

1. Jorge and Linda __have dinner__ (have dinner) at six o'clock.

2. Farah _____ (take a shower) every morning.

3. We _____ (start work) at nine o'clock in the morning.

4. Kira _____ (get up) at six o'clock every morning.

5. Isabel _____ (have lunch) every day.

B Write the sentences. Make them negative.

1. They finish work at five o'clock. _They don't finish work at 5 o'clock_____.

2. We eat lunch at one o'clock. _____.

3. Tina takes a shower in the evening. _____.

4. I get up at seven thirty every morning. _____.

5. She takes a nap on Sunday afternoon. _____.

C Complete the questions. Use the verbs in parentheses.

1. What time _____ _do you get up_____ (you/get up) in the morning?

2. What time _____ (Carlos/start work) every day?

3. What time _____ (they/have lunch)?

4. What time _____ (she/go to bed) on Saturday?

5. What time _____ (we/have dinner) in the evening?

D Write the questions for the sentences.

1. Ali gets up at nine o'clock on Sunday. _What time does Ali get up on Sunday_____?

2. She finishes work at four thirty. _____?

3. You start work at seven o'clock every day. _____?

4. He goes to bed at eleven o'clock. _____?

5. They have lunch every day at twelve thirty. _____?

E Complete the exchanges with questions.

1. A: _What time do you get up in the morning_____? B: I get up at eight o'clock in the morning.

2. A: _____ B: Eben takes a nap at four o'clock in the afternoon.

3. A: _____ B: Carmen finishes work at three o'clock.

Lesson C

A Complete the sentences with the verb in parentheses.

1. Elena _goes to the bank_ (go to the bank) every day.

2. Ivan _____ (travel) every week.

3. Anika and Neel _____ (go to the meetings) every day.

4. Eva _____ (meet clients) every day.

5. Leon _____ (make photocopies) every week.

B Write short answers to the questions. Use the cue in parentheses.

1. Does Ana talk to people on the phone? (no) _No, she doesn't_.

2. Do we go to meetings every day? (yes) _____.

3. Do they meet clients every week? (yes) _____.

4. Does he go to the bank every afternoon? (no) _____.

5. Do they travel every week? (yes) _____.

C Complete the sentences with *always*, *sometimes*, or *never*.

1. Valeska checks e-mail every morning. She _always_ checks e-mail.

2. They don't meet clients. They _____ meet clients.

3. I go to the bank every morning. I _____ go to the bank.

4. We write reports every year. We _____ write reports.

5. You talk to people on the phone every day. You _____ talk to people on the phone.

D Unscramble the sentences and questions.

1. sometimes / goes / to / Louis / meetings. _Louis sometimes goes to meetings_.

2. never / travel / they _____.

3. every / you / week / write reports / do _____?

4. my / every / evening / boss / checks e-mail _____.

5. Kia / does / make photocopies / day / every _____?

E Write the sentences as questions.

1. Dan goes to the bank every week. _Does Dan go to the bank every week_?

2. You make photocopies every day. _____?

3. Teng works on Saturdays. _____?

4. They talk to people on the phone every afternoon. _____?

5. She writes reports on Fridays. _____?

Unit 6: Getting There

Lesson A

A Look at the map. Complete each sentence with *on the corner of*, *across from*, or *between*.

1. The restaurant is __on the corner of__ Main Street and Oak Street.

2. The restaurant is _____ the park and the library.

3. The library is _____ the restaurant.

4. The bank is _____ the park.

5. The school is _____ the bank and the library.

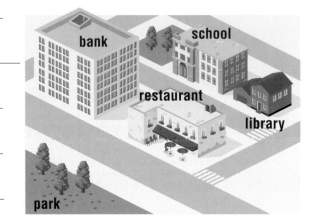

B Use the map and complete each sentence with *turn left*, *turn right*, or *cross*.

1. To walk to the bank from the restaurant __turn right__.

2. To walk to the library from the front of the restaurant _____.

3. To get to the park from the bank _____ the street.

4. To get to the restaurant from the school _____.

5. To get to the bank from the library _____ and _____.

C Write each phrase as an affirmative and a negative imperative sentence.

	Affirmative imperative	Negative imperative
1. go to the library	Go to the library.	Don't go to the library.
2. walk to school		
3. cross Elm Street		
4. turn left		
5. stop		

Lesson C

A Complete the sentences with the correct form of *have to* or *do*.

1. I ___have to___ buy a ticket for the train.

2. Do you _____ pay for the shuttle bus? No, it's free.

3. Amina _____ take a taxi to the airport.

4. _____ I _____ change trains?

5. _____ James _____ go to the meeting?

B Write each statement as a question.

1. Tam has to rent a car. ___Does Tam have to rent a car_____?

2. They have to take a bus to the subway station. _____?

3. We have to buy bus tickets. _____?

4. Diego has to travel by train to the meeting. _____?

5. You have to go to the meeting at 10 a.m. _____?

C Match the questions and answers.

1. Do you have to study on weekends? ___d___   **a.** Yes, she does.

2. Does Shumi have to write a report? _____   **b.** No, he doesn't.

3. Do your classmates have to take notes in class? _____   **c.** Yes, I do.

4. Do we have to write complete sentences? _____   **d.** Yes, they do.

5. Does Miguel have to walk to school? _____   **e.** Yes, you do.

D Write questions using *have to* and the words below.

1. Keiko / study / test ___Keiko has to study for a test_____.

2. Eli / take the bus / to school _____.

3. We / write reports / at work _____.

4. You / do your homework / tonight _____.

5. Cora and Lucy / cook dinner / Saturday _____.

E Write questions using *do* and *have to* and the words below.

1. Zara / study / this afternoon ___Does Zara have to study this afternoon_____?

2. You / finish / your homework / tonight _____?

3. Van / walk home / from school _____?

4. Eva / make dinner / for her family _____?

5. They / change trains / at Park Street Station _____?

Unit 7: Free Time

Lesson A

A Write the sentences in the present continuous tense.

1. She watches TV. _She is watching TV_____.

2. He reads the newspaper. _____.

3. My mother cooks dinner. _____.

4. I go to the movies. _____.

5. They shop at the mall. _____.

B Write questions using the present continuous tense and the cues below.

1. Jose / go for a walk. _Is Jose going for a walk_____?

2. they / watch TV _____?

3. Milan / play guitar _____?

4. you / study English _____?

5. Ada / do homework _____?

C Write responses to the questions using the present continuous tense and the words below.

1. What are you doing? (read / book) _I'm reading a book_____.

2. What is she doing? (write / report) _____.

3. What are they doing? (go for a walk) _____.

4. What are you doing? (shop) _____.

5. What is he doing? (listen to / music) _____.

D Write short answers to the questions.

1. Are you studying for the test? (yes) _Yes, I am____.

2. Is he watching TV? (no) _____.

3. Are they going to the movies? (no) _____.

4. Are we going for a walk? (yes) _____.

5. Is she cooking eggs? (yes) _____.

E Write answers to the questions using the cues.

1. Where are they going? (school) _They're going to school_____.

2. What are you doing? (work) _____.

3. Where is Vera going? (movies) _____.

4. What is your sister doing? (shop) _____.

5. What are they doing? (study) _____.

Lesson C

A Match the questions and answers.

1. Can you play tennis? ___b___
2. Can he ride a bike? _____
3. Can they play soccer? _____
4. Can Isla play golf? _____
5. Can we swim in the pool? _____

a. Yes, they can.
b. No, I can't.
c. Yes, we can.
d. Yes, he can.
e. No, she can't.

B Write statements using *can* or *can't* and the cues below.

1. Noor / swim (no) _Noor can't swim_____.
2. We / play volleyball _____.
3. My sister / ride a bike (no) _____.
4. We / play golf / today (no) _____.
5. They / ski _____.

C Write questions using *can* and the cues below.

1. you / ride a bike _Can you ride a bike_____?
2. they / ice skate _____?
3. John / play tennis _____?
4. Nasir / play soccer _____?
5. Sonja and Sarah / ski _____?

D Write short answers to the questions.

1. Can Ravi swim? (yes) _Yes, he can___.
2. Can they play volleyball? (yes) _____.
3. Can Iman play tennis?(yes) _____.
4. Can you ice skate? (no) _____.
5. Can we play soccer? (no) _____.

E Complete the conversations.

1. **A:** _____ play golf?
   B: No, I _____, but I _____ play tennis.
2. **A:** _____ Anita ride a bike?
   B: Yes, she _____, but she _____ swim.
3. **A:** _____ they ski?
   B: Yes, they _____ ski.

Unit 8: Clothes

Lesson A

A Unscramble the polite requests.

1. try on can jackets red I _Can I try on the red jacket_ ?

2. I buy blue can the please hat _____ ?

3. yellow the could I skirt try on _____ ?

4. you I can help _____ ?

5. me, you can please help _____ ?

B Match the polite requests and responses.

1. Can you help me __e__   **a.** this dress, please?

2. Can I pay for the sweater with _____   **b.** black pants?

3. Could I try on _____   **c.** a credit card?

4. Could you bring the _____   **d.** size 8?

5. Can I see a _____   **e.** , please?

C Write the polite requests.

1. You want to try on the red coat. _Can I try on the red coat, please_ ?

2. You want to see some blue ties. _____ ?

3. You want to try on the black jacket. _____ ?

4. You want the sales assistant to bring you a size 10. _____ ?

5. You want to pay by credit card. _____ ?

D Write polite requests using *can/could* and the words below.

1. try on / blue dress _Can I try on the blue dress_ ?

2. pay by / credit card _____ ?

3. you / help me _____ ?

4. you / bring / red shirt _____ ?

5. try on / size 7 _____ ?

Lesson C

Name	Love ☺☺	Like ☺	Don't like ☹	Hate ☹☹
Jackie	new clothes	red socks	brown shoes	black clothes
Ai	books	the color pink	white jackets	volleyball
Ridwan	hats	T-shirts	the color orange	credit cards
Paulo	soccer	jeans	ties	white socks

A Look at the chart. Complete the sentences.

1. Jackie __doesn't like__ brown shoes.

2. Ridwan _____ hats.

3. Paulo _____ jeans.

4. Ai _____ volleyball.

5. Ridwan _____ T-shirts.

B Look at the chart. Complete the conversations.

1. Ai: Jackie, do you like new clothes?

Jackie: Yes, I __love__ new clothes!

2. Ridwan: Paulo, do you like soccer?

Paulo: Yes, I _____ it.

3. Jackie: What clothes do you like, Ridwan?

Ridwan: I _____ T-shirts.

4. Paulo: Ai, do you like volleyball?

Ai: No, I _____ it.

5. Ridwan: Paulo, do you like red ties?

Paulo: No, I _____ ties.

C Answer the questions. Use the cues.

1. A: Do you like the color green?

B: ☺ ☺ __Yes, I love it!__

2. A: Do you like speaking English?

B: ☺ _____

3. A: Do you like skirts?

B: ☹ _____

4. A: Do you like hats?

B: ☹ ☹ _____

5. A: Do you like white clothes?

B: ☹ _____

Unit 9: Eat Well

Lesson A

A Circle *any* or *some*.

1. We don't have ((any) | some) milk.

2. There is (any | some) steak for dinner.

3. Do you have (any | some) ice cream?

4. Do we have (any | some) eggs?

5. Could I have (any | some) fish, please?

B Complete the sentences and questions with *any* or *some*.

1. Could I have _some_ tea, please?

2. There's _____ fruit juice in the refrigerator.

3. No, we don't have _____ salad.

4. Please buy _____ chicken at the store.

5. Do you have _____ pasta?

C Unscramble the words to write sentences and questions.

1. refrigerator. fish in the some there's _There's some fish in the refrigerator._

2. have do eggs? any you _____

3. juice. fruit I any have don't _____

4. some could , please? have cereal and milk I _____

5. for chocolate cake some there's dessert. _____

D Look at the food and the imperative *ask* or *order*. Write a question to ask about or order the food. Use *any* or *some*.

Example: **chicken** (ask): _Do you have any chicken?_

(order): _Could I have some chicken, please?_

1. **coffee** (order): _____

2. **chocolate cake** (ask): _____

3. **fish** (ask): _____

4. **salad** (order): _____

5. **fruit juice** (ask): _____

E Complete the conversation with *any* or *some*.

Monica: Carly, at the store can you buy (1) _____ tea and (2) _____ milk? Oh, and cereal. We don't have (3) _____ cereal.

Carly: OK.

Monica: Can you also buy (4) _____ eggs? We don't have (5) _____.

Carly: OK, Monica. Can I have (6) _____ money to pay for the food?

Monica: No, I don't have (7) _____!

Lesson C

A Circle *how much* or *how many* to complete the sentence.

1. ((How much)| How many) ice cream do you eat every week?

2. (How much | How many) milk does the baby drink every day?

3. (How much | How many) bottles of milk does the baby drink every day?

4. (How much | How many) yogurt do we need?

B Complete the sentences. Use *How much* or *How many*.

1. _How much_ coffee do you drink every day?

2. _____ apples do you eat every week?

3. _____ water do you drink every day?

4. _____ eggs do you eat for breakfast?

5. _____ vegetables do you eat every day?

C Complete the conversations with *how much* or *how many*.

1. **A**: _How much_ meat do vegetarians eat?   **B:** None! Vegetarians don't eat any meat!

2. **A**: _____ vegetables do vegetarians eat?   **B:** Vegetarians eat a lot of vegetables.

3. **A**: _____ rice do we have?   **B:** We don't have any rice.

4. **A**: _____ milk do you have?   **B:** I have two cartons.

5. **A**: _____ bags of beans do you have?   **B:** I don't have any beans.

D Complete the conversation with *how much* and *how many*.

Mother: We need rice and tomatoes.

Diane: (1) _How much_ rice and (2) _____ tomatoes?

Mother: Two bags of rice and four tomatoes.

Diane: (3) _____ butter do we have?

Mother: We don't have any butter. But we have some eggs.

Diane: So, (4) _____ butter do we need?

Mother: One stick of butter. And we need carrots.

Diane: OK. (5) _____ carrots do we need?

Mother: Three. That's all.

E Write questions asking about the food someone eats. Use *how much* or *how many* and the words below.

1. lettuce / eat / week _How much lettuce do you eat every week_?

2. potatoes / eat / week _____?

3. tea / drink / every day _____?

4. candy / eat / day _____?

5. eggs / eat / week _____?

Unit 10: Health

Lesson A

A Match the questions or statements and responses.

1. Do you feel OK? ___d___
2. How do you feel? _____
3. Does Kim look tired? _____
4. Does Martin have a stomachache? _____
5. Do you have a fever? _____

a. No, she doesn't.
b. No, I don't.
c. I feel fine.
d. Yes, I feel fine.
e. Yes, he does.

B Unscramble the questions.

1. feel / do / tired / you _Do you feel tired_____?
2. you / OK / do / feel _____?
3. do / you / how / feel _____?
4. are / feeling / you / how _____?
5. sick / does / look / he _____?

C Complete the sentences with the words given.

1. My mother (feel, not) _doesn't feel_ well.
2. Robin (feel) _____ fine today.
3. You (look, not) _____ well.
4. I (feel) _____ fine.
5. Cal (look) _____ tired.

D Rewrite the sentences as negative.

1. I feel sick. _I don't feel sick._____.
2. Juan feels great. _____.
3. You look tired. _____.
4. Cristina looks sick. _____.
5. He feels tired. _____.

E Complete the Yes/No questions and answers.

1. **A:** _Do you feel OK_____?
   B: Yes, I do.
2. **A:** Does he look tired?
   B: Yes, _____.
3. **A:** Do you _____ sick?
   B: No, _____.
4. **A:** _____ look sick?
   B: Yes, she does.
5. **A:** _____ feel tired?
   B: Yes, I do.

Lesson C

A Match the statements with the advice.

1. I have a cough. What should I do? __e__
2. Marie is tired. What should she do? _____
3. Abdi has a toothache. What should he do? _____
4. I have a headache. What should I do? _____
5. She has a fever. What should she do? _____

a. He should see a dentist.
b. You should take some pain reliever.
c. She should go to bed.
d. She should see a doctor.
e. You should take some cough medicine.

B Unscramble the statements and questions.

1. see / I / dentist / should / a _Should I see a dentist_____?
2. some / you / take / should / pain reliever _____.
3. today / go to / Dan / school / shouldn't _____.
4. shouldn't / you / no, _____.
5. she / what / should / do _____?

C For each statement give advice about what the person *should* and *shouldn't* do.

1. Jorge has a sore throat.

   _He should take some cough medicine_____.

   _He shouldn't see a dentist_____.

2. I have a fever.

   _____

   _____

3. She has a toothache.

   _____

   _____

4. My classmate has a headache.

   _____

   _____

5. You have the flu.

   _____

   _____

Unit 11: Making Plans

Lesson A

A Complete the sentences. Use the words in parentheses and *be going to*.

1. What _is he going to_ (he) do after school today?

2. _____ (you) have a family meal on Sunday?

3. _____ (they) go to the movies tonight.

4. _____ (we) study for the test.

5. I'm tired. _____ (I) go to bed.

B Write the sentence again. Make them negative.

1. Liz is going to the movies with me. _Liz is not going to the movies with me_ .

2. Will's family is having a big meal. _____ .

3. They are going to have a barbeque on Sunday. _____ .

4. We are going to have a party on Friday night. _____ .

5. You are going to a game tonight. _____ .

C Write the statements as questions.

1. We are going to have a party. _Are we going to have a party_ ?

2. They are going to have a family meal. _____ ?

3. Hafa is going to go to Miami. _____ ?

4. Milo is going to have a birthday party on Saturday. _____ ?

5. We are going to go to a soccer game. _____ ?

D Complete the conversations. Use the words in parentheses and *be going to*.

1. **A:** What _are you going to_ (you) do tonight?

   B: I'm _going to go_ to the movies.

2. **A:** What _____ (he) this afternoon?

   B: He is _____ a barbeque with friends.

3. **A:** What _____ (they) do on Sunday?

   B: They _____ have a family meal.

4. **A:** When _____ (she) have a party?

   B: She's _____ have a party on Saturday.

5. **A:** Where _____ (you) for vacation?

   B: I _____ go to the beach.

Lesson C

A Write short answers to the *Yes/No* questions.

1. Would you like to be a teacher? (yes) _____Yes, I would_____.

2. Would you like to study medicine? (no) _____.

3. Would you like to be an actor? (no) _____.

4. Would you like to study music? (yes) _____.

5. Would you like to be a nurse? (yes) _____.

B Complete the sentences and questions with *would like to*.

1. My sister _____would like to_____ study law.

2. I _____ be a doctor.

3. They _____ study acting.

4. _____ (you) be a lawyer?

5. _____ (James) study education?

C Use the cure to write sentences with *would like to* and *be*.

1. Adana, nurse _____Adana would like to be a nurse_____.

2. Sara, actor _____.

3. Ranjan, teacher _____.

4. medical students, doctors _____.

5. music students, musicians _____.

D Write questions using *would like to* and the words given.

1. you / study law _____Would you like to study law_____?

2. you / be a software engineer _____?

3. you / study information technology _____?

4. your son / be a teacher _____?

5. your daughter / be a nurse _____?

E Complete the questions and answers with *would* or *would like to*.

1. **A:** What _____would you like to_____ be?

   B: I _____ be an actor.

2. **A:** (you) _____ study engineering?

   B: Yes, I _____.

3. **A:** What (Jason) _____ study?

   B: Jason _____ study music.

Unit 12: On the Move

Lesson A

A Write the sentences in the simple past tense.

1. They go to school at 8 a.m. _They went to school at 8 a.m._

2. I return from school at 2 p.m. _____

3. The students arrive early. _____

4. He leaves work at 5 p.m. _____

5. We come from Canada. _____

B Complete the sentences with the simple past tense of the verb in parentheses.

1. Leo _____lived_____ (live) in Canada for two years.

2. The homework assignment _____ (be) difficult.

3. They _____ (go) to the library after school.

4. Maria _____ (move) from Madrid to Buenos Aires.

5. We _____ (stay) in a big hotel in Miami.

C Write the sentences in the negative.

1. We arrived on time. _We didn't arrive on time._

2. He went home after class. _____

3. I was in Chile for two years. _____

4. They did their homework. _____

5. You lived in a big apartment. _____

D Match the questions and answers.

1. Did your flight arrive on time? ___c___   **a.** I left at 4 o'clock.

2. Did you live in Toronto? _____   **b.** No, I stayed in my apartment.

3. Did you move to a new house? _____   **c.** No, it was late.

4. What time did you leave school? _____   **d.** In 2009.

5. When did you go to Germany? _____   **e.** No, I lived in Ottawa.

E Unscramble the questions.

1. to / did / Florida? / When / you / come _When did you come to Florida?_

2. did / What / leave / work? / they / time _____

3. you / Germany? / long / did / How / stay / in _____

4. after / did / do / class? / What / you _____

5. he / last / go / did / night? / Where _____

Lesson C

A Write the statements as simple past tense questions.

1. They left the library. _Did they leave the library?_

2. He sold his car. _____

3. He bought a bicycle. _____

4. Karen stopped the car. _____

5. Bill got tickets for the soccer game. _____

B Match the questions and answers.

1. Did the flight leave on time? __d__   **a.** Yes, I did.

2. Did you sell your house? _____   **b.** Yes, they did.

3. Did Marcos come to class yesterday? _____   **c.** Yes, she did.

4. Did they have a good time? _____   **d.** Yes, it did.

5. Did Li get a new phone? _____   **e.** No, he didn't.

C Complete the short answers in the simple past tense.

1. Did you get a new passport? Yes, _I did_.   4. Did Ivan pack his suitcase? Yes, _____.

2. Did Barbara buy the tickets online? Yes, _____.   5. Did your sister get a new job? No, _____.

3. Did they have a party? No, _____.

D Complete the questions and answers.

1. **A:** _____Did she_____ pack her books?   **B:** Yes, _____she did_____ .

2. **A:** _____ sell your car?   **B:** Yes, _____.

3. **A:** _____ close their bank account?   **B:** No, _____.

4. **A:** _____ do your homework?   **B:** Yes, _____.

5. **A:** _____ you get a passport?   **B:** No, _____.

E Read the paragraph and answer the questions. Use short answers.

Marta and Fredi are married. Last month they moved from Sao Paulo, Brazil, to New York, USA. They packed their suitcases and sold the car. They rented their house. They didn't sell it. Marta's family had a going-away party for them. They left Sao Paulo because they got new jobs in New York.

1. Did Marta and Fredi come from Argentina? _____.

2. Did they sell the car? _____.

3. Did they sell the house? _____.

4. Did they have a going-away party? _____.

5. Did they get new jobs in New York? _____.

UNIT 1 FRIENDS AND FAMILY

Lesson A

A. 2. am *or* 'm 3. is 4. are 5. are

B. 2. are 3. am 4. is 5. are

C. 2. Sarah's my classmate. 3. We're students. 4. They're David and Louis.
5. You're Carlos.

D. 2. e 3. a 4. b 5. c

E. 2. My 3. Their 4. Her 5. Your

Lesson C

A. 2. My brother is handsome. 3. We are married. 4. Are you single? 5. Is she attractive?

B. 2. are 3. am 4. is 5. are

C. 2. They are young with curly blond hair. 3. He is short with curly gray hair. 4. Anita is tall with wavy black hair. 5. Teng is young with straight black hair.

D. 2. e 3. a 4. b 5. c

E. 2. Is she married? 3. Are they married? 4. Is she young? 5. Is he short?

UNIT 2 JOBS AROUND THE WORLD

Lesson A

A. 2. isn't *or* is not 3. 're not *or* aren't 4. 're not *or* aren't 5. 'm not

B. 2. I am/I'm not a doctor. 3. They are/They're not artists. 4. We are/We're not teachers.
5. You are/You're not an architect.

C. 2. He's not a teacher. 3. We aren't students. 4. You are not an engineer. 5. They're not chefs.

D. 2. a 3. a 4. a 5. an

E. 1. isn't a 2. 're not *or* aren't 3. 're not *or* aren't 4. 'm not 5. 're not *or* aren't

Lesson C

A. 2. Indonesia is a hot, dry country. 3. Is Ecuador a small country? 4. Iceland is a cold country. 5. Is Ireland a wet country?

B. 2. No, it isn't. It's a dry country. 3. No, it isn't. It's a big country. 4. Yes, it is. 5. Yes, it is.

C. 2. Is Venezuela a hot country? 3. Is Asia a big continent? 4. Is England a wet country? 5. Is the UAE a hot, dry country?

D. 2. e 3. a 4. b 5. d

E. 2. Russia is a cold, dry country. 3. Australia is a big, dry continent. 4. Yemen is a small, hot country. 5. Ireland is a small, wet country.

UNIT 3 HOUSES AND APARTMENTS

Lesson A

A. 2. There is 3. There are 4. There is 5. There is

B. 2. There is 3. there is 4. There are 5. There is

C. 2. Is there a garage? 3. There is a small bathroom. 4. There are two closets downstairs. 5. Is there a garden?

D. 2. Are there cars in the garage? 3. Is there a bathroom downstairs? 4. Are there three bedrooms upstairs? 5. Is there a swimming pool in the backyard?

E. 2. Yes, there are. 3. No, there isn't. 4. No, there aren't. 5. Yes, there is.

Lesson C

A. 2. on 3. on 4. next to 5. next to 6. in

B. 2. under 3. in 4. next to 5. in

C. 2. F 3. T 4. T 5. F

UNIT 4 POSSESSIONS

Lesson A

A. 2. These 3. these 4. That 5. That

B. 2. Is this your notebook? 3. That's my phone. 4. Those are not my glasses.
5. This is your dictionary.

C. 2. a, b 3. c, d 4. a, b

D. 2. Those; these 3. That; this 4. this; that

E. 2. that 3. These 4. That 5. those

Lesson C

A. 2. Ploy's 3. Ana and Jane's 4. students' 5. passengers'

B. 2. have 3. have 4. has 5. have

C. 2. have 3. have 4. has 5. have

D. 2. Kia and Juana don't have bracelets. 3. You don't have a cell phone. 4. I don't have a book. 5. She doesn't have rings.

E. 2. Do you have keys? 3. Does the teacher have a dictionary? 4. Do they have a big house? 5. Does he have a cell phone?

F. 2. Yes, they do. 3. No, I don't. 4. No, we don't. 5. Yes, she does.

UNIT 5 DAILY ACTIVITIES

Lesson A

A. 2. takes a shower 3. start work 4. gets up 5. has lunch

B. 2. We don't eat lunch at one o'clock. 3. Tina doesn't take a shower in the evening.
4. I don't get up at seven thirty every morning. 5. She doesn't take a nap on Sunday afternoon.

C. 2. does Carlos start work 3. do they have lunch 4. does she go to bed 5. do we have dinner

D. 2. What time does she finish work? 3. What time do you start work every day?
4. What time does he go to bed? 5. What time do they have lunch every day?

E. 2. What time does Eben take a nap in the afternoon? 3. What time does Carmen finish work?

Lesson C

A. 2. travels 3. go to meetings 4. meets clients 5. makes photocopies

B. 2. Yes, we do. 3. Yes, they do. 4. No, he doesn't. 5. Yes, they do.

C. 2. never 3. always 4. sometimes 5. always

D. 2. They never travel. 3. Do you write reports every week? 4. My boss checks e-mail every evening. 5. Does Kia makes photocopies every day?

E. 2. Do you make photocopies every day? 3. Does Teng work on Saturdays? 4. Do they talk to people on the phone every afternoon? 5. Does she write reports on Fridays?

UNIT 6 GETTING THERE

Lesson A

A. 2. between 3. across from 4. across from 5. between

B. 2. turn left 3. cross 4. turn left 5. cross; turn right

C. 2. Walk to school. / Don't walk to school. 3. Cross Elm Street. / Don't cross Elm Street.
4. Turn left. / Don't turn left. 5. Stop. / Don't stop.

Lesson C

A. 2. have to 3. has to 4. Do; have to 5. Does; have to

B. 2. Do they have to take a bus to the subway station? 3. Do we have to buy bus tickets?
4. Does Diego have to travel by train to the meeting? 5. Do you have to go to the meeting at 10 a.m.?

C. 2. a 3. d 4. e 5. b

D. 2. Eli has to take the bus to school. 3. We have to write reports at work. 4. You have to do your homework tonight. 5. Cora and Lucy have to cook dinner Saturday night.

E. 2. Do you have to finish your homework tonight? 3. Does Van have to walk home from school? 4. Does Eva have to make dinner for her family? 5. Do they have to change trains at Park Street Station?

UNIT 7 FREE TIME

Lesson A

A. 2. He is reading the newspaper 3. My mother is cooking dinner. 4. I'm going to the movies. 5. They are shopping at the mall.

B. 2. Are they watching TV? 3. Is Milan playing guitar? 4. Are you studying English? 5. Is Ada doing her homework?

C. 2. She is writing a report. 3. They are going for a walk. 4. I'm shopping. 5. He is listening to music.

D. 2. No, he isn't. 3. No, they aren't. 4. Yes, we are. 5. Yes, she is.

E. 2. I'm working. 3. She's going to the movies. 4. She's shopping. 5. They're studying.

Lesson C

A. 2. d 3. a 4. e 5. c

B. 2. We can play volleyball. 3. My sister can't ride a bike. 4. We can't play golf today. 5. They can ski.

C. 2. Can they ice skate? 3. Can John play tennis? 4. Can Nasir play soccer? 5. Can Sonja and Sarah ski?

D. 2. Yes, they can. 3. Yes, she can. 4. No, I can't. 5. No, we can't.

E. 1. Can you; can't; can 2. Can; can; can't 3. Can; can

UNIT 8 CLOTHES

Lesson A

A. 2. Can I buy the blue hat, please? 3. Could I try on the yellow skirt? 4. Can I help you? 5. Can you help me, please?

B. 2. c 3. a 4. d 5. b

C. 1. Can/Could I try on the red coat, please? 2. Can/Could I see some blue ties, please? 3. Can/Could I try one the black jacket, please. 4. Can/Could you bring a size 10, please? 5. Can/Could I pay by credit card?

D. 1. Can/Could I try on the blue dress? 2. Can/Could I pay by credit card? 3. Can/Could you help me? 4. Can/Could you please bring a red shirt? 5. Can/Could you bring a size 7, please?

Lesson C

A. 2. loves 3. likes 4. hates 5. likes

B. 2. love 3. like 4. hate 5. don't like

C. 2. Yes, I like it. *or* I like speaking English. 3. No, I don't like them. *or* No, I don't like skirts. 4. No, I hate them. *or* No, I hate hats. 5. No, I don't like them. *or* No, I don't like white clothes.

UNIT 9 EAT WELL

Lesson A

A. 2. some 3. any 4. any 5. some

B. 2. some 3. any 4. some 5. any

C. 2. Do you have any eggs? 3. I don't have any fruit juice. 4. Could I have some cereal and milk, please? 5. There's some chocolate cake for dessert.

D. 1. Could I have some coffee, please? 2. Do you have any chocolate cake? 3. Do you have any fish? 4. Could I have some salad, please? 5. Do you have any fruit juice?

E. 1. some 2. some 3. any 4. some 5. any 6. some 7. any

Lesson C

A. 2. How much 3. How many 4. How much

B. 2. How many 3. How much 4. How many 5. How many

C. 2. How many 3. How much 4. How much 5. How many

D. 2. how many 3. How much 4. how much 5. How many

E. 2. How many potatoes do you eat every week? 3. How much tea do you drink every day? 4. How much candy do you eat every day? 5. How many eggs do you eat every week?

UNIT 10 HEALTH

Lesson A

A. 2. c 3. a 4. e 5. b

B. 2. Do you feel OK? 3. How do you feel? 4. How are you feeling? 5. Does he look sick?

C. 2. feels 3. don't look 4. feel 5. looks

D. 1. I don't feel sick. 2. Juan doesn't feel great. 3. You don't look tired. 4. Cristina doesn't look sick. 5. He doesn't feel tired.

E. 2. he does 3. feel; I don't 4. Does she 5. Do you

Lesson C

A. 2. c 3. a 4. b 5. d

B. 2. You should take some pain reliever. 3. Dan shouldn't go to school today. 4. No, you shouldn't. 5. What should she do?

C. *Answer will vary. Possible answers:* 1. He should take some cough medicine.; He shouldn't see a dentist. 2. You should go to bed.; You should not take any cough medicine. 3. She should see a dentist.; She should not see a doctor. 4. He/She should take some pain reliever.; He/She shouldn't see a doctor. 5. You should go to bed. You shouldn't go to school.

UNIT 11 MAKING PLANS

Lesson A

A. 2. Are you going to 3. They are going to go 4. We are going to 5. I'm going to

B. 2. Will's family is not having a big meal. 3. They are not going to have a barbeque on Sunday. 4. We are not going to have a party on Friday night. 5. You are not going to a game tonight.

C. 2. Are they going to have a family meal? 3. Is Hafa going to go to Miami? 4. Is Milo going to have a birthday party on Saturday? 5. Are we going to go to a soccer game?

D. 2. is he going to; he is going to 3. are they going to; are going to 4. is she going to; is going to 5. are you going to; am going to

Lesson C

A. 2. No, I wouldn't. 3. No, I wouldn't. 4. Yes, I would. 5. Yes, I would.

B. 2. would like to 3. would like to 4. Would you like to 5. Would James like to

C. 2. Sara would like to be an actor. 3. Ranjan would like to be a teacher. 4. Medical students would like to be doctors. 5. Music students would like to be musicians.

D. 2. Would you like to be a software engineer? 3. Would you like to study information technology? 4. Would your son like to be a teacher? 5. Would your daughter like to be a nurse?

E. 1. would like to 2. Would you like to; would 3. would you like to; would like to

UNIT 12 MIGRATIONS

Lesson A

A. 2. I returned from school at 2 p.m. 3. The students arrived early. 4. He left work at 5 p.m. 5. We came from Canada.

B. 2. was 3. went 4. moved 5. stayed

C. 2. He didn't go home after class. 3. I wasn't in Chile for two years. 4. They didn't do their homework. 5. You didn't live in a big apartment.

D. 2. e 3. b 4. a 5. d

E. 2. What time did they leave work? 3. How long did you stay in Germany? 4. What did you do after class? 5. Where did he go last night?

Lesson C

A. 2. Did he sell his car? 3. Did he buy a bicycle? 4. Did Karen stop the car? 5. Did Bill get tickets for the soccer game?

B. 2. a 3. e 4. b 5. c

C. 2. she did. 3. they didn't 4. he did. 5. she didn't.

D. 2. Did you; I did 3. Did they; they didn't 4. Did you; I did 5. Did; I didn't

E. 1. No, they didn't. 2. Yes, they did. 3. No, they didn't. 4. Yes, they did. 5. Yes, they did.